ADDITIONAL PRAISE FOR THIS WORK

"Richard Snoddy, author of a distinguished, recently published monograph The Soteriology of James Ussher: The Act and Object of Saving Faith (Oxford, 2014), has produced a splendid new edition of original texts, sermons and tractates on church government by this great 17th-century Irish scholar and bishop. Ussher is especially notable for his key role in drafting the Reformed Articles of Religion of the Church of Ireland (1615), a confessional formulary which constitutes a doctrinal bridge of sorts from the Thirty-Nine Articles (1571) to the Westminster Confession (1647). In Ussher's concerted endeavour to reconcile adherents of Reformed divinity to the institution of episcopal government, these writings perform a function for ecclesiology analogous to the Irish Articles in matters of doctrine. This scholarly edition should be of considerable interest and edification to all who are students of the Reformed Episcopal tradition."

—W.J. Torrance Kirby, *Professor of Ecclesiastical History,* *McGill University*

"Richard Snoddy has done the church a great service by bringing back into accessible print these sermons and treatises of the great Archbishop James Ussher. They will both edify and provoke readers to rethink and reapply Reformed Anglican ecclesiology for our own days."

—Rev. Dr. Lee Gatiss, *Director, Church Society*

"The publication of this volume represents the first fruits of a noble and ambitious project - the Library of Early English Protestantism. This selection of Archbishop James Ussher's key writings on the Church and ministry will help to make this brilliant seventeenth-century divine - an irenic and constructive thinker - better known to all who have an interest in the legacy of early Anglican theology and a concern for the well-being and flourishing of Anglicanism today. We still have much to learn from Ussher."

—Professor Paul Avis, Universities of Durham and Exeter, UK; **Editor-in-Chief of Ecclesiology**

James Ussher

and a

Reformed Episcopal Church

James Ussher

and a

Reformed Episcopal Church: Sermons and Treatises on Ecclesiology

Edited by Richard Snoddy

TABLE OF CONTENTS

ACKNOWLEDGEMENTS

I am grateful to Dr. Chris Fletcher, Keeper of Special Collections at the Bodleian Library, Oxford for permission to reproduce the Temple Church sermon from MS Perrot 9. I am also grateful to Northamptonshire Record Office for their *nihil obstat* in regard to the Greenwich sermon recorded in NRO Finch Hatton MS 247.

I must thank Daniel Schwartz, Constantine Campbell, Edward Holt, Eric Hutchinson, and Michael Lynch for advice on points of translation, and also Harrison Perkins for general banter on all things Ussher.

This is a good opportunity to belatedly acknowledge my gratitude to Michael McClenahan who must shoulder much of the blame for pointing me in the direction of Ussher many years ago as I considered options for doctoral research.

Words would fail to express my thanks to and gratitude for Sarah, Samuel, Lydia, and Reuben.

ABBREVIATIONS

ACO   *Acta Conciliorum Oecumenicorum*, ed. E. Schwartz and J. Straub, 4 tomes in 15 vols (Berlin: de Gruyter, 1914–)

ACW   *Ancient Christian Writers: The Works of the Fathers in Translation*, 63 vols (Mahwah, NJ: Paulist Press, 1946–)

ANF   *The Ante-Nicene Fathers*, ed. Alexander Roberts and James Donaldson, 9 vols (Buffalo and New York: Christian Literature Company, 1885–96)

CCSL   *Corpus Christianorum, Series Latina*, 212 vols (Turnhout: Brepols, 1953–)

CO   John Calvin, *Ioannis Calvini Opera Quae Supersunt Omnia*, ed. G. Baum, E. Cunitz and E. Reuss, 59 vols (Brunswick and Berlin: C.A. Schwetschke, 1863–1900)

FoC   *The Fathers of the Church (Patristic Series)*, 138 vols (Washington, DC: Catholic University of America Press, 1947–)

KJV   King James Version, 1611

LCL   *Loeb Classical Library*, 534 vols (Cambridge, MA: Harvard University Press, 1911–)

LF   *A Library of Fathers of the Holy Catholic Church*, ed. E. B. Pusey et al, 51 vols (London: G. & F. Rivington, and Oxford: John Henry Parker, 1838–85)

NPNF1   *A Select Library of the Nicene and Post-Nicene Fathers of the Christian Church*, ed. Philip Schaff, 14 vols (Buffalo and New York: Christian Literature Company, 1886–90)

NPNF2   *A Select Library of the Nicene and Post-Nicene Fathers of the Christian Church, Second Series*, ed. Philip Schaff and Henry Wace, 14 vols

(Buffalo and New York: Christian Literature Company, 1890–1900)

ODCC   *The Oxford Dictionary of the Christian Church*, ed. F. L. Cross, 3rd edn, rev. by E. A. Livingstone (Oxford: Oxford University Press, 2005)

ODNB   *Oxford Dictionary of National Biography*, ed. H. C. G. Matthew and Brian Howard Harrison, 60 vols (Oxford: Oxford University Press, 2004)

PG   *Patrologia Graeca*, ed. J.-P. Migne, 161 vols (Paris, 1857–66)

PL   *Patrologia Latina*, ed. J.-P. Migne, 221 vols (Paris, 1844–64) [where a revised volume was issued page/column numbers in the revised version are given within { } following the original]

WJU   *The Whole Works of the Most Rev. James Ussher, D.D., Lord Archbishop of Armagh, and Primate of All Ireland*, ed. Charles R. Elrington and J. H. Todd, 17 vols (Dublin: Hodges and Smith, 1829–64)

CONVENTIONS

The spelling and punctuation of the texts has been lightly modernized, with i/j, u/v, and thorns modified in line with modern orthography, and ampersands expanded to 'and'. Capitalization has been modernized and italics have generally been removed except where their use for emphasis seemed helpful.

Bibliographical references in the footnotes have been modernized and some of Ussher's text critical comments summarized in translation. Where he has given a fair paraphrase of a Latin or Greek source in the text no additional translation is given in the footnote.

The place of publication is London unless otherwise indicated. Dates are given old style but the year taken to have begun on 1 January.

GENERAL INTRODUCTION

RECENT YEARS have seen an increasing interest in James Ussher, Archbishop of Armagh. On the one hand historians have recognized his importance in the ecclesiological and theological debates of the seventeenth century and his stature as one of the great scholarly intellects of early modern Europe. On the other, at a popular level, the insertion of dates from his biblical chronology into many editions of the King James Version of the Bible since 1701 has guaranteed his place as the poster-boy of young earth creationism. This volume seeks to introduce four of Ussher's sermons and two treatises on church government to a new readership in the confessionally Reformed churches and the wider evangelical community.[1] These pieces all in some way deal with the theme of the Church—its nature, its unity, its purity, its government, and how it must deal with difference—and they should stimulate theological reflection, especially for those within the Anglican tradition. A brief introduction to Ussher's life and career precedes an introduction to each work in turn.

James Ussher

James Ussher was born to Arland and Margaret Ussher in Dublin on 4 January 1581, the fifth of their ten children. This prominent Anglo-Irish family embodied in miniature the religious divisions of late sixteenth-

---

[1] For other publications directed to these constituencies, see *The Puritan Pulpit: James Ussher, 1581–1656* (Orlando: Soli Deo Gloria Publications, 2006), which reproduces the sermons found in *WJU*, 13:1–191, 209–334; *A Body of Divinity* (Birmingham, AL: Solid Ground Christian Books, 2007), a major handbook of Christian doctrine attributed to Ussher which is not included in *WJU*; Crawford Gribben, *The Irish Puritans: James Ussher and the Reformation of the Church* (Darlington: Evangelical Press, 2003); The editor is also preparing a volume of Ussher's previously unpublished sermons from the 1620s. On the contested authorship of *A Body of Divinity*, see Harrison Perkins, "Manuscript and Material Evidence for James Ussher's Authorship of 'A Body of Divinitie' (1645)," *Evangelical Quarterly* 89 (2018): 133–61.

century Ireland. His uncle, Henry Ussher, was the Protestant Archbishop of Armagh from 1595 until his death in 1613. On the maternal side, his uncle Richard Stanihurst was an advocate on the continent for the Irish Catholic cause, and his cousin Henry Fitzsimon was a Jesuit controversialist active in the Irish mission. According to his first biographer, Nicholas Bernard, Ussher's mother was "seduced by some of the Popish Priests to the Roman Religion" whilst Ussher was in England, and she never returned to the Protestant faith, a cause of much anguish for her son.[2]

As a young man Ussher was a promising scholar. He entered Trinity College, Dublin in 1593, one year after it opened. He obtained his B.A. by 1599, his M.A. by 1601, and was awarded the degrees B.D. in 1607 and D.D. in 1613. He was a fellow of the college from 1600, and was appointed Professor of Theological Controversies in 1607, and Vice-Chancellor in 1615. Ussher was ordained in 1602, and after three years' preaching and catechising from various pulpits in the city, he became Chancellor of St. Patrick's Cathedral, Dublin. This office carried with it the prebend of Finglas, where Ussher preached in the church every Lord's day. Despite rumors about his puritan inclinations, Ussher impressed King James VI and I, who elevated him to the see of Meath in 1621. He was nominated Archbishop of Armagh in the last days of James's reign in 1625, an office which he held until his death in 1656.

age 12 [handwritten annotation in margin]

---

[2] Nicholas Bernard, *The Life & Death of the Most Reverend and Learned Father of Our Church Dr. James Usher, Late Arch-Bishop of Armagh, and Primate of All Ireland* (London: E.Tyler, 1656), 19–20; Other biographical accounts can be found in Richard Parr, *The Life of the Most Reverend Father in God, James Usher, Late Lord Arch-Bishop of Armagh, Primate and Metropolitan of all Ireland* (London: Nathanael Ranew, 1686); Charles R. Elrington, "The Life of James Ussher, D.D., Archbishop of Armagh," in *WJU*, 1:1–324; R. Buick Knox, *James Ussher: Archbishop of Armagh* (Cardiff: University of Wales Press, 1967); Hugh Trevor-Roper, "James Ussher, Archbishop of Armagh," in *Catholics, Anglicans and Puritans: Seventeenth Century Essays* (London: Secker & Warburg, 1987), 120–65; Alan Ford, *James Ussher: Theology, History, and Politics in Early-Modern Ireland and England* (Oxford: Oxford University Press, 2007). The correspondence in *WJU*, vols 15–16 has now been superseded by *The Correspondence of James Ussher, 1600–1656*, ed. Elizabethanne Boran, 3 vols (Dublin: Irish Manuscripts Commission, 2015). For Ussher's irenic, moderate Reformed theology, see Richard Snoddy, *The Soteriology of James Ussher: The Act and Object of Saving Faith* (New York: Oxford University Press, 2014).

The Reformation in Ireland was incomplete and precarious.[3] The English authorities had control of only a small portion of the island and even here it was difficult to enforce religious change. An illegal Catholic episcopate operated in the shadows of the established church and this was reinforced by waves of priests educated in the seminaries of continental Europe. Early seventeenth-century Irish Protestants were thus an embattled minority. These pressures helped to forge a distinct Irish Protestant identity, marked by fierce anti-Catholicism and an awareness of being locked in a deadly struggle. This is reflected in Ussher's professorial title; not "Professor of Divinity" as it would have been at other universities in the British Isles, but "Professor of Theological Controversies." His successor in that role, Joshua Hoyle, put it succinctly: the Protestant theologian's duty is to "love God, and hate the Pope."[4]

Ussher would certainly have played a leading role in drafting the Irish Articles of 1615, a confessional document which expresses this Irish Protestant perspective. Article 80 brands the Bishop of Rome as "that man of sin" (2 Thess. 2:3), raising belief in the identity of the pope as Antichrist to the level of an article of faith.[5] The Articles are strongly predestinarian and Sabbatarian, and whilst incorporating much of the substance of the Thirty-nine Articles of the Church of England they are conspicuously silent on the subject of episcopacy—the only bishop mentioned is that of Rome. This is a strongly Reformed confessional document that would appeal to those with puritan inclinations and which would keep them within the fold, maintaining unity against the papist enemy. This concern for Protestant unity was also manifested at the practical level. The need for a capable preaching ministry was such that considerable latitude was given to Scottish Presbyterian ministers in the diocese of Down and Connor in the early years of Ussher's primacy.[6]

---

[3] On the Reformation in Ireland, see Henry A. Jefferies, *The Irish Church and the Tudor Reformations* (Dublin: Four Courts Press, 2010); Alan Ford, *The Protestant Reformation in Ireland, 1590–1641*, 2nd impression (Frankfurt am Main: Peter Lang, 1987); Karl S. Bottigheimer and Ute Lotz-Heumann, "The Irish Reformation in European Perspective," *Archiv für Reformationsgeschichte* 87 (1998): 268–309.

[4] Joshua Hoyle, *A Reioynder to Master Malone's Reply Concerning Reall Presence* (Dublin: Societie of Stationers, 1641), sig. a4v.

[5] *The Creeds of Christendom: With a History and Critical Notes*, ed. Philip Schaff, 6th ed., 3 vols (New York: Harper, 1931; repr. Grand Rapids, MI: Baker, 1998), 3:540.

[6] Ford, *James Ussher*, 164–73.

The independence and flexibility of the Irish church jarred with the vision of ecclesiastical uniformity pursued by King Charles I and William Laud, Archbishop of Canterbury from 1633. Their agents in Ireland, Thomas Wentworth, Lord Deputy from 1633 and later Earl of Strafford, and John Bramhall, Bishop of Derry, set about remodelling the church to reflect the discipline and ceremonialism of the English Arminian party.[7] They sought to impose the English Articles and the canons of 1604 on the Church of Ireland in the Convocation of 1634. Ussher and others found the English form of subscription abhorrent and resisted, but a new set of Irish canons were drafted, following the English precedent. The English Articles were adopted but the more explicitly Reformed Irish Articles were not thereby overturned and Ussher henceforth insisted that clergy assent to both at ordination.[8] The Irish Articles would thus, in a sense, interpret the

---

[7] What is often dubbed English Arminianism cannot be simply equated with the theology of Arminius and the Dutch Remonstrants. The latter could be regarded as a humanist and liberalizing movement, their distinctives centred on issues of soteriology. The former were more interested in ceremonial, sacramentalism, the aesthetics of worship, and discipline within the church. Their sacramental theology did have implications for the doctrine of grace, so it was easy for their opponents to brand them as Arminians and gain much polemical mileage in doing so. The literature on the phenomenon is extensive, but important works include Nicholas Tyacke, "Puritanism, Arminianism and Counter-Revolution," in *The Origins of the English Civil War*, ed. Conrad Russell (London: Macmillan, 1973), 119–43; idem, *Anti-Calvinists: The Rise of English Arminianism c.1590–1640* (Oxford: Clarendon Press, 1987); Peter White, "The Rise of Arminianism Reconsidered," *Past & Present* 101 (1983): 34–53; idem, *Predestination, Policy and Polemic: Conflict and Consensus in the English Church from the Reformation to the Civil War* (Cambridge: Cambridge University Press, 1992); idem, "The *Via Media* in the Early Stuart Church," in *The Early Stuart Church, 1603–1642*, ed. Kenneth Fincham (Basingstoke: Macmillan, 1993), 211–30; Kevin Sharpe, *The Personal Rule of Charles I* (New Haven, CT: Yale University Press, 1992), 275–402, 731–65; Peter Lake, "The Laudian Style: Order, Uniformity and the Pursuit of the Beauty of Holiness in the 1630s," in *The Early Stuart Church, 1603–1642*, ed. Kenneth Fincham (Basingstoke: Macmillan, 1993), 161–85; Anthony Milton, "The Creation of Laudianism: A New Approach," in *Politics, Religion and Popularity in Early Stuart Britain*, ed. Thomas Cogswell, Richard Cust, and Peter Lake (Cambridge: Cambridge University Press, 2002), 162–84. For perceptive reappraisal of certain aspects, see Jay T. Collier, *Debating Perseverance: The Augustinian Tradition in Post-Reformation England* (New York: Oxford University Press, 2018).

[8] Amanda Louise Capern, "The Caroline Church: James Ussher and the Irish Dimension," *Historical Journal* 39 (1996): 57–85; Alan Ford, "Dependent or Independent? The Church of Ireland and Its Colonial Context, 1536–1649," *Seventeenth Century* 10 (1995): 163–87.

potential ambiguities of the English Articles for the Irish clergy. The appointment of William Chappell as provost of Trinity College in 1634 was another indication of the growing strength of Arminianism in Ireland and the changing ethos of its institutions.[9] By 1635, though still primate, Ussher had lost effective control of the Irish church. He withdrew from public affairs into scholarly seclusion.

Ussher's scholarly output was considerable. His first published work, *Gravissimae quaestionis, de Christianarum ecclesiarum … continua successione et statu, historica explicatio* (London, 1613) chronicled the succession of the Christian Church from the earliest times to the twelfth century through the lens of Revelation 20. He traced the continuity of truth in the proto-Protestantism of various fringe and heretical groups in the medieval period, dismissing evidence of their heterodoxy as Catholic distortion, and charted the rise of Antichrist in Rome.[10] Another important work was published in 1621 appended to a tract by Christopher Sibthorp, and later expanded and published separately as *A Discourse of the Religion Anciently Professed by the Irish and British*. Here Ussher attempted to demonstrate the essential harmony between the reformed Irish church and a pristine Celtic Christianity untainted by popery.[11] *An Answer to a Challenge Made by a Iesuite in Ireland* (Dublin, 1624) soon followed, arguing that Rome had strayed from its early purity on

---

[9] Alan Ford, "'That Bugbear Arminianism': Archbishop Laud and Trinity College, Dublin," in *British Interventions in Early Modern Ireland*, ed. Ciaran Brady and Jane Ohlmeyer (Cambridge: Cambridge University Press, 2005), 135–60.

[10] *WJU*, 2:1–413 (from revised edition, 1687); an unpublished English translation by Ambrose Ussher, his brother, can be found in Trinity College Dublin, MS 2940; On this work and Ussher's apocalypticism more broadly, see Crawford Gribben, *The Puritan Millennium: Literature & Theology, 1550–1682* (Dublin: Four Courts Press, 2000), 80–100; Ford, *James Ussher*, 70–84.

[11] Ussher, *An epistle [...] concerning the religion anciently professed by the Irish and Scottish; Shewing it to be for substance the same with that which at this day is by publick authoritie established in the Church of England*, in Christopher Sibthorp, *A Friendly Advertisement to the pretended Catholickes of Ireland* (Dublin, 1622); Ussher, *A Discourse of the Religion Anciently Professed by the Irish and British*, in *The Workes of the Most Reverend Father in God, Iames Vssher* (London, 1631). This is the version found in *WJU*, 4:235–381. On this, see Ute Lotz-Heumann, "The Protestant Interpretation of History in Ireland: The Case of James Ussher's *Discourse*," in *Protestant History and Identity in Sixteenth-Century Europe*, ed. Bruce Gordon, 2 vols (Aldershot: Scolar Press, 1996), 2:107–20; Alan Ford, "James Ussher and the Creation of an Irish Protestant Identity," in *British Consciousness and Identity: The Making of Britain, 1533–1707*, ed. Brendan Bradshaw and Peter Roberts (Cambridge: Cambridge University Press, 1998), 185–212.

issues such as real presence, confession, purgatory, prayer for the dead, images, free will, and merit.[12] This was still regarded as a useful guide to these controversies in the nineteenth century.[13]

Ussher's publications in the 1630s indicate serious concern about Arminianism but with increasing censorship there were limits on what could be stated in print. His *Gotteschalci historia* (1631) was, on the surface, a historical treatment of Gottschalk of Orbais (*c.*804–*c.*869), but the Saxon monk's strident anti-Pelagianism implicitly spoke into the controversies of the 1630s.[14] Ussher was able to take a similar oblique approach in *Britannicarum ecclesiarum antiquitates* (1639), which traced the progress of Christianity in the British Isles down to the seventh century with an account of attempts to eradicate Pelagianism.[15]

As a regular visitor to England, initially to buy books for the fledgling college and later for scholarly pursuits, Ussher built up a network of friends and acquaintances that included great scholars such as William Camden and Sir Henry Savile, and puritan clergy such as John Preston and Richard Sibbes.[16] This extensive network meant that when he returned to England in 1640 after a long absence he had friends on both sides of the deepening political divide between king and parliament. His principled royalism meant that when forced to choose he had to side with the king even though he had so much in common with the theologians and preachers who aligned themselves with parliament. In April 1642 Ussher was nominated by the Commons to represent Oxford University at the synod which would become the Westminster Assembly but he could not attend a gathering proscribed by the king.[17] Prior to this parting of the ways he had attempted to act as a mediator, especially on the difficult question of the government of the church, as discussed below.

---

[12] *WJU*, vol. 3.

[13] Ford, *James Ussher*, 70.

[14] *WJU*, 4:1–233.

[15] *WJU*, vols 5–6.

[16] On Ussher's Puritan connections, see Elizabethanne Boran, "An Early Friendship Network of James Ussher, Archbishop of Armagh, 1626–1656," in *European Universities in the Age of Reformation and Counter Reformation*, ed. Helga Robinson-Hammerstein (Dublin: Four Courts Press, 1998), 116–34.

[17] *Journal of the House of Commons: Volume 2, 1640–1643* (London, 1802), 540.

Ussher fled from Oxford in 1645 as the parliamentarian armies advanced. After sojourning in Wales he returned to London in 1647 and was appointed Lecturer at Lincoln's Inn. Approval for this appointment was only passed by a narrow majority in the House of Commons,[18] so whilst some held him in high regard, to others he was still suspect on account of his royalist and episcopalian inclinations. He preached regularly until 1654 when his health began to fail, and from then only occasionally. In these final years in London he continued to work on his biblical and historical chronology, including the famous *Annales* which calculated the date of creation as Sunday 23 October 4004 BC.[19]

James Ussher died on 21 March 1656 at the home of the Countess of Peterborough at Reigate. His friends intended a private burial at Reigate but Oliver Cromwell insisted on a state funeral at Westminster Abbey, and the ceremony followed the liturgy of the banned Book of Common Prayer.[20]

At the Temple Church, 1620

Ussher's sermon at the Temple Church on 2 July 1620 is printed here for the first time. The Temple Church is a round church, originally built in the twelfth century by the Knights Templar. By the seventeenth century it was serving as the chapel for Inner Temple and Middle Temple, two of the Inns of Court, large institutions where barristers trained, lodged, and practiced their profession. Ussher's auditors on this occasion were predominantly lawyers, men of affairs, some of whom would have been actively involved in the political life of the nation. The religious ethos would have inclined towards moderate Puritanism and sympathy for the European Reformed churches in their afflictions.[21]

The sermon was preached in the wider context of Europe's descent into one of the most destructive wars of its history. In 1618 the Protestant

---

[18] *Journal of the House of Commons: Volume 5, 1646–1648* (London, 1802), 393.

[19] See *WJU*, vols 8–11. Also available in a revised English translation as *The Annals of the World: James Ussher's Classic Survey of World History*, ed. Larry Pierce and Marion Pierce (Green Forest: Master Books, 2003).

[20] Parr, *Life*, 78–79.

[21] Hugh Adlington, "Gospel, Law, and *Ars Prædicandi* at the Inns of Court," in *The Intellectual and Cultural World of the Early Modern Inns of Court*, ed. Jayne Archer, Elizabeth Goldring, and Sarah Knight (Manchester: Manchester University Press, 2011), 51–74.

nobility of Bohemia rebelled against Ferdinand of Styria, the newly-elected king of Bohemia and Hungary. Ferdinand was a Jesuit-educated Catholic and member of the Habsburg dynasty, which had for centuries held the Bohemian throne, a Habsburg being the only candidate in what had become largely a ceremonial election. In August 1619 the nobles offered the crown to Frederick, Elector Palatine, a Reformed Protestant and son-in-law to King James. He rashly accepted. Two days after this offer was made, Ferdinand was elected Holy Roman Emperor. Even as Emperor, Ferdinand lacked the strength to reclaim Bohemia. He offered the Upper Palatinate and Frederick's electoral title to Maximilian of Bavaria in return for assistance in subduing Bohemia, and he offered the Lower Palatinate to the Spanish Habsburgs for their help in launching a diversionary attack on the Palatinate. The tangled web of allegiances would make mediation in this dispute impossible.[22]

Many English Protestants viewed the rebellion in Bohemia as the first shots fired in the apocalyptic last battle, a conflict which would escalate and see the final overthrow of the papal Antichrist. Sir Edward Herbert, later Lord Herbert of Cherbury, was ambassador in Paris in 1619. He hoped that Frederick, the new Protestant champion, would accept the proffered crown: "God forbid he should refuse it, being the apparent way His [God's] providence hath opened to the ruin of the Papacy." He hoped that King James would "assist in this great work" and spend the winter preparing "against the next summer."[23] George Abbot, Archbishop of Canterbury, likewise saw Frederick's acceptance of the crown as a harbinger of apocalyptic events: "the work of God, that piece by piece, the Kings of the Earth that gave their power unto the Beast (all the word of God must be fulfilled) shall now tear the Whore, and make her desolate, as St. John in his Revelation hath foretold."[24] There was a strong "Bohemian party" which believed that England had a duty, through religion and through familial bonds, to

---

[22] For a detailed account see Peter Wilson, *Europe's Tragedy: A History of the Thirty Years' War* (London: Allen Lane, 2009); In briefer compass, see Mark Greengrass, *Christendom Destroyed: Europe 1517–1648* (London: Allen Lane, 2014), 596–643.

[23] Sir Edward Herbert to Sir Robert Naunton, 9 Sept. 1619, in *Letters and Other Documents Illustrating the Relations Between England and Germany at the Commencement of the Thirty Years' War: Second Series*, ed. S. R. Gardiner (London: Camden Society, 1868), 12–13.

[24] George Abbot to Sir Robert Naunton, 12 Sept. 1619, in Bodleian Library, MS Tanner 74, fols. 221–22.

support Frederick.[25] Many preachers aligned with this hawkish faction and played a significant role in the shaping of public opinion. Their influence was so great that James, increasingly reluctant to recognise and support Frederick's claim, would have to issue directions in December 1620, and again in 1622, to order preachers not to meddle in matters of state. He would also find it necessary to ban public prayers for Frederick and Elizabeth as King and Queen of Bohemia.[26]

For his sermon at the Temple Church, Ussher took Revelation 19:20 as his text: "And the beast was taken, and with him the false prophet that wrought miracles before him ... These both were cast alive into a fiery lake burning with brimstone." Ussher began with the insidious rise of the "mystery of iniquity," a lying, hypocritical religion which covers its false doctrines with "a veil of piety," pointing to clerical celibacy and abstaining from certain meats as examples of this pseudo-spirituality. Ussher recognized that some would wonder at his choice of subject—"you may say the minister hath a great want of matter when he brings controversies into the pulpit"—but it is the duty of a good minister to warn the flock "when we are in the midst of these evil devices of Satan." Some of his hearers might think he spoke "censoriously" but he was speaking plainly from Scripture. These were the last days and the Book of Revelation spoke to the Church just as the Old Testament prophecies spoke to God's people of old. John is a "perpetual prophet and nothing shall fall unto the Church of God unto the end of the world, but this book shall reveal it," a statement reflecting Ussher's historicist reading of Revelation.[27]

What John reveals is a sobering spectacle: the judgement that will come down on the whore of Babylon. Ussher warned,

> though men think it a small matter to join with popery, yet those that are branded with this mark of the beast and worship his image, professing this religion and following

---

[25] W. B. Patterson, *King James VI and I and the Reunion of Christendom* (Cambridge: Cambridge University Press, 1997), 293–338; S. L. Adams, "The Protestant Cause: Religious Alliance with the West European Calvinist Communities as a Political Issue in England, 1585–1630" (unpublished doctoral dissertation, University of Oxford, 1973).

[26] Adams, "The Protestant Cause," 290.

[27] For an excellent introduction to this field, see Katherine R. Firth, *The Apocalyptic Tradition in Reformation Britain, 1530–1645* (Oxford: Oxford University Press, 1979).

this spirit, they must go together with the man of sin into
the lake of fire burning with brimstone.

Ussher then spent much of the sermon unpacking several passages from Revelation and explaining the identity of the whore, the beast, and the false prophet. He handled the question of false miracles raised by his text, and also the fate of English Protestants' forefathers who had died in the days of popery before the gospel was proclaimed openly again by the Reformers. This clear gospel proclamation dealt a blow to the papacy. "Then comes popery tumbling down," and Ussher reckoned that Rome had already lost half its adherents. "Now the hour of the judgement of popery is come," Ussher insisted, and he urged his hearers not to suffer the everlasting punishment that would befall the followers of the beast. As belligerent as he might have sounded at times, there is an unmistakable note of sadness in his closing comment:

> I take no delight to revile any. I speak the bare truth, and
> have great sorrow of heart and am much afflicted for my
> countrymen's sake who most of them live in the darkness
> of popery yet where God says that there is danger, we
> must speak and not hold our peace, else shall their blood
> be required at our hands.

Before the Commons, St. Margaret's Church, 1621

On 5 February 1621, just weeks after being nominated for the see of Meath, Ussher was appointed to preach at a special communion service for the House of Commons. The occasion would have a clear purpose, to expose crypto-papists amongst the members, acting as "a touchstone to try their faith."[28] Two of the members moving the motion were close associates of Ussher: Sir Francis Barrington, who regarded Ussher as his "most noble friend,"[29] and Sir James Perrot, illegitimate son of a former Lord Deputy of Ireland. It seems that John Williams, Dean of Westminster, who would have expected to preach himself or to nominate another divine to do so in his place, felt snubbed and forbade such a gathering within his precincts. A

---

[28] *Journal of the House of Commons: Volume 1, 1547–1629* (London, 1802), 508.

[29] *Barrington Family Letters, 1628–1632*, ed. Arthur Searle, Camden Society, 4th series, 28 (London: Royal Historical Society, 1983), 12.

number of venues were then considered, but King James intervened to ensure that the service went ahead on 18 February in St. Margaret's Church, which lies between the Houses of Parliament and Westminster Abbey.[30]

John Chamberlain, in one of his gossipy letters, reported that "Dr. Usher ... made as I hear but a dry sermon and kept them so long, that it was very near two o'clock before they had all done."[31] Long and boring to some, perhaps, but it was well-received and later published by command of the Commons. The sermon is an early illustration of the competition between king and parliament for Ussher's allegiance, a tension that would rise to breaking point in the 1640s. A sizeable majority of the Commons would have held strongly anti-papal views and they would have expected a fiery Protestant message. The king expected his new bishop to help him obtain parliamentary subsidies, vital financial support that had to be secured before the true direction of royal foreign policy became publicly known. The king warned Ussher that he "had charge of an unruly flock," even questioning whether there was sufficient charity in the hearts of the members to consider them prepared to receive the sacrament. Ussher was to exhort the members "to look to the urgent necessities of the times, and the miserable state of Christendom with *Bis dat, qui cito dat* [he gives twice who gives quickly]."[32] The pressure on Ussher eased when the Commons granted subsidies two days before he was due to address them.

Ussher took as his text 1 Corinthians 10:17: "We being many, are one bread and one body: for we are all partakers of one bread." His discourse contrasted union and disunion, communion and segregation, knitting together and separating out. Against the unity of the faithful with each other and with Christ their head, he set the urgent need for distance from all false and idolatrous worship. The sacrament that was to follow would concretize these dynamics: those united in the truth would join in one body and partake in the same communion, an act which would seal their participation in

---

[30] Godfrey Goodman, *The Court of King James the First*, ed. J. S. Brewer, 2 vols (London: Richard Bentley, 1839), 2:199–200; *The Letters of John Chamberlain*, ed. Norman E. McClure, 2 vols (Philadelphia: The American Philosophical Society, 1939), 2:341; Thomas Smith, *V[iri] Cl[arissimi] Guilielmi Camdeni et Illustrium Virorum ad G. Camdenum Epistolae* (London, 1691), in the appended *Annales*, 67.

[31] McClure, ed., *The Letters of John Chamberlain*, 2:347.

[32] Parr, *Life*, 17–18.

one mystical body, whilst "such as adhere to false worship, may be discovered and avoided." To them the sacrament would be a trial by fire.

A major theme of the sermon was the unity of the Church. God has established order in his Church, but because of the disorder of our sinful nature there is a constant risk of internal division. Many will be inclined to "break rank," often "the watchmen themselves," the very same men who have been appointed to protect and defend the Church. The recent events in the Netherlands should serve as a warning against complacency, and having raised the spectre of Arminianism Ussher called for a unity rooted in Scripture and the doctrine of the Thirty-nine Articles. A further application was found in the need for "mutual sympathy" which the members of the body should have for one another. Ussher directed his hearers to look upon "the face of Christendom, so miserably rent and torn." What a pitiful sight, a spectacle that must move true members of the body to compassion, and indeed to action on behalf of their suffering brethren. The complacent would fall under the same curse as did Meroz, a town or city that failed to heed God's call to war against the Canaanites.[33] Ussher commended the members on their vote for subsidies, a thing done in "fit time" as "the season of the year is approaching, wherein 'kings go forth to battle'."[34] Clearly Ussher and the members expected that this money would fund military intervention on behalf of beleaguered Protestant states on the continent. The Bohemian forces under Christian of Anhalt had suffered a crushing defeat by imperial forces at the Battle of White Mountain several months previously and Frederick's Palatinate was now threatened.

Not only was the Lord's Supper a "seal of our conjunction" with one another and with Christ, but it was "evidence of our disjunction from idolators," setting apart true and false worshippers. Rome's worship is idolatrous. In the adoration of the host the sacrament is "made the object of the grossest idolatry that ever hath been practised by any." Protestants must not associate with papists in their false worship or they risk falling under divine punishment: "if we will be partakers of Babylon's sins, we must look to receive of her plagues." But Ussher went further. We must not only ourselves

---

[33] Judg. 5:23. For examples of similarly militant references to this text in the antecedent literature, see its use at Paul's Cross as the text for R[oger] H[acket], *A Sermon Needful for These Times* (Oxford, 1591); and see Edward Topsell, *Times Lamentation* (London, 1599), 417.

[34] See 2 Sam. 11:1.

"refrain" from worshipping idols but "restrain, as much as in us lieth, the practice thereof in others." Ussher's application, as Alan Ford notes, is driving towards a complete rejection of any notion of tolerating the practice of Catholicism. The king would never go so far, and indeed was at this time under pressure from Spain to relax civil penalties against Catholics. "As if realizing this," Ford writes, "Ussher abruptly broke off his argument, limiting the necessary action against Catholics to the suppression of 'open idolatries'—something James was quite happy to endorse."[35] The laws already on the statute books were sufficient to this end "if they were duly put in execution." He concluded by quoting 1 Corinthians 10:15, "I speak as to wise men; judge ye what I say."

Ussher pushed towards the limits of decorum in this sermon and pulled back. He had played to the gallery, but not in such a manner as to rouse the ire of the king. Ussher protested that he did not intend to "exasperate" his audience against "these persons" but his litany of Catholic idolatry, duplicity, and treachery was calculated to stoke their Romophobia.

Before King James at Wanstead, 1624

In June 1624 Ussher preached before the King at Wanstead House in Essex. This was a favourite hunting lodge of Henry VII but passed out of royal hands during the reign of Edward VI. Since 1619 it had been the home of Sir Henry Mildmay, and James had also enjoyed the hospitality of its previous owners: Charles Blount, Lord Mountjoy; his son, Sir Mountjoy Blount; and George Villiers, Earl (subsequently Marquess, and later Duke) of Buckingham. It was apparently the private house most frequented by James and he stayed there over forty times, usually in the summer months, but only once on royal progress. His fondness for it is perhaps reflected in his spending six of his last seven birthdays there (1618–21, 1623–24; he arrived from Theobalds the next day in 1622). Wanstead gave James a degree of seclusion but it still allowed the operation of functions of the court such as the reception of foreign ambassadors. On this occasion James travelled up from Greenwich and was at Wanstead from 19 to 23 June, Ussher preaching on 20 June, the day after the King's birthday.[36]

---

[35] Ford, *James Ussher*, 114.

[36] Emily V. Cole, "The State Apartment in the Jacobean Country House, 1603–1625" (unpublished doctoral dissertation, University of Sussex, 2010).

Ussher's text was Ephesians 4:13 and his theme the "unity of faith" and the universality of the Church. The Church is a "spiritual edifice," built up of living stones. It is found where believers are baptized by one Spirit into one body. The catholic or universal Church "is not be sought for in any one angle or quarter of the world," but among all who call on the name of Jesus Christ the Lord. It is a body, one and entire, comprising all the faithful. They stand in relation to the Church universal as parts to the whole, and it follows that "neither particular persons, nor particular churches, are to work as several divided bodies by themselves (which is the ground of all schism), but are to teach, and to be taught, and to do all other Christian duties, as parts conjoined unto the whole." Ussher spoke against "the new separatists" who were either completely indifferent to catholic communion, or who "dote so much upon the perfection of their own part" that they refuse to join in fellowship with the rest of the body. Worse still were the "Romanists ... authors of the most cruel schism that ever hath been seen in the Church of God," a rupture in comparison to which the Novatian and Donatist schisms were "but petty rents." Rome "scorning any longer to be accounted one of the branches of the catholic Church, would fain be acknowledged to be the root of it." Now all other churches must confess their dependence on Rome or be cast aside as dead branches.

The papists talked much of the Church catholic, but "they obtrude their own piece unto us, circumscribing the Church of Christ within the precincts of the Romish jurisdiction." In doing so they placed the churches of the east and of Asia, the Greek and Russian Orthodox, the Christians of Africa, and the Protestants of Europe, beyond the bounds of the catholic Church, outside of which there is no salvation. They are not recognized as Christ's subjects simply because they are not the pope's subjects, and are therefore damned in the eyes of Rome. Reformed Protestants might not talk so much of the universality of the church "but hold to the truth of it" and "cannot find in our hearts to pass such a bloody sentence upon so many poor souls that have given their names to Christ."

The unity of the Church lies in the "unity of faith," but how is this unity of faith preserved, one might ask, if there is no one church set above all the rest, and one bishop above all others? Ussher responded that unity must not be rooted in "any politic tricks of man's devising," but rather "compassed by such means as God hath ordained." Those means lie in the teaching office of the church, the prophets, apostles, evangelists, pastors and teachers. Scripture speaks of these as a plurality, and it is beyond belief that maintenance of unity depends on a single person overlooked in Ephesians 4:11. That a multitude of teachers, scattered all over the world, should agree in the foundations of the faith is a special work of God's Spirit. Ussher then proceeded to a discussion of these foundations. These are a rule of faith, common to all, capable of being grasped by "common Christians" since heaven was not "prepared for deep clerks only." These propositions are few and "of so much weight and moment" that they will be sufficient to make one wise unto salvation.[37] Ussher found these fundamentals in the early creeds which the ancient church used in catechesis prior to baptism and admission to the fellowship of the Church. It is worth noting that they do not include episcopal succession. These foundations can be obscured or perhaps even overturned by the superstructure which is subsequently built on them.

This led Ussher to deal again with the question of "our forefathers, who lived in the communion of the church of Rome" before the Reformation. This was a pastoral issue, the question being one that troubled many. Ussher reassured the court that "we have no reason to think otherwise, but that they lived and died under the mercy of God." He insisted that the papacy must be distinguished from the church it dwells in, just as the "man of sin" is distinguished from the temple of God in which he sits in 2 Thessalonians 2:4. Antichrist might build "with vile and pernicious matter" and threaten the foundations, but many of the laity lived in ignorance of these perversions. The foundations were so deeply imprinted and reinforced through the liturgical calendar with its commemoration of Trinity, nativity, passion, resurrection, and ascension, that the memory of these things continued. Ussher could point to the literature of the medieval *ars moriendi* ("art of dying") where one finds examples of men and women on their deathbed being instructed to place all their confidence in Christ's death only, and hope to come to glory through his merits, not their own. Where the foundations were held and the most dangerous errors were not known or accepted, then one must trust that "God had fitted a subject for his mercy to work upon." "Members of the Roman Church perhaps they

---

[37] On attempts to establish the fundamental points of religion, see Graham Windsor, "The Reunion Views of Archbishop Ussher and his Circle," *The Churchman* 77 (1963): 163–74.

were," Ussher concluded, "but such as by God's goodness were preserved from the mortality of popery that reigned there."

A second question was "Where was your church before Luther?" "Our church," Ussher answered, "was even there where it now is," in all places where the ancient foundations were retained. Taking this line, Ussher had no need to seek gospel succession in fringe groups. Protestants brought no new faith and no new church. They preached the same catholic faith that had always been preached and rather than beginning a new church had sought to reform the old. A tree pruned is not another tree, "neither is the Church *reformed* in our days another Church than that which was *deformed* in the days of our forefathers; though it hath no agreement, for all that, with popery." God's great power is manifested in his preservation of his Church even through the dark days of popery.

Ussher believed that ignorance of the foundations of the faith had done even more harm in Ireland than "the vulgar superstitions of popery." He had urged those on the other side of the confessional divide, whatever their differences in other matters, to join with him in teaching "those main points, the knowledge whereof was so necessary unto salvation, and of the truth whereof there was no controversy betwixt us." Little came of this, perhaps due to the "jealousies" bred by religious differences, and the people were still living in ignorance. No doubt Ussher made capital here from depicting his opponents as uncharitable and unreasonable, but this passage of the sermon also resonates with the thesis that much missional effort in the sixteenth and seventeenth centuries was dedicated to primary Christianization rather than simply competing for confessional allegiance.[38] The situation in England was different, and Ussher could praise "your Majesty's care" in ordering that regular catechizing be part of the ordinary ministry. This laid the foundation, and Ussher wished that the order was executed everywhere. Learned scholars may think it beneath them to teach the rudiments of the faith, but to make an ignorant man understand these is a great test of skill and is essential: "Let us preach never so many sermons unto the people, our labour is but lost, as long as the foundation is unlaid, and the first principles untaught, upon which all other doctrine must be builded."

---

[38] See, for example, the argument in Scott H. Hendrix, *Recultivating the Vineyard: The Reformation Agendas of Christianization* (Louisville, KY: Westminster John Knox Press, 2004).

Ussher's text rises higher than the foundations, anticipating the believer's growth and maturity. The perfection of which the Apostle speaks is not absolute. No Christian will attain that state in this life. It points to maturity rather than childhood. It is an "imperfect kind of perfection." Ussher closes the sermon with an exhortation to proceed from "faith to faith," with the expectation that the other graces will thence "ripen." The tone that Ussher has taken is more moderate and irenic than in the previous sermons included here. There are recurring polemical notes. The papacy is clearly identified with Antichrist, and Ussher longs to see English-style catechesis dispelling the Romish darkness in Ireland. The emphasis, however, is on that which unites the faithful, the common foundations on which a diversity of superstructures may be erected. The sermon would surely have pleased a king who had long hoped to see reconciliation and the peace of Christendom.[39] It was also highly topical, delivered at the height of controversy around John Percy, or "Fisher the Jesuit," and dealing with the issues thrown up during that controversy.[40]

The sermon was answered in *A Briefe Confutation* by the turbulent priest Paul Harris, an often humorous mix of reasoned argument, misrepresentation, and *ad hominem* attacks. He likened Ussher's "new" church, gathered from the four corners of the earth to the "enchanted castles in the air, made by the art, and spell, of cunning wizards" in romance novels. He expected more: "I doubt not but at your next pulpitting, you will pluck in the Jews, and the Turks also." The basic argument was that Jews and Muslims differed less from a "Geneva Puritan" than churches such as the Greek and Russian Orthodox, a point which might perhaps appear more plausible once Luther and Calvin have been represented as decidedly shaky on the doctrine of the Trinity. On many important criteria the Greek and Russian churches were closer to Rome, and the Reformed religion closer to Judaism and Islam. Ussher's church was indeed "no Church, but a meer *ens rationis*,

---

[39] For an excellent overview of James's aspirations and efforts in this regard, see Patterson, *King James*.

[40] For the context, see Timothy H. Wadkins, "The Percy-'Fisher' Controversies and the Ecclesiastical Politics of Jacobean Anti-Catholicism, 1622–1625," *Church History* 57 (1988): 153–69; Peter Milward, *Religious Controversies of the Jacobean Age: A Survey of Printed Sources* (London: Scolar Press, 1978), 216–27.

composed of shadows, negations, privations."[41] Harris moved towards a close with an uncomfortably personal plea:

> I understand, M. Usher, that you have a virtuous matron to your mother yet living in Ireland, who daily laments your wilfulness, and with wet eyes, prays to heaven for your conversion. O let not the son of so many tears, go longer astray, to the grief, and discomfort of the natural mother, the scandal of our spiritual mother, the Catholic Church, and the utter ruin and damnation of your own soul.[42]

Ussher did not condescend to reply.

Before King Charles at Greenwich, 1626

The final sermon included here was preached at Greenwich before King Charles on 25 June 1626 in much altered circumstances. Charles had come to the throne in 1625 upon the death of King James. He was reassuringly hostile towards Spain after the fiasco of courting Maria Anna, the Spanish Infanta. His marriage to the French princess Henrietta Maria, however, gave rise to fears that he might prove more tolerant towards Catholics than his father had been. Bitter controversy had also erupted over the writings of Richard Montagu, an English clergyman who was widely denounced as an Arminian. He was perceived to be distancing the Church of England from a distinctively Reformed theology, situating it as a *via media* between Geneva and Rome, though in reality he was simply defending certain minority positions for which the Reformed tradition had more latitude before the Synod of Dort.[43] It was not yet clear how fully the new king's sympathies lay with

---

[41] Paulus Veridicus [Paul Harris], *A Briefe Confutation of Certaine Absurd, Hereticall and Damnable Doctrines, delivered by Mr. James Usher, in a sermon, preached before King James our late soveraigne, at Wansted, Iune 20. anno domini 1624* (St. Omer, 1627; republished in *English Recusant Literature 1558–1640*, vol. 161 (Menston: Scolar Press, 1973); and a second edition at Antwerp (1639), esp. 3, 8, 18–19, 31, 40; *Ens rationis*, lit. a being of reason, an abstraction having no existence outside the mind.

[42] *Briefe Confutation*, 71. Harris followed this with a paraphrase on Baruch 4:2, *Convertere Iacob* ... ("Turn thee, O Jacob ..." in KJV), Ussher's name "James" being *Iacobus* in Latin.

[43] For a reading of Montagu's theology as broadly Reformed, see Collier, *Debating Perseverance*, 93–123.

the Arminian party but Buckingham's refusal to endorse the articles of the Synod of Dort at the York House Conference in February 1626 gave an early indication of the way the political winds might be blowing.

Ussher's sermons around this time often sound a sombre warning note. Preaching alongside John Preston at the end of 1625 during a fast at Hatfield Broad Oak in Essex, the home of the influential Barrington family, Ussher warned the godly that like Christ they would have to suffer outside the camp and that they must "be content to suffer all manner of reproaches for his name's sake."[44] On 27 March 1626, the first anniversary of King James's death, Ussher preached in St. Mary's, Cambridge on 1 Sam. 12:24–25: "Only fear the LORD, and serve him in truth with all your heart: for consider how great things he hath done for you. But if ye shall still do wickedly, ye shall be consumed, both ye and your king."[45] This was one of a number of occasions on which Ussher was later deemed to have spoken prophetically of national calamity.[46] Just a week after the Greenwich sermon, shortly before his return to Ireland, Ussher preached on 1 Peter 4:17 at Islington, echoing the caution that "judgement must begin with the house of God." The godly should not be surprised at the "fiery trial" that they are experiencing (v. 12), and worse was likely to come: "Take that for a rule, when God hath suffered the gospel to be preached to a nation and coming to look for fruit he finds none ... then it is the time." God has been patient and looked for fruit year after year, but soon the axe of judgement will fall.[47]

The sermon before Charles was no doubt preached in the Chapel Royal of Greenwich Palace, on the banks of the Thames downstream from London. The chapel had been extensively renovated between 1623 and 1625 under the supervision of Lancelot Andrewes, Dean of the Chapel Royal, and the architect Inigo Jones. The imagery of the chapel was a concession to Catholic aesthetic preferences at a time when King James still

---

[44] See Heb. 13:11–13; Essex Record Office, D/DBa F5/1, fol. 4r. The notes are in the hand of John Kendall, steward to Sir Thomas Barrington.

[45] Bodleian Library, MS Rawlinson D1290, fol. 63v.

[46] Bernard, *Life*, 86; See also Ute Lotz-Heumann, "'The Spirit of Prophecy Has Not Wholly Left the World': The Stylisation of Archbishop James Ussher as a Prophet," in *Religion and Superstition in Reformation Europe*, ed. Helen Parish and W. G. Naphy (Manchester: Manchester University Press, 2002), 119–32.

[47] Bodleian Library, MS Eng.th.e.25, fols 125r, 137v–138v.

sought an *entente* with Spain. The colourful decoration of the east end probably included a life-size mural series of the prophets and apostles, and silver
crucifixes were seen in royal chapels from the early 1620s. Perhaps the most
striking feature, however, was the royal closet at the west end, facing and
elevated above the preacher, thus asserting royal supremacy in the Church
of England.[48]

Ussher took as his text 1 Corinthians 14:33: "For God is not the author of confusion, but of peace, as in all the churches of the saints." Ussher
applied Paul's instructions on order in prophesying to the problem of ecclesiastical disputes and the locus of authority. Discord and sedition arise in
the Church when men teach as they please "without control." There must
be order and the Apostle urges "let the spirit of the prophets be subject
unto the prophets." Two or three may speak and the others judge what they
say. They have liberty in speaking but must not imagine that they can be
without censure. They must be content to submit to the greater number of
the company.

So often the root of contention in the Church can be found in
"worldly respects" and "temporal ends." This was certainly the case in the
Netherlands, riven and almost destroyed by faction, and now held up as a
warning. Contention had already begun in England, however, over the same
matters, and there was a danger that things would spiral out of control before people realized the gravity of situation: "We see the prognostication of
our ruin before our eyes and yet we are not sensible of it. We see distemper
in the state and dissention in the Church and yet persuade ourselves all will
be well, and that wisdom and policy will hold us out. Beloved, this may not
be." Ussher was conscious that his address was becoming more direct than
court decorum permitted and that he was now touching on matters of state.
He insisted "I intrude not. Far be it from me to meddle with matters of
state. I leave that to my superiors to whom it doth belong. But my text
leads me to all the churches of the saints. Here I am sure I am within my
own element." It was his duty as a preacher to follow and apply his text.

Ussher pleaded for an end to name-calling. He was particularly ag-
grieved that "that odious and contemptible name of Puritans" had been
foisted on conforming Calvinists in an attempt to paint them in the colours

---

[48] On the architectural setting, see Peter E. McCullough, *Sermons at Court: Politics and
Religion in Elizabethan and Jacobean Preaching* (Cambridge: Cambridge University Press,
1998), 32–35.

of sedition. Their doctrine was the same, "no more, no less," as that maintained by King James and who would dare call him "Puritan"? Those who opposed the incursion of Arminian ideas were not the seditious fringe but the mainstream. Their doctrine was not innovation but the faith they were raised in, the teaching of the national church and their late sovereign. He also urged those who had brought in "new doctrine" and thus disturbed the peace to submit to the majority. They might feel they had right on their side but they should hold their peace for the sake of order. The matters in question did not concern the foundations of the faith, the essential truths without which none can be saved, so they could safely submit to the greater number. Ussher insisted that if he himself were an Arminian this was the course he would take. This is God's means of preserving order in the Church and the principle upon which councils are founded.

Having insisted that he would "intrude not" on matters of state, as Ussher moved to conclude he directly questioned the wisdom of the recent royal proclamation banning both sides from discussion of the controverted points:[49] "it was not so good advice given as might have been, that both sides should be stopped. It is not an easy matter to silence a multitude in that they have been born, bred, and taught in, as to keep in order a few." Aware of the risk he was taking he added, "I need not make an apology for myself, my heart being upright, and it being the last time perhaps that I may ever speak unto you." It was not the last time that Ussher would speak with Charles. Ussher would attend Charles's belated Scottish coronation in July 1633, settle in Royalist Oxford during the first civil war, and counsel and preach before Charles in his captivity on the Isle of Wight in 1648. His absence from England from 1626 until 1640, however, did serve to vindicate his fears that such outspokenness before the king would force a move from the centre to the margins. When he did return in 1640, it would be to witness the destruction that he had predicted.

The account of the sermon reproduced here is based on a manuscript witness, the version appearing in Elrington's edition of the *Works*, the only published account so far, being somewhat shorter and likely redacted by Elrington.[50] The sermon is strikingly frank as Ussher seeks to persuade king

---

[49] *A Proclamation for the Establishing of the Peace and Quiet of the Church of England* (1626).

[50] See the footnotes to the text for specific instances of suspected editorial intervention. For a discussion of Elrington's high-church prejudices and their impact on *WJU*, see Jamie Blake-Knox, "High-Church History: C. R. Elrington and His Edi-

and court. The words "you see" occur 20 times (21 including the interrogative "Will you see…?") as Ussher attempts to demonstrate the truth of his argument by the standard of Scripture. It is also remarkably plain in style and features only two references to extra-biblical authorities (one to Jerome, the other to Augustine). This is in noticeable contrast to the other sermons gathered here. The sermons preached before the Commons and before King James may have been embellished somewhat as Ussher prepared them for the press, but his preparatory notes are laden with classical, patristic, medieval and early modern citations, and the Temple Church manuscript, probably derived from an auditor's notes, contains its fair share. It seems that on this occasion, despite the elite audience, Ussher wanted his argument to be as clear, as forceful, and as scriptural as possible.

Episcopacy

Ussher returned to England in May 1640 in much-changed circumstances. It was a time of high political tension.[51] Charles, in pursuit of a vision of ecclesiastical uniformity across his dominions, had attempted to impose a Book of Common Prayer on his Scottish kingdom in 1637. This led to riots and rebellion, and formal opposition under a National Covenant. The General Assembly which met in Glasgow in November 1638 not only abolished the new liturgy but also voted to depose the bishops, episcopacy having been rather awkwardly grafted onto the Scottish presbyterian system by King James in 1584. Charles tried to cow the Scots with a show of force, but his expedition northwards was inconclusive and he failed to engage beyond minor skirmishes. A peace was agreed in 1639, referring disputed questions to a forthcoming General Assembly and a meeting of the Parliament of Scotland, but this General Assembly declared itself free of royal control and upheld the decisions of 1638.

Charles would require a parliamentary grant in England to raise the sums of money needed to subdue Scotland militarily, so after eleven years

---

tion of James Ussher's Works," in *The Church of Ireland and its Past: History, Interpretation and Identity*, ed. Mark Empey, Alan Ford, and Miriam Moffitt (Dublin: Four Courts Press, 2017), 74–94.

[51] For a concise account of this period, see David Scott, *Politics and War in the Three Stuart Kingdoms, 1637–49* (Basingstoke: Palgrave Macmillan, 2004), 1–67; and also Austin Woolrych, *Britain in Revolution, 1625–1660* (Oxford: Oxford University Press, 2002), 85–233.

of personal rule in the absence of a parliament he was forced to call one. Charles could not manage this parliament as eleven years of grievances sought a voice, and he dissolved the Short Parliament on 5 May, after only three weeks' sitting. Not least among these grievances was the matter of religion. There was unrest over innovations in ceremonies and the government of the church, particularly the heavy-handed manner of dealing with those who evidenced traits of Puritanism. The conduct of the bishops over the last fifteen years prompted many to question episcopacy itself and the government of the church would emerge as one of the major debates of the 1640s.

Ussher had close associates on both sides of the political divide and was respected by both the king and his opponents. To parliamentarians Ussher was a model bishop, a stark contrast to the Laudian prelates. He was a Calvinist, a preacher, a scholar, and something of a martyr at the hands of Wentworth and Laud. During this period he was in regular contact with leading godly parliamentarians such as the Earl of Warwick, John Pym, Sir Simmonds D'Ewes, and Sir Edward Dering, all active leaders of the opposition to the King in the Long Parliament which sat from 3 November 1640. At the same time, however, as a loyal subject, Ussher was meeting with Charles and counselling him. The political situation had not yet reached the point where Ussher would effectively have to choose a side, and he can be viewed as a mediating figure at this time.[52]

The petition signed by many citizens "in and about the City of London" and submitted to the Commons on 11 December 1640 is a useful barometer of the animus against episcopacy in some quarters. Subsequently known as the "root and branch petition" it opposed "the government of archbishops and lord bishops, deans and archdeacons, &c," and insisted that "the said government, with all its dependencies, roots and branches, may be abolished" and government established "according to God's word."[53] Other Reformed churches had with the Pope, "cast the prelates out also as members of the beast."[54] A motion to impeach Laud was moved just a few days later. The Laudian regime would clearly have to go, but a more difficult question presented itself: What type of ecclesiastical govern-

---

[52] For this phase of his career, see Ford, *James Ussher*, 223–56.

[53] S. R. Gardiner, *Constitutional Documents of the Puritan Revolution, 1625–1660*, 3rd ed. (Oxford: Clarendon Press, 1906), 137–38.

[54] Gardiner, *Constitutional Documents*, 140.

ment should replace it? The Commons were reluctant to proceed far in this direction as difference of opinion over the preferred replacement could reveal divisions within the parliamentary alliance. Some would go so far as presbyterian settlement with the Scots, others inclined towards a congregationalist polity, whilst others favoured an Erastian settlement with the church firmly under the control of Parliament. Many wanted to preserve episcopacy, returning to the Calvinist episcopate of Elizabeth and James. They would turn back the clock to the time before the Laudian innovations, but others would go further still, seeking to return to the primitive episcopacy of the early church.

Ussher was advocating this latter position soon after his return to England. In December 1640, Robert Baillie recognised Ussher "and a great faction with him" as being in favour of "a limited good, and ... calked episcopacy."[55] In January, reported Sir John Temple, Ussher, along with Ralph Brownrigg and Richard Holdsworth, were to appear before the King: "My Lord Primate desires much to have them [bishops] moulded into the ancient primitive way, and to see them reduced into the same state wherein they continued many hundred years after Christ." Ussher would make a "proposition" in this matter which "hath been very little understood of late by any of our divines."[56]

Ussher had two aims in his writings on episcopacy at this time: to establish its antiquity and to apply the early model to the contemporary situation. His research on the letters of Ignatius would provide a central strand of his argument for the antiquity of episcopacy. The authority of these epistles was disputed. It was unclear which of the twelve letters attributed to Ignatius were authentic and to what extent later interpolations had tainted the genuine ones. Conformists happily cited them as proof of the early, even apostolic, origin of episcopacy, whilst puritans dismissed them as pseudepigraphal, as misleading fakes. One of Ussher's greatest scholarly achievements was unravelling this textual tangle. By identifying two manuscripts which contained accurate texts he was able to establish the Ignatian

---

[55] *The Letters and Journals of Robert Baillie*, ed. David Laing, 3 vols (Edinburgh: Bannatyne Club, 1841–43), 1:287.

[56] *Report on the Manuscripts of the Right Honourable Viscount De L'Isle & Dudley*, 6 vols (London: Historical Manuscripts Commission, 1925–66), 6:368; Bernard states that the *Reduction of Episcopacy* was presented to the King in 1641. Bernard, *Clavi Trabales; or, Nailes Fastned by some Great Masters of Assemblyes* (1661), 54.

canon.[57] The modern scholarly consensus is that Ussher was mistaken in jettisoning the genuine epistle to Polycarp but otherwise his insights have stood up well to the scrutiny of the succeeding centuries. He was able to confirm that episcopacy was not a late development but can be traced back to the earliest days of the Christian church.

The Original of Bishops and Metropolitans

Ussher's contribution to the pamphlet war over church government began in late May 1641 with the publication of *The Judgement of Doctor Rainoldes Touching the Original of Episcopacy*. Later the same year, his *Original of Bishops and Metropolitans* was published in *Certain Brief Treatises Written by Diverse Learned Men, Concerning the Ancient and Modern Government of the Church*. This was expanded by folding in much of *The Judgement of Doctor Rainoldes* and published in *Confessions and Proofes of Protestant Divines of Reformed Churches, that Episcopacy is in respect of Office according to the Word of God, and in respect of the Use the Best* (1644). It is in this latter form that *Original of Bishops and Metropolitans* appears here in this volume.

Ussher began by arguing that "the ground of episcopacy is derived partly from the pattern prescribed by God in the Old Testament, and partly from the imitation thereof brought in by the apostles, and confirmed by Christ himself in the time of the New." Episcopacy arises not as an innovation of post-Apostolic times but as the outworking of a "pattern prescribed by God" in the Old Testament. There was no parity among priests and Levites, but a hierarchy, with both orders governed by heads and rulers. Ussher points out that these heads were even given the title of ἐπίσκοπος (*episcopos*) or "bishop" in the Septuagint (Neh. 11:14, 22). Ministers of the gospel are successors of the priests and Levites, not in serving at the altar as that typological role has ceased with Christ's once for all sacrifice, but as teachers of the people (1 Tim. 3:2; cf. Deut. 33:10) who are given maintenance in their sacred duty (1 Cor. 9:13–14). The important differences between ministers of the Old and New Covenants should not obscure all similarity. Why, Ussher asked, may the principle of hierarchical ordering not continue?

---

[57] James Ussher, *Polycarpi et Ignatii Epistolae* (Oxford, 1644), in part reproduced in *WJU*, 7:87–267; See also Hugh de Quehen, "Politics and Scholarship in the Ignatian Controversy," *Seventeenth Century* 13 (1998): 69–84.

With what show of reason then can any man imagine, that what was instituted by God in the Law, for mere matter of government and preservation of good order, without all respect of type or ceremony, should now be rejected in the Gospel, as a device of Antichrist? that what was by the Lord once "planted a noble vine, wholly a right seed," should now be so "turned into the degenerate plant of a strange vine"; that no purging or pruning of it will serve the turn, but it must be cut down root and branch, as "a plant which our heavenly Father had never planted?" But nothing being so familiar nowadays, as to father upon Antichrist, whatsoever in church matters we do not find to suit with our own humours: the safest way will be, to consult with Christ himself herein, and hear what he delivers in the cause.[58]

Ussher proceeded to argue that the pattern is indeed confirmed by Christ and his Apostles. When the risen Christ addresses the seven angels of the seven churches of Asia in the opening chapters of Revelation, he addresses not the presbyters collectively but the bishops of those churches. Ussher conceded that there was a plurality of elders in the church at Ephesus, and the name "elder" was then interchangeable with "bishop" (Acts 20:17, 28). But in addressing one as the "angel" (Rev. 2:1) he signals the "eminency" of one above the others. Whilst ἄγγελος (*angelos*) is usually rendered as "angel" in Bible translations, it does not always denote a supernatural being. The word simply means "messenger" and can be used of humans: indeed Ussher went on to state that the other elders were "in their own several stations accounted angels or messengers of the Lord of Hosts," but Christ singles out one as he addresses each church.

Ignatius of Antioch, writing no more than twelve years after John, addressed the president of the presbyters as "bishop." To the church of Ephesus he wrote that their presbytery were "so conjoined with their bishop, as the strings are with a harp" and went on to exhort them to "obey both the bishop and the presbytery, with an undivided mind." Similarly, he wrote to the church at Smyrna, urging them to "follow their bishop, as

---

[58] Quotations are from Jer. 2:21 and Matt. 15:13; The expression "root and branch" likely reflects the radical language of the root and branch petition, etc. On the practice of labelling one's episcopal opponents as "Antichrist," see Christopher Hill, *Antichrist in Seventeenth-Century England* (London: Oxford University Press, 1971), esp. 69–77.

Christ Jesus did his Father, and the presbytery, as the apostles." The bishop of Smyrna at this time was Polycarp, who had been instituted there by the apostles. As bishop of Smyrna at the time John wrote Revelation he was "the angel" of the church of Smyrna. Similar arguments posit Timothy as "the angel" of the church at Ephesus. Ignatius himself was reported to have been ordained bishop by Peter. Ussher set forth many other testimonies to apostolic ordination of bishops from early writers such as Irenaeus and Tertullian. Episcopal ordination can then be seen to operate in succession down through the centuries, though Ussher's tying of its institution in England to the peregrinations of Peter is somewhat tenuous.

Ussher then developed his case to support the metropolitan jurisdiction and thus a more elaborate hierarchy. John, after his return from Patmos, governed the church in the metropolis of Ephesus, assisted by seven bishops, and ordaining bishops in other churches. Surely this pattern was already in operation. When John had written to the churches in Asia, he addressed seven by name, not because there were only seven churches, but because these seven had a "degree of eminency" among the others. They did "in some sort ... comprehend all the rest under them." All the other churches were understood to be in some manner standing in relation to these seven. Ussher shows that the seven churches were located in metropolitical centres of secular government, cities from which justice was administered over the surrounding regions. The churches of these cities naturally took a lead in the ecclesiastical affairs of those regions.[59] These seven churches were not "bare parochial ones" or simply particular congregations, but "diocesan churches ... if not metropolitical."

Again, Ussher could produce examples of such authority from early in the history of the church. Ignatius wrote a letter to the church "which had presidency in the place of the region of the Romans." This was not simply the congregation at Rome, but a church which stood pre-eminent in a particular region. At one point in the letter Ignatius styled himself bishop of Syria, suggesting that his authority was similarly not limited to Antioch but extended over a province. After further examples Ussher returned to

[59] This argument was supported by another piece from Ussher, *A Geographicall and Historicall Disquisition, touching the Lydian or Proconsular Asia; and the seven Metropolitical Churches contained therein*, first published in *Certain Briefe Treatises* (1641), 76–96. This was issued separately (Oxford, 1643) and also later accompanying *The Original of Bishops and Metropolitans* in Latin translation in *Jacobi Usserii Archiepiscopi Armachani, Opuscula Duo* (1687, 1688). It can be found in *WJU*, 7:1–39.

the Apostolic age, to Titus and his commission to ordain elders in every city in Crete, his authority encompassing the whole island. He echoes John Jewel's question: "Having the government of many bishops, what may we call him but an archbishop?" Going further back in time, into the Old Testament and the hierarchy of priests and Levites, he notes Eleazar's status as "the president of the presidents of the Levites" (Num. 3:32). Surely none giving this serious attention "would much stick to afford unto him the name of an archbishop."

Ussher has argued that the pattern of episcopal government can be seen in the Old Testament, in the ministry of Christ and the Apostles, and in the history the age following. Episcopacy is not simply the best form of church government or the one most suited to the circumstances of the Church of England. It is scriptural. The argument of *Original of Bishops and Metropolitans* is dense, but its cumulative case for the consistency of episcopacy with biblical revelation is impressive and bears careful consideration.

The Reduction of Episcopacy

Ussher's other major contribution to seventeenth-century debates about church government was *The Reduction of Episcopacy* which was probably composed in early 1641, but not appearing in print until after his death in 1656. This was an attempt to implement his vision of primitive episcopacy in the Church of England and was proposed as a mediating position between presbyterian and more conservative episcopalian polities. It opens in a manner familiar to readers of *The Original of Bishops and Metropolitans*, conceding a plurality of elders equal in status but observing that one was singled out as pre-eminent. In the course of time it would become the custom to call this presiding elder by the name of "bishop." The *Reduction* explains how bishop and presbyters could work together in such a way that they produced the harmony of which Ignatius wrote and reflected the practice of the earliest centuries of the Church.

Bishops were to preside over but operate with their clergy in a more consensual fashion than the prelatical manner which had become the norm. They were not to hear or judge any cause without the presbyters and any sentence pronounced would be void in their absence. Ussher admits that "this kind of presbyterial government hath been long disused," but, he continues:

how easily this ancient form of government by the united suffrages of the clergy might be revived again, and with what little show of alteration the synodical conventions of the pastors of every parish might be accorded with the presidency of the bishops of each diocese and province, the indifferent reader may quickly perceive by the perusal of the ensuing propositions.

Ussher then proceeds to describe a tiered structure, rising from the pastor administering discipline at the parish level, up through deanery, diocesan and national synods. The pastor or rector exercises a ministry of word, sacrament, and discipline in the parish. The right to administer discipline should be restored to the pastor who, with church wardens and sidesmen, will meet weekly to admonish those who "live scandalously." If they do not repent and mend their ways they can be barred from the Lord's Supper and presented at the next monthly synod. Suffragan bishops preside over these monthly synods which bring together all the pastors from an area equivalent to a rural deanery. The synod can pronounce the sentence of excommunication on unrepentant offenders and hold the parish ministers to account for their doctrine and conduct. Appeal may be made from this synod to a diocesan synod, meeting once or twice a year and chaired by "the bishop, or superintendent (call him whether you will)" or a deputed suffragan serving as "moderator." More difficult matters could be referred to two provincial synods, Canterbury in the south and York in the north, which would comprise the bishops, suffragans, and elected clergy from every diocese, with an archbishop presiding. These should meet every third year, and if parliament is sitting they could join as one national synod.

This scheme was constructed from the ground up, rather than top down as in the papal hierarchy. It decentralized authority and provided some safeguards against dictatorial prelacy. The tract was irenic in its tone. Ussher sought to win over those Puritans who leaned towards a presbyterian position by ensuring that discipline in the parish is foundational. He makes a terminological concession on "the bishop, or superintendent, call him whether you will," because for him the function of the office rather than the name was the matter worth contending for. Words such as "assembly" and "moderator" are also calculated to resonate with such readers. The side notes in the first edition map the elements of his scheme onto the equivalent Scottish structures in order to demonstrate that the distance between them is not so great. There are differences, however. Whilst the pastor meets with the wardens and sidesmen for the exercise of discipline, there is nothing to suggest that their role equates to that of Scottish lay elders. In Scotland the role of moderator rotated, but in Ussher's scheme the moderator would continue in post just as English bishops did. There were a number of important points which were not addressed, perhaps intentionally, not least how this scheme would account for the royal supremacy in the Church of England. Alan Ford observes that it is "undeniable" that the *Reduction of Episcopacy* "raised a whole host of unanswered practical questions, such as the role of clergy in ordination and the king in selecting bishops, the fate of the church courts, and the precise location of authority within the new structures."[60]

Although the concept of a reformed or reduced episcopacy has become associated with Ussher's name, such ideas had precedent in the schemes of moderate episcopacy proposed by Francis Mason and others during the reigns of Elizabeth and James.[61] There were other variations on this theme proposed in the early 1640s.[62] Ussher probably circulated the *Reduction* in manuscript in early 1641. Little is known about its distribution and reception, but hard evidence for widespread circulation is lacking. William Abbott notes that considering Ussher's stature and the interest in other proposals for modified episcopacy at this time it is remarkable how the existence of Ussher's manuscript leaves almost no trace in contemporary documents such as diaries and letters. Nor can awareness of the manuscript be inferred from polemical tracts such as Baillie's *Unlawfulness and Danger of Limited Episcopacie*, where the content and terminology give no indication that he was responding to Ussher's proposals. Abbott insists that "such

---

[60] Ford, *James Ussher*, 251.

[61] Patrick Collinson, "Episcopacy and Reform in England in the Later Sixteenth Century," in *Godly People: Essays on English Protestantism and Puritanism* (London: Hambledon Press, 1983), 155–89.

[62] James C. Spalding and Maynard F. Brass, "Reduction of Episcopacy as a Means to Unity in England, 1640–1662," *Church History* 30 (1961): 414–32; Maynard F. Brass, "Moderate Episcopacy, 1640–1662" (unpublished doctoral dissertation, State University of Iowa, 1962); William M. Abbott, "The Issue of Episcopacy in the Long Parliament, 1640–1648: The Reasons for Abolition" (unpublished doctoral dissertation, University of Oxford, 1981).

references are similarly missing from all of the contemporary pamphlets that deal with the episcopal issue."[63]

The *Reduction* did not fare well as the parties polarized on this issue. The Scots were firmly opposed to any form of episcopacy and Parliament would become increasingly reliant on their support and unable to pursue such a compromise settlement. The King also signalled that a scheme such as Ussher's would not be acceptable. Speaking at Whitehall on 25 January 1641, Charles stated his intention to reduce "all Matters of Religion and Government to what they were in the purest Times of Queen Elizabeth's Days." He warned against petitions that would pull down episcopacy and proposals that would have bishops "no better than Cyphers."[64] In October he would again affirm that "I am constant for the doctrine and discipline of the Church of England as it was established by Queene Elis. and my father."[65] In all likelihood it was the King's disapproval of such reforms that prevented Ussher from distributing the manuscript of the *Reduction* more widely. For example, from March 1641 Ussher was called to consult a House of Lords committee on religion and there is no evidence that he submitted his scheme to the committee, whilst reform proposals from Sir Edward Dering, MP for Kent, and John Williams, Bishop of Lincoln, were debated in Parliament and the focus of much interest.

It seems that Ussher continued to harbour hopes that the *Reduction* would provide a way forward through the debates over polity. As late as May 1641 he was discussing the details of his plan with the Dutch ambassador.[66] It seems that the King did give further consideration to Ussher's ideas and reduced episcopacy is reflected in the royal response to

---

[63] William M. Abbot, "James Ussher and 'Ussherian' Episcopacy, 1640–1656: The Primate and His Reduction Manuscript," *Albion* 22 (1990): 237–59 (248); *contra* Jack P. Cunningham, "The *Eirenicon* and the 'Primitive Episcopacy' of James Ussher: An Irish Panacea for Britannia's Ailment," *Reformation and Renaissance Review* 8 (2006): 128–46 (131), who claims that Ussher's proposals were directly answered by Alexander Henderson, *The Unlawfulness and Danger of Limited Prelacie, or Perpetual Precidencie in the Church, Briefly Discovered* (s.l. [London?], 1641).

[64] *Journal of the House of Lords: Volume IV, 1629–42* (London, 1771), 142.

[65] *Diary and Correspondence of John Evelyn*, ed. William Bray, 4 vols (London, 1859–62), 4:88.

[66] *Archives ou Correspondance inédite de la Maison d'Orange-Nassau, Deuxième Série, Tome III, 1625–1642*, ed. G. Groen van Prinsterer (Utrecht: Kemink et Fils, 1859), 439–40.

parliamentarian clergy during the negotiations at Newport on the Isle of Wight in September to November 1648, a response that was drafted before Ussher's arrival at Newport.[67] Alan Ford notes the irony: "royal stubbournness and political ineptitude meant that, when Ussher's proposal had the best opportunity for widespread acceptance, in 1641, Charles rejected it, and when it had little hope of success, in 1648, he endorsed it." In 1640 the King had missed the opportunity to occupy the middle ground so carefully prepared by Ussher.[68]

Are the *Reduction of Episcopacy* and *The Original of Bishops and Metropolitans* compatible? Or did Ussher execute an abrupt *volte face*, either in deference to the King's conservatism or out of fear of more radical positions that might be taken by parliamentarians? Did he offer a path of conciliation incorporating elements of a presbyterian polity but then fall back to a dogged defence of the status quo, his real belief all along?[69] There is nothing frankly incompatible between these two tracts, but there are certainly differences of tone and emphasis. The former is persuasive and practical, the latter defensive and polemical. The former insists that the bishop must not act without the presbyters, whilst the latter echoes Ignatius in demanding that the presbyters do nothing without the bishop. Whilst the first says little about the institution of bishops other than that they "obtained this honour … by good report," the latter foregrounds their apostolic appointment.

Despite these contrasts, there is a consistent picture of a bishop working with the presbyters to govern the flock, a man pre-eminent among the elders. In private conversation Ussher explicitly affirmed his conviction

---

[67] *The Kings Majesties Answer to the Paper Delivered in by the Reverend Divines* (1648), 13.

[68] Ford, *James Ussher*, 255.

[69] Writing after the Restoration, Nicholas Bernard claimed that Ussher had made concessions, an "accommodation" as the state faced a "total shipwreck" in 1641: "The merchant parts with that in a storm, that he would not have done in a calm, and at shore recruits himself with the like goods again." Bernard added that he had only published *The Reduction* in 1656 after "an imperfect copy invited unto it." Of course, in the altered circumstances of 1661 it was advantageous for Bernard to distance Ussher, and thus himself, from Presbyterianism. Bernard, *Clavi Trabales*, 54–55.

that their difference is one of degree not of order.[70] The presbyters could therefore work with the bishop in the exercise of powers which Laudians considered to be limited to the episcopal office. The Laudian elevation of the episcopal office also placed the Church of England at greater distance from the continental Reformed churches. Ussher's levelling made it easier to regard their ordination and sacraments as valid in the absence of an episcopate.[71] They were "true members of the Church universal," albeit "very much defective."[72]

The modern-day Church of England with a total of nearly one hundred diocesans and suffragans is closer to Ussher's vision than the Church of England of early 1641, but still falls a long way short, and at a time of falling attendance there is talk of merging dioceses. There have, however, been calls for devolution and the transformation of deaneries into small dioceses of twenty-five to thirty-five parishes to make the episcopal role more manageable and more pastoral. With appropriate support the bishop would remain fully functional in parish ministry himself. Citing Ussher in support, Michael Keulemans insists that this could be seen "as nothing more revolutionary than a return to something like the original function of the episcopate in the city dioceses scattered across the Roman Empire of the 4th century."[73] Others have found Ussher's writings to be helpful today. Wallace Benn, former Bishop of Lewes, found in Ussher's defence of episcopacy an antidote to the functional congregationalism so often encountered amongst evangelicals in the Church of England. Ussher's writings encouraged a broader ecclesiological view of a "Reformed Catholicism," an

---

[70] Van Prinsterer, ed., *Archives ou Correspondance inédite de la Maison d'Orange-Nassau … 1625–1642*, 439–40; See Bernard, *Clavi Trabales*, 56–57; *The Judgement of the Late Arch-Bishop of Armagh and Primate of Ireland, 1. Of the extent of Christs death and satisfaction, &c. 2. Of the Sabbath, and observation of the Lords day. 3. Of the ordination in other reformed churches*, ed. Nicholas Bernard (1658), 112.

[71] On the tension between *iure divino* episcopacy and the political necessity of affirming the validity of the ministry of the Reformed continental churches, see Anthony Milton, *Catholic and Reformed: The Roman and Protestant Churches in English Protestant Thought, 1600–1640* (Cambridge: Cambridge University Press, 1995), 465–66, 475–94.

[72] Bernard, ed., *The Judgement of the Late Arch-Bishop of Armagh*, 112–13.

[73] Michael Keulemans, *Bishops: The Changing Nature of the Anglican Episcopate in Mainland Britain* (Bloomington, IN: Xlibris, 2012), 257–59.

appreciation of episcopal government and motivation to work for its reform.[74] The scholarly discussion of these issues has, of course, moved on, but Ussher's writings on episcopacy remain stimulating and useful.[75]

---

[74] Wallace Benn, *Ussher on Bishops: A Reforming Ecclesiology* (London: St. Antholin's Lectureship Charity, 2002).

[75] See, for example, Alistair C. Stewart, *The Original Bishops: Office and Order in the First Christian Communities* (Grand Rapids: Baker Academic, 2014), with its self-conscious nod towards Ussher in the title (p. x); At a more introductory level, see Roger Beckwith, *Elders in Every City: The Origin and Role of the Ordained Ministry* (Carlisle: Paternoster, 2003).

A SERMON AT TEMPLE CHURCH (1620)

Notes taken of Doctor Ussher's Sermon at Temple Church 2nd July 1620.[1]

Revelation 19th chap. 20th v: And the beast was taken etc. [insertion: & with him the false prophet that wrought miracles before him. &c: These both were cast alive into a fiery lake burning with brimstone.]

THE APOSTLE Paul in the first Epistle of Timothy, the third and the end, having propounded the great mystery of godliness, which is great without all controversy, in the beginninge of the next chapter following parallels it with the mystery of iniquity. And having showed before the rule of faith, and this mystery of God manifested in the flesh, justified in the Spirit, seen of angels, preached unto the Gentiles, believed on in the world, received up into glory:[2] this is universal faith believed in the whole world, which all the fury of the enemy could never suppress. But where God builds his church, the devil will be sure to have his chapel. And because the mystery of godli-

---

[1] All footnotes to this sermon are editorial, there being none in the manuscript source. Square brackets around editorial footnotes have been dispensed with. All quotation marks are supplied by the editor. This sermon survives in Bodleian Library, MS Perrot 9 and has never been published before. Whilst this manuscript witness has its problems, the occasion and the nature of the material are such that its publication would seem to be warranted. Although there is no other known record of the sermon, some of its substance can also be found in Ussher's papers in Bodleian, MS Barlow 13, fols 85v–86r, in which he drafts a response to Edward Warren's request, in a letter of 14 Oct. 1617, for an explanation of Rev. 17:8, 11 (fol. 85r; *CJU*, 1:134–35). A neater manuscript copy of the response in another hand is preserved in Bodleian, MS Add. C299, fol. 108 (date unknown) and Ussher's views were published in *The Judgement of the Late Arch-Bishop of Armagh, and Primate of Ireland, of Babylon (Rev. 18.4.) being the present See of Rome*, ed. Nicholas Bernard (London, 1659), 13–20 (*WJU*, 12:545–50).

[2] 1 Tim. 3:16.

ness was great indeed, therefore the foundation must be laid deep in the earth and sure. For if popery had lifted itself up in the ancient fathers' time, they would have been the first that would have torn the flesh of the whore and burnt her with fire. But then popery wrought underground; whereas now it is as a leprosy in their foreheads, that a man may run and read it in their faces.[3] Yet in those times it was thought the part of a good minister of Jesus Christ to forearm the people and put them in mind of these things.[4] Therefore the Apostle warns them, and the Spirit speaks expressly and evidently, that in the latter time there should be a departure from the faith, and that there would be a controversy and giving heed to seducing spirits.[5] And as the church of Rome say, that we have made the revolt, so we say, it is they: and therefore because we have an evidence to discern of what so[rt][6] the error is, let us consider where the defection lieth. The Apostle saith that such should come as should speak lies in hypocrisy;[7] such as should come and preach lies openly, as Marcion,[8] and Arius, but lies in hypocrisy, lies guilded over as a cup full of fornica[tion][9] presented in a gilded bowl: that some false doctrines might have a veil of piety cast over them. And what are those? The Apostle sets down, that the simplest may understand. The Apostle names not the most dangerous and deep doctrines, such as were the disputations of the schoolmen, and the like, but the most evident, such as the simplest may understand and cannot baulk, as forbidding marriage, and making a difference of meats, which God hath created to be received

---

[3] This point is developed at greater length in Ussher, *An Answer to a Challenge Made by a Iesuite in Ireland* (Dublin, 1624), 1–3 (see *WJU*, 3:9–10), where Ussher responds to William Malone's challenge to specifically name the pope in whose reign the Christian faith was overthrown in Rome. Just as Ussher did not believe that Rome had been built in a day, he did not hold that "the great dunghill of errors, which now we see in it" was erected within the reign of any single pope. Rome's errors were not the type of flagrant heresies that would have been instantly recognisable in their frank opposition to the foundations of the faith. They were, rather, a manifestation of the "mystery of iniquity" (2 Thess. 2:7), wickedness cloaked by the semblance of piety. Their rise was insidious, their origins forgotten.

[4] 1 Tim. 4:6.

[5] 1 Tim. 4:1.

[6] Ending lost to binding.

[7] 1 Tim. 4:2.

[8] "Martins" in MS.

[9] See Rev. 17:4. Ending lost to binding.

with thanksgiving that they might believe and know the truth.[10] The simple cannot comprehend the mystery of transubstantiation and other high school points: but every one can discern and conceive the doctrine named by the Apostle: as forbidding marriage, and commanding to abstain from meats, etc.

Why then, is marriage absolutely forbidden? Or to abstain from meats absolutely? No certainly, it is not so meant, for then the seducers shall have few followers. But it is meant of those, that under the colour of religion, for the taming of the flesh do teach these doctrines.

Fasting is a duty, not a thing left to a man's liberty but a thing enjoined, but under colour of fasting only to change our dishes and to make a choice of meats, which God hath commanded to be received with thanksgiving, every creature being good and sanctified by the word of God and prayer.[11]

But this may be thought a matter not pertinent for this place and time, and you may say the minister hath a great want of matter when he brings controversies into the pulpit. But I see this error is spread abroad so far, and many have so favourable a conceit of these things, that if the Apostle to Timothy speaking of the same things said, "If thou put thy brethren in remembrance of these things, thou shalt be a good minister of Jesus Christ nourished up in the words of faith and of good doctrine where unto thou hast attained": If then Timothy did discharge his duty well in the beginning to put the brethren in remembrance when no such danger was, how much more now is it the part of a good minister when we are in the midst of these evil devices of Satan.

The man of God ought not to strive, nor to be contentious. If any man contend, we have no such custom, nor the Church of God.[12] For in matters indifferent, the man of God ought not to be so eager. There be great matters in the service of God for him to spend his spirits in.

These are the last days: let the adversary show me a matter of thirteen hundred years old: yet if it fall from the apostles' time the longer it holds, the worse it smells. For the truth was but once delivered unto the Church, if it comes afterward it comes into the Church too late to be received by a Christian from a very angel.

---

[10] 1 Tim. 4:3.

[11] 1 Tim. 4:3–5.

[12] 1 Cor. 11:16.

This Book of the Revelation unto the Church now, is instead of the prophesies of the Old Testament to the Church of old.

I choose this place to show, what should become of this whore that shall after so long time perish.

Here is the people deceived.

Here is the means, by which they were deceived.

And the number of them that were deceived.

And the issue: these both were cast into a lake of fire burning with brimstone. That though men think it a small matter to join with popery, yet those that are branded with this mark of the beast and worship his image, professing this religion and following this spirit, they must go together with the man of sin into a lake of fire burning with brimstone. You may think we speak somewhat censoriously: but when we find it recorded plainly in the word of God who shall then bid the minister hold his peace? John is a perpetual prophet and nothing shall fall unto the Church of God unto the end of the world, but this book shall reveal it.

In the 10th of the Revelation after John had eaten the book it is said, "Thou must prophesy again before many people, and nations, and tongues and kings."[13] That whereas before John was as it were tongue-tied, and as if he had not been, because the people understood him not, yet now God stirs up the hearts and eye[s][14] of men to discern the words of this prophecy better than formerly, and blessed are they that read and hear the words of this prophecy and keep those things which are written therein, for the time is at hand. And happy had many that had lived in the darkness of popery been, if they had read the book of the Revelation well, they had been in a blessed and happy case, and had not been then so enticed with the whore, as they have been. There is the beast that was taken and with him the false prophet. And mark in the former parts of the chapter, how they bind themselves together, and the kings of the earth their armies gathered together. There was great armies and great provision, to make war against him that sat on the horse.[15] Now, say they, we shall devour them at once. But against whom are they gathered? It is against the Lord and against his Christ. In the former part of this chapter, saith John: "I saw heaven opened, and behold a white horse, and he that sat upon him was called faithful and true; and in

---

[13] Rev. 10:11.

[14] Ending lost to binding.

[15] Rev. 19:19.

righteousness he doth judge and make war. His eyes were as a flame of fire, and on his head were many crowns, and he had a name written, that no man knew but he himself, and he was clothed with a vesture dipped in blood, and his name is called the word of God. And the armies which were in heaven followed him upon white horses clothed in fine linen, white and clean. And out of his mouth a sharp sword, that with it he should smite the nations; and he shall rule them with a rod of iron, and he treadeth the winepress of the fierceness of the anger of the wrath of Almighty God. And he hath on his vesture and on his thigh a name written, King of Kings, and Lord of Lords."[16]

To prove that he that sits upon the white horse here is Christ, look in the 6th of the Revelation, the 2nd verse where there is mention made again of the white horse: "And I saw, and behold a white horse, and he that sat on him had a bow, and a crown was given unto him, and he went forth conquering, and to conquer."

Ancient interpreters and the papists themselves confess, that Christ riding on this horse, &c. signifieth the victory that Christ made over the heathen.[17] Now the second time, in the chapter of my text, where Christ comes on a white horse, he comes to conquer another enemy worse than heathenism which is popery and Antichristianism. And as Christ is brought in upon a white horse, so the Pope when he goes abroad must be carried on a white horse in imitation of Christ. This doctrine is the doctrine of devils, yet look to his authority, it is like the Lamb, so though he be the beast yet he hath two horns like the Lamb, but Christ comes to take him. Here in my text, in which first is set down, how they rustle in the church, and how they prevail and what a do they make.

Secondly, their end.

Hence are the seducers beast and false prophet. The people seduced, which are those that receive the mark of the beast, and worshipped his image. These that received not the love of the truth to be saved, it was just with God to make them a prey unto seducers, the false prophet that

---

[16] Rev. 19:11–16.

[17] The identification of the rider of the white horse in Rev. 6:2 with the victorious Christ, or the triumph of the gospel, goes back as far as Irenaeus in *Adversus Haereses* 4.21.3 (*PG* 7:1045A; *ANF* 1:493). See Primasius, *Commentaria in Apocalypsim* 2.6 (*PL* 68:836B–C). For an early modern example, see Francisco Ribera, *In Sacram b. Iohannis Apostoli & Euangelistae Apocalypsin Commentarii* (Salamanca, 1591), 101–103.

wrought miracles, and the beast. "Evil men," saith the Apostle, "wax worse and worse deceiving and being deceived."[18] It is certain that at this day popery is brought to as high a degree of abomination as ever.

There is new orders of seducers and never known of before in former ages.

But when they are in they are in the height of their jollity and pride then the Word[19] comes and takes the beast and the false prophet, both these are cast alive into a lake of fire, burning with brimstone.

A beast. What, are there any beasts in the Church of God?

Consider this book is written with the style of the prophets in the Old Testament where the church afflicted is called Zion, and Jerusalem. And the afflicting church is called Babel and Babylon, because they of the north afflicted the Church of old.[20] So here, in this place, the affl[icting][21] church is called Babel and the delivery of the true[22] Church from the tyranny of the church of Rome, and so we see by beast in the old prophets in the seventh of Daniel, the third verse, it is showed where the prophet saw a rising of four great beasts. Afterward the Spirit of God in the seventeenth verse saith that these four beasts are four great kings, or states, or potentates, not meaning four individual kings. For all the world knows the meaning is four monarchies so that though the word be kings, yet by it is meant four kingdoms or monarchies. In the Book of the Revelation there is set down unto us two beasts and here we must well consider which of them is taken and cast into the lake of fire. 13th Revelation, 1: "And I saw a beast rise up out of the sea having seven heads and ten horns, and upon his horns ten crowns, and upon his head the name of blasphemy. And the beast which I saw was like a leopard, and his feet were as the feet of a bear, and his mouth as the mouth of a lion, and the dragon gave him his power and his seat[23] and great authority. And I beheld another beast," verse 11, "coming up out of the earth, and he had two horns like a lamb, and he spake as a dragon. And he exerciseth all the power of the first beast before him, and

---

[18] 2 Tim. 3:13.

[19] Clearly "worlde" in MS but should almost certainly be read as "Word" in light of Rev. 19:13.

[20] For example, Jer. 1:14–15; 4:6; 6:1; 10:22; 46:20; 50:3; Ezek. 26:7.

[21] Ending lost; "afflicting" assumed.

[22] "true" repeated in MS.

[23] "and his seat" repeated in MS.

causeth the earth, and them that dwell therein to worship the first beast. And he doeth great wonders, for he makes fire come down from heaven on earth in the sight of men."[24]

So that this second beast is wholly compounded of the first beast: as in the seventh of Daniel the beast[s] came up divers one from another. The first like a lion, the second like a bear, the third like a leopard, and the fourth was "dreadful and terrible," and "devoured and brake empires and stamped the residue with the feet of it etc., and was divers from all the beasts that were before it, and had ten horns etc."[25]

This prophecy of Daniel was in the days of Belshazzar, last king of Persia, so that that was not a prophecy of Persia. For that monarchy was now to end and to go out of the world: but that showeth the Roman state and goverment, which is compounded of all the rest because it trod down all that went before, and so is compounded of them all and is described as a great empire, compounded of all the other kingdoms, in regard it had mastered them. Then in the 13th Revelation, 11, after he had described the first beast to rise out of the sea, then he saith, another beast came "up out of the earth and had two horns like a lamb, and he spake as the dragon and exercised all the power of the first beast before him," so the second beast must come to be where the first beast was in the Roman state. And what shall he do? He shall do great miracles and wonders, and deceiveth them that dwell on the earth by the means of those miracles which he had power to do in the sight of the beast:

The first beast is the Roman state.

The second is that which is spoken of in the text, for the same things are said of this beast, that are spoken of the first beast.

The first beast.[26]

The last beast that steps up, and thrusts the emperor out of his seat, is a number of the grand beast, and for his extraordinary power is a beast by himself. That this is so, consider the 17th Revelation, where it is said, that "the seven heads are seven mountains, on which the woman sitteth. And there are seven kings: five are fallen, one is, and the other is not yet come, and when he cometh, he must continue a short space, and the beast that was and is not, even he is the eighth and is of the seventh, and goeth into

---

[24] Rev. 13:1–2, 11–13.

[25] Dan. 7:3–7.

[26] Some text may have been lost following this or it could be erroneous repetition.

perdition."[27] Here is the mind of him that hath wisdom, so the second beast is parcel[28] of the first and the woman sits upon this beast.

Now for the better understanding of this, you must consider that there are four things distinguished in the Revelation.

1: The harlot.

2: The first beast.

3: The second beast.

4: The false prophet.

The harlot or woman is plainly set down, verse 17 [17:18], to be "the great city, which reigneth over the kings of the earth."

So it is a city and a great city, that rules over the kings of the earth.

So then there is the woman, and the witch, etc.

As it is *urbs* [city], or as it is *civitas* [state]:[29] If you regard it as it is *urbs*: so the seven heads signify seven mountains on which the woman sits. But if you regard it as it is *civitas* in respect of the government, then it is seven kings, which are seven such regiments, as have no superior above them, not subordinate offices, but high offices, having none above them.

The woman sits upon the beast.

The woman is so described, that no city can be meant but Rome. What he that was so infallible, that if you missed of any doctrine, you shall surely have it at Rome?[30] Is she a harlot? Therefore it is rather a prejudice.

I will not stand to prove that Rome stands on seven hills.

The very description of Rome doth plainly prove it. But I will tell you an argument that I myself have seen the papists stand amazed at. The heathen writers that never knew Scriptures have described Rome in the same manner, as the Spirit of God hath described it in the Revelation in the place

---

[27] Rev. 17:9–11.

[28] An integral portion.

[29] This distinction between *urbs* and *civitas*, between the physical city and the political entity, can be found in Cicero. In a sermon on Rev. 18:4, preached at Lincoln's Inn in 1650, Ussher attributes this "difference" to "the master of words, Tully," i.e. Marcus Tullius Cicero (CUL, MS Mm.6.55, fol. 183v). Clear examples include *Pro Sestio* 42.91 (*LCL* 309:160–61) and *Academica* 2.45.137 (*LCL* 268:646–47).

[30] The sentence as given is difficult, perhaps mangled in copying. The general idea is clear enough. Ussher ventriloquizes an opponent who complains that it is Reformed prejudice to assume that Rome is the fount of theological heterodoxy and thus identify her with the harlot.

before mentioned, where it is called the great city that reigneth over the kings of the earth:

Antonius Pius, an heathen emperor, did describe Rome in a piece of coin by a city or woman crowned being seated upon seven hills, etc.[31]

And that they may not think that it is any of our own coining[32] Ortelius a writer of their own hath it, and it stands printed in a corner of Ortelius over his old map of Italy, so that Rome is printed out precisely by the heathen writers that know not the Scriptures, as it is in the Revelation.[33] As a woman sitting on seven hills and ruling the whole world, and *Roma* written under it. As the ancient poet: *Septem urbs alta jugis totam quae regulat orbem*,[34] which proofs are so plain, that he hath no wisdom (but puts out voluntarily his own eyes) that will not lay this for a ground, that by the harlot in the Revelation is meant the city of Rome.

So now you have found the place where the beast is, but where's the time when the beast shall reign? For if you can make both time and place to concur, then the matter is done.

Rome must be the mistress of seduction. Why then, say the papists, that time of Rome is past, for that is Rome in the days of St. John in the heathenish time, before it professed Christianity. It[35] could not be Rome in her first days, because this prophecy is revealed unto John as a wonderful thing, and when John saw it he marvelled with a very great marvel to see Rome bloody, with the blood of the saints, and to see Rome bloody with

---

[31] An apparent slip. It has not been possible to identify a coin from the reign of Antoninus Pius (138–161 AD) that matches this description. The Ortelius map (see below) indicates Vespasian (69–79 AD) on the legend and there are coins issued in his reign which precisely match the iconography found there. One example is reproduced in Caroline Vout, *The Hills of Rome: Signature of an Eternal City* (Cambridge: Cambridge University Press, 2012), 129.

[32] A rare Ussher pun.

[33] See, for example, Abraham Ortelius, *Parergon, sive Veteris Geographiae Aliquot Tabulae* (Antwerp, 1601), xviii, "Italia."

[34] Propertius, *Elegies* 3.11. Ussher's quotation does not quite match the original *Septem urbs alta jugis, toti quae praesidet orbi* ("The city set high on seven hills which presides over the whole world"; *LCL* 18:260–61, rev. ed. 1990). The text is given correctly in *The Judgement of the Late Arch-Bishop of Armagh, and Primate of Ireland, of Babylon (Rev. 18.4.) being the present See of Rome* (London, 1659), 4 (*WJU*, 12:540), so perhaps on this occasion Ussher was quoting from memory.

[35] "In" in MS.

the blood of the martyrs of Jesus would John have wondered, that heathen Rome should have presented[?]

This is a thing subject to sense, and he could not marvel at it. But that Rome Christian should imbrue[36] her hands in the blood of Christians this was a greater marvel. Revelation 18:2: "An angel came down from heaven having great power, and the earth was lightened with his glory. And they cried mightily with a strong voice saying Babylon the great is fallen, it is fallen, and is become the habitation of devils, and the hold of every foul spirit, and a cage of every unclean and hateful bird." Admit that it were meant that heathenish Rome was fallen and destroyed: what consequence is this, or what marvel is there that there should be such a change.

But will you have a third demonstration.

This propehecy must be here plainly meant of Rome in the last days, and that Rome must be a harlot then. For this Rome, this Babylon here spoken of by John, God hath foretold that in this prophecy it shall be over-thrown and destroyed, that it shall be never re-edified again. For though Rome hath been sacked and taken many times, yet it never end that calami-ty and utter ruin, as not to be built again. But in the Revelation, the 18th, 22v, it is said that "a mighty angel took up a stone like a great millstone, and cast it into the sea, saying thus with violence shall that great city Babylon be thrown down, and shall be found no more at all, and the voice of harpers and musicians and of pipers and trumpeters shall be heard no more at all in thee. And no craftsman of whatsoever craft he be shall be found any more in thee. And the sound of a millstone shall be heard no more at all in thee. And the light of a candle shall shine no more at all in thee. And the voice of the bridegroom and of the bride shall be heard no more in thee."[37]

So then by these words I prove that Rome shall be restored again, and that her fornication shall continue unto the end, and to the last hour of the destruction of Rome as it is Revelation 18, 9 v, where it is said: "And the kings of the earth who have committed fornication and lived deliciously with her shall bewail her and lament for her when they shall [see] the smoke of her burning standing afar off for the fear of her torment saying, Alas, Alas, the great city Babylon, that mighty city. For in one hour is thy judge-ment come."[38] So they shall bemoan her, that did commit fornication and

---

[36] Drench or soak.

[37] Rev. 18:21–23.

[38] Rev. 18:9–10.

even at the last hour when they shall see the smoke of her burning. But the heathen emperor shall never be revived again to bewail her: but the kings of the earth that have committed fornication and lived deliciously with her, the great kings that now support her, they shall bewail her fall, which shows that it is Rome in her last days, that is meant in the Revelation, and not Rome in the time of the heathen emperors.

When the papists are pressed by this and the like arguments, when they confess that Antichrist surely shall be in Rome, but that it shall be as they would make us believe, three years and a half before the end of the world, when the pope shall go out of Rome, and that then Antichrist shall take his place.[39] Of this there is no great likelihood, but this their assertion, doth prove this much, that the strumpet is Rome and not in her beginning but in the end. But when did the faithful city become an harlot, an enchantress and a witch?

The Apostle in the second of the Thessalonians sets it down warily for in the second of the Thessalonians the 2nd chapter, 3. 4. v, having spoken of "the man of sin" and "the son of perdition" and in the 5th verse he saith, "Remember ye not when I was yet with you, I told you of these things?"

But they might have said, "Why did not the Apostle tell us of these things? And set it down plainly in his epistle?" Because in those days when the Apostle wrote it, was a matter of state, and perhaps in the emperors' time might have cost him his life.

As Tertullian saith we pray for the emperor, for when he loseth his place, Antichrist shall come in, but as long as the emperor stands the other must crouch, for two suns cannot be in the firmament, at one time.[40]

And the Apostle saith, in the 6th verse of the 2nd of the Thessalonians, "And now you know what withholdeth that he might be revealed in his

---

[39] For a classic expression of this futurist reading, see the work of the Jesuit Francisco Ribera, *In Apocalypsin Commentarii* (Salamanca, 1591). By taking the months and days of Rev. 11:2–3 literally he is able to posit an individual Antichrist just before Christ's return (see pp. 163–64). Robert Bellarmine took the same approach in *De Summo Pontifice* 3.8, in *Opera Omnia*, 6 vols (Naples: Giuliano, 1856–1862), 1:436–38; idem, *De Controversiis: On the Roman Pontiff*, trans. Ryan Grant (Mediatrix Press, 2016), 363–64.

[40] Tertullian, *De Resurrectione Carnis* 24 (PL 2:829A–830A {875A–877A}; *ANF* 3:42–43); *Apologeticus Adversus Gentes Pro Christianis* 32 (PL 1:508B–509A {447A–448A}; *ANF* 3:563).

time." The word "withholdeth" hath a double signification, either he which now holdeth the empire and is lord and chief governor, and when he loseth his hold then shall the wicked one be revealed.

"For the mystery of iniquity doth already work," saith the Apostle, "only he which now letteth or holdeth the place of empire shall hold that place till he be taken out of the way, there shall the wicked one be revealed."[41] So when he that withholdeth the empire is taken away, then look to him that sits in Rome, for that is the time when the wicked one shall be revealed and in that place.

For it is plain, Revelation 17, 10th verse, where it is said, "And there are seven kings." "Five are fallen," saith the prophet John. There were five head governors of Rome fallen before the prophecy came. Let anybody read the beginning of the 6th book of Livy in his first decades,[42] or the first book of Tacitus's *Annals*,[43] and you shall see that just before the governement of the emperor, there were five head governments past in Rome:

1. The first was: the governement of kings.
2. Consuls.
3. Dictators.
4. Then *decemviri*.[44]
5. And lastly *tribuni plebis*.[45]

And these five were fallen before the time of the prophecy. "One is." What is that? Who can miss that? It was the emperor. For in the emperor's time this prophecy was made.

And the Apostle in the Thessalonians speaking of the emperor saith, "only he which now letteth, will let, until he be taken out of the way and then shall the wicked one be revealed";[46] when the emperor is gone out of Rome then Antichrist shall come in. And now the emperor hath no more to do in Rome than I have. Therefore it is plain that Antichrist is in Rome. Was it not a very plain prophecy that when the sceptre shall be taken from

---

[41] 2 Thess. 2:7–8.

[42] Livy, *History of Rome* 6 (*LCL* 172:194–95): *sub regibus primum, consulibus deinde ac dictatoribus decemvirisque ac tribunis consularibus gessere* ("at first under kings and afterwards under consuls and dictators, decemvirs and consular tribunes").

[43] Tacitus, *Annals* 1 (*LCL* 249:242–43), presents a similar abbreviated history.

[44] The decemvirate, or "ten men."

[45] "the tribunes of the people."

[46] 2 Thess. 2:7–8.

the empire, then Antichrist shall come? And is not <space> drawn over our eyes, that when the emperor is taken away, out of Rome, we should not see that now Antichrist is there?

And when there were six heads or governments fallen, then the 7th must be Antichrist.

But here remains another thing: "And here," saith John, "is the mind of him, that hath wisdom. The beast which thou sawest was, and is not, even he is the eighth, and is of the seventh and goeth into perdition."[47]

I will deliver unto you what I take to be the true and natural meaning of the place: although, that I must needs confess, the interpreters that I have read, give me no satisfaction.[48]

There was a government in Rome, for ecclesiastical matters, in the time of heathens, the head whereof was called *Pontifex Maximus*,[49] so the place that saith, there are seven heads, that is seven temporal heads, and the pope is the seventh in that respect.

But you must understand that *Pontifices Romani*,[50] that looked to ecclesiastical matters, they were exempt persons, from all other authority and jurisdiction. As now, if a priest should do never so treasonable an act, and yet should be so exempt from authority as he should be accounted no traitor. So were the *Pontifici* in the time of the ancient Romans exempt. Neither the senate nor any other power had to do with them, but only the *Pontifex Maximus*, and this was the great bishop, that was appointed to give answer in matters of religion, by Numa Pompilius.[51] But when the emperors had in their own hands all the great liberties of former times then they bethought themselves that it were not safe for them to let so great a matter as the office of *Pontifex Maximus* to be out of their own hands and power. And therefore the emperors from Julius Caesar downwards were themselves *Pontifices Maximi*, and every one did write himself *Pontifex Maximus*. It was a title of the emperor. To make this more plain, I will instance in something in our own kingdom as if a prophecy should be of the Dukes of Lancaster, of some great things, that they should do, and it should be described as the

---

[47] Rev. 17:9, 11.

[48] See *The Judgement* (1659), 15 (Bodl., MS Barlow 13, fol. 85v; *WJU*, 12:548): "My conceit of this is singular, but such as it is, I will not conceal from you."

[49] Lit. "the greatest bridge-builder." The greatest of the *pontifices* (priests).

[50] "Priests of the Romans."

[51] Legendary successor to Romulus, reigning as king 715–673 BC.

prophecy here is laid down in the text (*vilt*)[52] "the beast that was, and is not and yet is."[53]

"That was," for the Dukes of Lancaster were great, and they have done many valiant acts in former times. "And is not," because the Duchy of Lancaster is now annexed to the crown. "And yet is," for the Duchy remains and they have their chancellors, their Duchy courts and their attorney of the Duchy and the like, which shows that the Duchy remains as yet.

So in this prophecy the beast "that was," that is the *Pontifex Maximus*. And "is not," for it is annexed to the empire and drowned in that government. And "yet is." For the empires call the sev[enth][54] *Pontifices Maximi*, and have the courts, power and jurisdiction, that the *Pontifex Maximus* had. And the beast that was and is not, even he is the eighth, which is the papal jurisdiction, and is of the seventh in regard of the ecclesiastical power, and he shall be the seventh head and he shall extend it further than ever it was before.[55] For before the *Pontifex Maximus* had but one hundred miles in

---

[52] A contraction of *videlicet*. In effect, "that is to say."

[53] Rev. 17:8.

[54] Ending lost to binding.

[55] This interpretive scheme of types of government, with variations on the details, was already established in the Reformed commentary tradition. See, for example, Benedictus Aretius, *Commentarii in Apocalypsin D. Joannis Apostoli* (Morges, 1581), 385–87; John Napier, *A Plaine Discovery of the Whole Revelation of S. John* (London, 1611), 254–55; Thomas Brightman, *A Revelation of the Revelation* (Amsterdam, 1615), 594–600; David Paraeus, *In Divinam Apocalypsin S. Apostoli et Evangelistae Johannis Commentarius* (Heidelberg, 1618), 902–11. Citations of both Livy (Aretius) and Tacitus (Brightman, Paraeus) are found. Paraeus develops his scheme with a discussion of the *Pontifex Maximus* in relation to the eighth head. Unlike Ussher, Paraeus regards the seventh as the Christian emperors (and not part of Antichrist) so that in the eighth spiritual and temporal power are brought together. Ussher sees the pope taking civil power (with an appended local religious jurisdiction) in the seventh head, and an overweening global spiritual power in the eighth. This reading is confirmed in *The Judgement* (1659), 18–20 (see *WJU*, 12:549–50): "The Pope in regard of his civil power over the woman (i.e.) his regal power over the city of Rome, orderly succeedeth the six heads that went before him, and so becometh the seventh, claiming that respect in higher headship than did his predecessors. But not content with that ... the Pope raised it [the state of Pontifex Maximus] again out of the grave and took it to himself, and after he had gotten to be the seventh head, retained not the pontificality as an appendant of his regal power (as did the emperors before him) but advanced the head thereof far above any of the seven civil supreme governments, making himself by that means an eighth head distinct from any of the former, which in respect of his civil power was one of the seven." Ussher goes on

compass round about the city, but this beast shall advance his power above all governments on earth and become the most supreme and greatest power on earth, yea, the most supreme godhead upon earth as Stapleton calls him.[56]

And the beast was taken, and so goeth into perdition, even he is the eighth, and is of the seventh that is the seventh head, in regard of the temporal sword, is the eighth head because he hath another sword, that was never found in the world before this beast came. But the issue is, that this beast is taken and with him the false prophet, all shall be taken with the beast even the false prophet, that wrought miracles before him which is *Clerus Romanus*.[57]

1. Here is first the woman, that is, *Urbs Romana*.[58]
2. And then the first beast, which is *Imperium Romanum*.[59]
3. And thirdly the second beast, which is *Pontifex Romanus*.
4. Lastly the false prophet, which is *Clerus Romanus*.

The second beast, that is, Antichrist doth great wonders and it is said that the false prophet which was the *Clerus Romanus* did likewise great miracles before the beast. We may remember the Bull that Pope Pius Quinctus caused to be hung up at the Bishop of London's gate,[60] against our late Queen Elizabeth of famous memory, and how when she heard of it, she

---

to argue that it was in his universal ambitions, striving to be recognized as *Summus Pontifex Orbis*, that the pope "became not only a head of the former beast, but also a several beast by himself."

[56] Dedicatory epistle to Pope Gregory XIII, in Thomas Stapleton, *Principiorum Fidei Doctrinalium Demonstratio Methodica* (Paris, 1582), sig. ã iiii v: *et sub tui amplissimi nominis planeque supremi in terris numenis tutela atque auspiciis in lucem emissum.*

[57] "the Roman clergy."

[58] "the city of Rome."

[59] "the Roman empire."

[60] Pius V's bull *Regnans in Excelsis* excommunicating Elizabeth, declaring her a heretic and releasing her subjects from obedience, was fixed to the gates of the bishop of London's palace on 25 May 1570. On the offender and his gruesome death as a traitor, see *ODNB*, "Felton, John (*d.* 1570)."

used the words of the Psalmist: "when they curse, thou wilt bless."[61] So it angered them, when we took it no more to heart, but Bristow could say[62]

The beast and the false prophet do work miracles.

They will tell us of such things as are either in themselves false or else the whole scope of them, though it be true is to establish a false doctrine. So they will tell us of divers strange things done in our country which we never heard of there.

But if they work miracles I will say as Solomon saith, there is a time for all things.[63]

The time was appointed when miracles should be done but now they are ceased. The papists cannot deny but it is a thousand times easier to discern a true doctrine than a true miracle.

We have seen men […]

Vespasian cured both the lame and blind yet Bellarmine himself will not admit that these are true miracles. For it may be as Bellarmine saith that they were not truly lame, not truly blind, but the devil sat in the eye[64] and so hindered the sight that the party could not see or else the devil sat in the hip and so contracted the hip that the party could not go which might make it a false miracle and not a true miracle.[65]

---

[61] Ps. 109:28. See, for example, 'De Iure Regis Ecclesiastico', in Edward Coke, *Quinta Pars Relationum Edwardi Coke Equitis Aurati, Regii Atturnati Generalis* (London, 1607), fol. 35r.

[62] A space equivalent to one line of text after this line (and also after the next short line) as well as the evident loss of continuity signals loss of content. This is the most obvious defect of this manuscript witness. The reference is likely to Richard Bristow, *A Briefe Treatise of Diverse Plaine and Sure Wayes to find out the Truthe in this Doubtful and Dangerous Time of Heresie* [often referred to as Bristow's *Motives* from the subtitle] (Antwerp, 1574), fols 31v–32r, where the author writes, "it is manifest that they do miserably forget themselves, who fear not the excommunication of Pius Quintus, of holy memory: in whom Christ himself to have spoken and excommunicated ... they might consider by the miracles, that Christ by him, as by S. Paul, did work: he with his prayers and signing of the cross casting devils out of five women, in open procession, as very many *oculati testes* ['eye witnesses'] do to this day bear witness."

[63] Eccl. 3:1.

[64] This is followed by "or in the hip / in the eye," clearly an error in copying.

[65] Robert Bellarmine, *De Notis Ecclesiae* 14, in *Opera Omnia*, 2:136; idem, *De Notis Ecclesiae: On the Marks of the Church*, trans. Ryan Grant (Mediatrix Press, 2015), 137–38.

The same may be said of the papists' lying miracles. Who can tell if the devil were not at Mont-aigu or at Halle[66] and the devil hath not forgot his old tricks now.

Therefore for the discerning of a miracle the only way is to look to the doctrine for which the miracle is brought.

The 13th of Deuteronomy, the 1st verse: "If there arise among you a prophet or a dreamer of dreams and giveth thee a sign or wonder, and the sign or the wonder come to pass whereof he spake unto thee, saying, Let us go after other gods (which thou hast not known), and let us serve them; thou shalt not harken unto the word of that prophet, or that dreamer of dreams for the Lord your God proveth you to know whether you love the lord your God with all your heart and with all your soul. You shall walk after the Lord your God and fear him and keep his commandments and obey his voice and you shall serve him and cleave unto him, and that prophet or dreamer of dreams shall be put to death because he hath spoken to turn you away from the Lord your God."[67]

So, this worker of miracles for the confirmation of a false doctrine, shall I believe him? No, I will stone him first as is commanded in the text. Nay, if an angel of heaven should come and deliver any thing, as the Apostle saith, contrary to true doctrine let him be accursed. So miracles are now out of date and are rather a seal of a false religion than of a true. And it is said that the working of Satan shall be with powers and signs and lying wonders.

Some of the ancient fathers as Gregory upon the forenamed place saith that then there shall be great affliction in the Church of God and the cause is because it now falls out that the Lord will not have us to oppose

---

[66] Given in MS as "att Mountague or att Hall." For Mont-aigu (Scherpenheuvel) and Halle, see Pieter Geyl, *The Netherlands in the Seventeenth Century, 1609–1648* (London: E. Benn, 1961), 29; For examples of the claims being made for miracles at these shrines in counter-Reformation literature, see Philippe Numan, *Miracles Lately Wrought by the Intercession of the Glorious Virgin Marie, at Mont-aigu, nere unto Siché in Brabant* (Antwerp, 1606), a work which the translator, Richard Chambers, dedicated to King James I; Justus Lipsius, *Diva Virgo Hallensis: beneficia eius et miracula fide atque ordine descripta* (Antwerp, 1604), available in translation as *Miracles of the B. Virgin. Or, An historical account of the original, and stupendious performances of the image, entituled, Our Blessed Lady of Halle* (London, 1688); On miracles in contemporary polemic, see Alexandra Walsham, "Miracles in Post-Reformation England," *Studies in Church History* 41 (2005): 273–306.

[67] Deut. 13:1–5.

miracle with miracles as Moses did with Jannes and Jambres, but now the Lord will try whether the Church will love him and will believe in him with all their heart and with all their soul.[68] Now follows in the text who they were that should be seduced, those that received the mark of the beast and worshipped his image. The word mark is a thing taken from bondslaves that are branded with some character deep in the flesh, with which mark or brand those that follow Antichrist shall be marked. But only contrariwise it is said that God sets his seal in his children and servants. Revelation 7th ch., 3rd verse: "Hurt not the earth nor the sea nor the trees till we have sealed the servants of our God[69] in their foreheads."

But Antichrist will have a character, to be set on his followers, that will take deep impression in their flesh, like unto those that I read of, that would have their emperor's names ingraven deep in their bodies,[70] these that have so received the mark shall together with the beast be cast into a lake that burneth with fire and brimstone which is the last point, that is to say, the issue and end of the beast, etc.

It is a lake of fire and brimstone[71] because the city of Rome is spiritually called Sodom. Now what was the end of Sodom? The Lord poured down fire and brimstone upon it and destroyed it, leaving it a sulphurous lake unto this day.[72]

But divers will object that we should receive in charity a good opinion of our ancestors. For if the beast be Antichrist and the pope of Rome and all them that follow the religion shall be cast into the lake of fire and brimstone together with Antichrist then we must conclude that all our ancestors were damned.

---

[68] Seemingly a reference to Gregory, *Moralia in Job* 28.4 (*PL* 76:454A; *LF* 23:270), see 19.7 (*PL* 76:104B; *LF* 21:404).

[69] "gods" in MS.

[70] It has not been possible to identify an exact parallel but for the practice of branding in antiquity, see 3 Macc. 2:28–29; Herodotus, *The Persian Wars* 2.113; 7.233 (*LCL* 117:402–403; 119:548–49); Plutarch, *Pericles* 26 (*LCL* 65:76–77); Lucian, *De Syria Dea* 59 (*LCL* 162:408–409).

[71] Followed by "~~which is the last point~~" (see previous paragraph), a clear error in copying.

[72] Gen. 19:24–25; Josephus gives the Dead Sea as the site of the destroyed city. Josephus, *Antiquities of the Jews* 1.9 (*LCL* 242:86–87).

The papists themselves do confess that ignorance is the mother of devotion,[73] and certainly that rule may thus far hold true, and be confirmed in a good sense, that many of our ancestors [that][74] lived in the time of popery were no doubt ignorant of the deep mysteries of iniquity and ever retained substance of religion according to that which Wyclif said in his time, that who said that the true faith of the Eucharist was always preserved amongst the laity in his days when the church was in the midst of the darkness of popery but now they begin to instruct the people and learn from us to catechise them in particular,[75] so that though we cannot justify those that now live in popery yet[76] we hope wondrous well of our ancestors for the time was when the light of the Gospel was not so clear as now it is. But now it is preached in the midst of heaven according to that Revelation, the fourteenth ch., and the seventh verse, where three angels came flying one after another, the words are, "And I saw another angel flying in the midst of heaven having the everlasting Gospel to preach to them that dwell on the earth, to every nation, and kindred, tongue, and people, saying with a loud voice, Fear God, and give glory to him, for the hour of his judgement is come, and worship him that made heaven and earth, and the sea and the fountains of waters. And there followed another angel saying Babylon is fallen, is fallen, that great city, because she made all nations drink of the wine of the wrath of her fornication. And the third angel followed them, saying with a loud voice, If any man worship the beast and his image and receive his mark in his forehead or in his hand, the same shall drink of the wine of the wrath of God which is poured out without mixture into the cup of his indignation and still[77] shall be tormented with fire and brimstone in

---

[73] John Jewel alleged that Henry Cole, Dean of St. Paul's, at the accession of Elizabeth, made this claim during a disputation at Westminster. See Jewel's comments in *The Works of John Jewel, D.D., Bishop of Salisbury*, ed. Richard William Jelf, 8 vols (Oxford: Oxford University Press, 1848), 1:93; see 1:32; 3:485; 8:115.

[74] Superscript insertion after "lived."

[75] See the "Confession" of John Tissington against John Wyclif, reproduced in *Fasciculi Zizaniorum Magistri Johannis Wyclif cum tritico*, ed. Rev. Walter W. Shirley, Rolls Series (London: Longman, Brown, Green, Longmans, and Roberts, 1858), 145. The original manuscript of this piece carries annotations in Ussher's hand and can be found in Bodleian, MS e Mus. 86 (in which see fol. 42v).

[76] "that" in MS. Probable transcription error, with the letter "y" being taken as a thorn.

[77] Probable transcription error.

the presence of the holy angels and the lamb and the smoke of the[ir] torment ascendeth up for ever and ever."[78]

So this angel that preacheth the gospel doth not teach in corners as Wyclif did but openly in the midst of heaven and our gospel is not here called a new gospel as the papists would have it, but it is called an everlasting gospel such as was before popery and shall stand when popery should be drowned in fire and brimstone. And what is this doctrine of the gospel? "Fear God and give glory unto him and worship him that made heaven and earth and the sea and the fountains of water." So it is a proclamation against idolatry which is the substance of the everlasting gospel which they call new, which was before theirs and shall survive it.

Then "there followed another angel, saying, Babylon is fallen, that great city because she made all nations drink of the wine of the wrath of her fornication," so that presently after the everlasting gospel is preached then comes popery tumbling down as now since the preaching of the gospel it is so shaken that it hath lost half her predecessors, I dare say half of them if you tell them by the poll[79] and she is fallen lower and lower. The angel that preached the gospel cried with a loud voice and did cry in the midst of heaven. And therefore what do you talk of predecessors for they were in darkness when the light of the gospel did not so plainly appear as now it doth. But after the light of the gospel appears, and therefore now when the third angel cometh he crieth and saith, "If any man worship the beast and his image and receive his mark on his forehead or in his hand the same shall drink of the wine of the wrath of God which is poured out without mixture into the cup of his indignation and he shall be tormented with fire and brimstone in the presence of the holy angels and in the presence of the lamb and the smoke of the torment ascendeth up for ever and ever. And they have no rest day or night who worship the beast and his image and who soever receiveth the mark of his name."

So that after the gospel was published and the true service of god made known in the midst of heaven now the hour of the judgement of popery is come and therefore now look to it. And as for the times of former ignorance that shall not justify you, for now the case is altered in regard that they knew not the mystery of iniquity in those days as you do now and therefore if now you will fully refuse the truth so plainly manifested to you

---

[78] Rev. 14:6–11.

[79] "Pole" in MS. The number of people assembled, counted one by one.

by the preaching of the gospel and worship the beast and his image suffering yourselves to be seduced by them, both the seducers and the seduced must go together and this must be their woeful case that they shall be cast alive into a lake of fire burning with brimstone. Willful opposers of the truth made known unto them that have the spirit of fornication and cannot be drawn from it:[80] "because they received not the love of the truth that they might be saved for this cause God shall send them strong delusions that they should believe a lie: that they all might be damned who believed not the truth but had pleasure in unrighteousness."[81]

Yet I am very much persuaded concerning those that lived before the truth was so plainly revealed that there was so much truth in popery then that if a man could receive it without those gross errors and the depths of the malice of popery that they then held as transubstantiation and the rest of the points in schools that such men living in those days might be saved.[82]

But concerning papists that live in these our times, that do not only know popery, but believe it to be true, and are instructed in the mysteries and all depths of it, and whereas they might be instructed in the truth yet had they rather die than alter their religion: the case is altered for such, their damnation is just. They delight in unrighteousness and will not come forth out of Babel therefore is their case dangerous. But of all others the reconciled papists are in a fearful case especially those that come from the truth to adhere to popery coming out of the light and so go into the darkness. As for such men heaven and hell: the lake that burneth with fire and brimstone, and the heavenly Jerusalem shall first meet before a man dying in such a case shall be saved. Therefore the harlot shall be taken and shall be burnt alive.[83]

I take no delight to revile any. I speak but the bare truth, and have great sorrow of heart and am much afflicted for my countrymen's sake who most of them live in the darkness of popery yet where God says that there is danger, we must speak and not hold our peace, else shall their blood be required at our hands.

---

[80] Superscript: 'according as it is 2 Thess: 2, 10'.

[81] 2 Thess. 2:10–12.

[82] For a discussion of the range of opinions expressed on this issue by contemporary authors, see Anthony Milton, *Catholic and Reformed: The Roman and Protestant Churches in English Protestant Thought, 1600–1640* (Cambridge: Cambridge University Press, 1995), 283–95.

[83] Rev. 18:8.

A SERMON AT ST. MARGARET'S CHURCH (1621)

A Sermon Preached Before the Commons House
of Parliament, in St. Margaret's Church, at Westminster,
the 18th of February, 1620 [1621].[1]

[Epistle Dedicatory, from 1621 edn.]

To the Honourable Assembly of the Commons House of
Parliament.

IT PLEASED this honourable assembly to require my service, in preaching at that late religious meeting of yours, for the receiving of the holy sacrament of the Lord's Supper. I was afterward also sent unto by the like authority, to publish that which (according to my poor ability) I then delivered. And although in respect of myself, and of my want of time to prosecute such a subject, I could wish I had been spared from such a task, yet rather than the expectation, and express signification of the desire of the representative body of the whole commonality of the kingdom should rest unsatisfied, I have yielded to commit this unto the disposing and direction of them, for whose sakes it was at first undertaken. *Opprimi enim me onere*

---

[1] [The text followed here is that of 1631. The sermon was first published in 1621, and again in 1624. "The second edition corrected and amended by the author" appeared in 1631 and is included in *The Workes of the Most Reverend Father in God, Iames Vssher, Archbishop of Armagh, and Primate of Ireland* (1631), with its own frontispiece and separate pagination, but lacking the dedicatory epistle to the Commons which precedes the sermon in the earlier editions. This early collection of Ussher's works was a composite of pieces produced on several presses. The sermon was published again in 1681 and can also be found in *WJU*, 2:415–57. Ussher's preparatory notes survive in Bodleian, MS Rawlinson D1290, fols 49r–53r. The account found in Balliol College, Oxford, MS 259, fols 71r–97v is probably copied from a printed edition.]

officii malui, quam id, quod mihi cum fide semel impositum fuit, propter infirmitatem animi deponere.[2] The very words which then I uttered, I am not able to present unto you. The substance of the matter I have truly laid down, though in some places, as it fell out, somewhat contracted, in others a little more enlarged. Whatsoever it is, I wholly submit it unto your grave censures, and so beseeching the Lord to give you prosperous success in all your worthy endeavours for the service of God, his Majesty and your country, I rest

Yours in all Christian duty to be commanded,

James Ussher.

---

1 Cor. 10. Vers. 17

We being many, are one bread, and one body: for we are all partakers of that one bread.

Other entrance I need not make unto my speech at this time, than that which the Apostle himself presenteth unto me in the verse next but one going before my text: "I speak to wise men." The more unwise might I deem myself to be, who, being so conscious unto myself of my great weakness, durst[3] adventure to discover the same before so grave and judicious an auditory; but that this consideration doth somewhat support me, that no great blame can light herein upon me, but some aspersion thereof must reflect upon yourselves, who happened to make so evil a choice; the more facile[4] I expect you to be in a cause, wherein you yourselves are someways interested.

The special cause of your assembling at this time is, first, that you, who profess the same truth, may join in one body, and partake together of

---

[2] ["I preferred to be overwhelmed by the burden of duty rather than to renounce that which was once imposed on me with faith, because of weakness of the spirit." Adapted from Cicero, *Pro Sexto Roscio Amerino* 10 (*LCL* 240:130–31).]

[3] ["dared."]

[4] ["lenient."]

the same blessed communion, and then, that such as adhere unto false worship, may be discovered and avoided; you in your

wisdom discerning this holy sacrament to be, as it were, *ignis probationis* [a trial by fire], which would both *congregare homogenea*, and *segregare heterogenea*, as in philosophy we use to speak, both conjoin those that be of the same, and disjoin such as be of a differing kind and disposition. And to this purpose have I made choice of this present text, wherein the Apostle maketh our partaking of the Lord's table to be a testimony, not only of the union and communion which we have betwixt ourselves, and with our head (which he doth in the express words which I have read), but also of our dis-union and separation from all idolatrous worship, as appeareth by the application hereof unto his main drift and intendment, laid down in the 14 and 21 verses.

The effect therefore of that, which Saint Paul in express terms here delivereth, is the communion of saints, which consisteth of two parts: the fellowship which they have with the body, laid down in the beginning, and the fellowship which they have with the head, laid down in the end of the verse, both which are thus explained by St. John. "That which we have seen and heard, declare we unto you, that ye also may have fellowship with us; and truly our fellowship is with the Father, and with his Son Jesus Christ," 1 John 1. 3. Let them therefore, that walk in darkness, brag as much as they list of their good-fellowship. This blessed Apostle assureth us that such only, as do walk in the light, "have fellowship one with another," even as they have fellowship with God, and Jesus Christ his Son, whose blood shall cleanse them from all sin.[5] And to what better company can a man come, than "to the general assembly and church of the first born which are enrolled in heaven, and to God the judge of all, and to the spirits of just men made perfect, and to Jesus the mediator of the new covenant, and to the blood of sprinkling, which speaketh better things than that of Abel?"[6] No fellowship, doubtless, is comparable to this communion of saints.

To begin therefore with the first part thereof; as the Apostle in the third to the Galatians maketh our being "baptized into Christ" to be a testimony that we "are all one in Christ,"[7] so doth he here make our "partaking of that one bread" to be an evidence that we also are all "one bread, and

---

[5] 1 John 1:6–7.

[6] Heb. 12:23–24.

[7] Gal. 3:27–28.

one body" in him. And to the same purpose, in the twelfth chapter following, he propoundeth both our baptism and our drinking of the Lord's cup,
as seals of the spiritual conjunction of us all into one mystical body. "For as
the body is one," saith he, "and hath many members, and all the members
of that one body, being many, are one body: so also is Christ. For by one
Spirit are we all baptized into one body, whether we be Jews or Gentiles,
whether we be bond or free: and have been all made to drink into one Spirit."[8] Afterwards he addeth, that we "are the body of Christ, and members in
particular";[9] and in another place also, that "We being many, are one body
in Christ, and every one members one of another."[10]

Now the use which he teacheth us to make of this wonderful conjunction, whereby we are made members of Christ, and members one of
another, is twofold: 1. "That there should be no schism in the body." 2.
"That the members should have the same care one for another." 1 Corinthians 12. 25. For preventing of schism, he exhorteth us in the fourth to the
Ephesians, "to keep the unity of the Spirit in the bond of peace"; and to
make this bond the firmer, he putteth us in mind of "one body, one Spirit,
one hope, one Lord, one faith, one baptism, one God and Father of all,
who is above all, and through all, and in us all";[11] by this multiplication of
unities declaring unto us that the knots whereby we are tied together, are
both in number more, and of far greater moment, than that matters of
smaller consequence should dissever us, and therefore that we should
"stand fast in one spirit, with one mind, striving together for the faith of the
Gospel, and in nothing terrified by our adversaries," Philippians 1. 27, 28.

But howsoever God hath thus marshalled his Church in a goodly order, "terrible as an army with banners,"[12] yet such is the disorder of our
nature, that many for all this break rank, and the enemy laboureth to breed
division in God's house, that so his kingdom might not stand. Nay, oftentimes it cometh to pass, that the watchmen themselves, who were appointed for the safeguarding of the Church, prove in this kind to be the smiters

---

[8] 1 Cor. 12:12–13.

[9] 1 Cor. 12:27.

[10] Rom. 12:5.

[11] Eph. 4:3–6.

[12] Cant. 6:4.

and wounders of her;[13] and from among them who were purposely ordained in the Church, for the bringing of men "into the unity of the faith,
and of the knowledge of the Son of God,"[14] even from among those some
do arise, that "speak perverse things, to draw away disciples after them."[15]

Thus we find in the Ecclesiastical History, that after the death of Jul-
ian the apostate, "questions and disputes concerning matters of doctrine
were freshly set afoot by those who were set over the Churches." Whereupon Sozomen maketh this grave observation: that "the disposition of men
is such that when they are wronged by others, they are at agreement among
themselves; but when they are freed of evils from abroad, then they make
insurrections one against another."[16] Which as we find to be too true by the
late experience of our neighbour churches in the Low Countries, so are we
to consider with the wise man, that "what hath been, is now, and that which
is to be, hath already been";[17] and be not so inquisitive, why "the former
days were better than these? for we do not enquire wisely concerning
this."[18] When like troubles were in the Church heretofore, Isodorus Pelu-
siota, an ancient father, moveth the question, "What a man should do" in
this case, and maketh answer that, "If it be possible we should mend it, but
if that may not be, we should hold our peace."[19]

The Apostle's resolution, I think, may give sufficient satisfaction in
this point, to all that have moderate and peaceable minds. "If in any thing

---

[13] Cant. 5:7. *Veteres scripturas scrutans, invenire non possum, scidisse Ecclesiam, et de domo
Dei populos seduxisse; praeter illos qui sacerdotes a Deo positi fuerant et prophetae* ["On examining the ancient scriptures, I am unable to find the division of the church and the
people led away from the house of God; more than those who had been appointed
priests and prophets by God"]. Jerome, *Commentariorum in Osee Prophetam*, on Hos.
9:8–9 [cf. *PL* 25:895B–C].

[14] Eph. 4:13.

[15] Acts 20:30.

[16] αἱ περὶ τῶν δογμάτων ζητήσεις τε καὶ διαλέξεις πάλιν ἀνεκινοῦντο τοῖς
προεστῶσι τῶν ἐκκλησιῶν ... οὕτω πῆ τοῖς ἀνθρώποις φίλον, παρ' ἑτέρων μὲν
ἀδικουμένοις, πρὸς τὸ ὁμόφυλον ὁμονοεῖν ἀπηλλαγμένοις δὲ τῶν ἔξωθεν κακῶν
πρὸς σφᾶς αὐτοὺς στασιάζειν. Sozomen, *Historia Ecclesiastica* 6.4 [*PG* 67:1300B–
1301A; *NPNF2* 2:348].

[17] Eccl. 3:15.

[18] Eccl. 7:10.

[19] Τί οὖν ποιητέον; φῇς. Εἰ μὲν δυνατόν, διορθωτέον· εἰ δὲ μη, ἡσυχαστέον. Isi-
dore of Pelusium, *Epistolae* 4.133 [*PG* 78:1216B].

ye be otherwise minded, God shall reveal even this unto you: nevertheless, whereto we have already attained, let us walk by the same rule, let us mind the same thing."[20] It is not to be looked for, that all good men should agree in all things: neither is it fit that we should, as our adversaries do, put the truth unto compromise, and to the saying of an Achitophel, whose counsel must be accepted, "as if a man had enquired at the oracle of God."[21] We all agree that the scriptures of God are the perfect rule of our faith; we all consent in the main grounds of religion drawn from thence; we all subscribe to the articles of doctrine agreed upon in the synod of the year 1562, "for the avoiding of diversities of opinions, and the establishing of consent touching true Religion."[22] Hitherto, by God's mercy, have we already attained; thus far therefore let us mind the same thing: let not every wanton wit be permitted to bring what fancies he list into the pulpit, and to disturb things that have been well ordered. "I beseech you, brethren," saith the Apostle, "mark them which cause divisions and offences, contrary to the doctrine which ye have learned, and avoid them."[23]

If in some other things we be otherwise minded, than others of our brethren are, let us bear one with another, until God shall reveal the same thing unto us; and howsoever we may see cause why we should dissent from others in matter of opinion, yet let us remember, that that is no cause why we should break the King's peace, and make a rent in the Church of God. A thing deeply to be thought of by the Ishmaels of our time, whose "hand is against every man and every man's hand against them";[24] who "bite and devour one another," until they "be consumed one of another";[25] who forsake the fellowship of the saints, and by a sacrilegious separation break this bond of peace.[26] Little do these men consider, how precious the

---

[20] Phil. 3:15–16.

[21] [2 Sam. 16:23.]

[22] [The reference is to the "Thirty-Nine Articles of Religion of the Church of England" and the citation is from the preface to the first English edition of 1571. *The Creeds of Christendom*, ed. Philip Schaff, 3 vols (1931; repr., Grand Rapids: Baker Books, 1983), 3:487.]

[23] Rom. 16:17.

[24] Gen. 16:12.

[25] Gal. 5:15.

[26] *Vos ergo quare separatione sacrilega pacis vinculum disrupistis.* Augustine, *De Baptismo contra Donatistas* 2.6 [PL 43:130; NPNF1 4:428]. Λέγω καὶ διαμαρτύρομαι ὅτι τοῦ εἰς αἵρεσιν ἐμπεσεῖν, τὸ τὴν ἐκκλησίαν σχίσαι οὐκ ἔλαττόν ἐστι κακόν. "I say

peace of the Church ought to be in our eyes, to be redeemed with a thousand of our lives, and of what dangerous consequence the matter of schism is unto their own souls. For howsoever the schismatic *secundum affectum*, as the schoolmen speak, in his intention and wicked purpose, taketh away unity from the Church, even as he that hateth God doth take away goodness from him, as much as in him lieth; yet *secundum effectum*, in truth and in very deed, he taketh away the unity of the Church only from himself. That is, he cutteth himself off from being united with the rest of the body; and being dissevered from the body, how is it possible that he should retain communion with the head?[27]

To conclude therefore this first use which we are to make of our communion with the body, let us call to mind the exhortation of the Apostle: "above all things put on love, which is the bond of perfectness, and let the peace of God rule in your hearts, to the which also ye are called in one body."[28] Behold how good and pleasant a thing it is for brethren to dwell together in unity.[29] What a goodly thing it is to behold such an honourable assembly as this is, to be as a house that is "compact together" in itself,[30] holding fit correspondence with the other part of this great body,[31] and due subordination unto their and our head! Such as wish not well to the public

---

and protest, that to make schism in the Church is no less evil, than to fall into heresy." Chrysostom, *In Epist. Ad Ephes.*, Hom. 11 [*PG* 62:87; *NPNF1* 13:107].

[27] [*secundum affectum ... secundum effectum.* A scholastic distinction used with reference to intentional and unintentional actions. For example, Aquinas's distinction between a man killing another who, unknown to him, is his father, being a parricide in effect, but not in affect, because this was not his intention (a deed arising from his affections or passions). Aquinas, *Summa Theologiae*, ed. Thomas Gilby, Blackfriars edition, 61 vols (London: Eyre & Spottiswoode, 1964–81), 44:122–23 (IIa-IIae, q. 162, a. 2, ad 2).]

[28] Col. 3:14–15.

[29] Ps. 133:1.

[30] Ps. 122:3.

[31] [Elrington emends "part" to "parts" in *WJU*, 2:422 which would be consistent with Pauline imagery, but the first and second editions agree on the singular. Ussher appears to be referring to the upper chamber, the Lords, as "the other part," and to Parliament as a whole as "this great body." This reading is entirely consistent with the point he is making about enemies who "would rejoice at the ruin of our state" longing to see "that dissensions should arise here, betwixt the members mutually, and betwixt them and the head" (emphasis added). The Pauline imagery is mapped onto the harmony of relations between Parliamentarians and their submission to their earthly king.]

good, and would rejoice at the ruin of our state, long for nothing more, than that dissensions should arise here, betwixt the members mutually, and betwixt them and the head.

Hoc Ithacus velit, et magno mercentur Atridae.[32] They know full well, that "every kingdom divided against itself is brought to desolation; and every house divided against itself, shall not stand."[33] Nor do they forget the politician's old rule, *Divide et impera*, make a division, and get the dominion.[34] The more need have we to look herein unto ourselves; who cannot be ignorant how dolorous *solutio continui*,[35] and how dangerous ruptures prove to be unto our bodies. If therefore there be any comfort of love, if any fellowship of the Spirit, fulfil our joy: "that ye be like-minded, having the same love, being of one accord, of one mind"; and doing "nothing through strife or vain glory."[36] Remember that as oft as we come unto the Lord's table, so oft do we enter into new bonds of peace, and tie ourselves with firmer knots of love together, this blessed communion being a sacred seal, not only of the union which we have with our head by faith, but also of our conjunction with the other members of the body by love.

Whereby as we are admonished to maintain unity among ourselves, "that there be no schism or division in the body," so are we also further put

---

[32] ["This the Ithacan would wish and the sons of Atreus buy at a great price!" Virgil, *Aeneid* 2.104 (*LCL* 63:322–23, rev. ed. 1999). A common Latin tag on the desirability of a bit of Schadenfreude.]

[33] Matt. 12:25.

[34] [It is uncertain whether Ussher had a specific individual in mind here. Elrington renders it as "politician's" but all seventeenth-century texts give as "Politicians," with no apostrophe to indicate singular or plural. The capitalization may not be especially significant as many nouns were capitalized in early modern print. Even if the apostrophe is placed to indicate the singular, this could be read generically. The "divide and conquer" maxim was a commonplace in antiquity. If Ussher has a specific individual in mind, Cicero, Livy, even Machiavelli, would all be potential candidates.]

[35] [*solutio continui*, lit. "solution of continuity." A medical term denoting loss of cohesion in the solid parts of the body. Sometimes used in early modern literature in reference to the separation of normally contiguous parts, such as schism in the Church. See, for example, "Of unity in religion," in *Sir Francis Bacon: The Essayes or Counsels, Civill and Morall*, ed. M. Kiernan (Oxford: Clarendon Press, 1985), 12. The expression can also be found in the sermons of Lancelot Andrewes, John Donne, and Edward Reynolds.]

[36] Phil. 2:1–3.

in mind, "that the members should have the same care one for another."[37]
For that is the second use which Saint Paul teacheth us to make hereof, in 1
Corinthians 12. 26. which he further amplifieth in the verse next following,
by the mutual sympathy and fellow-feeling which the members of the same
body have one with another. For "whether one member suffer, all the
members suffer with it; or one member be honoured, all the members rejoice with it." And then he addeth: "Now ye are the body of Christ, and
members in particular," showing unto us thereby, that as we are all
σύσσωμοι καὶ συμμέτοχοι τῆς ἐπαγγελίας, concorporated, as it were, and
made copartners of the promise in Christ,[38] so we should have one another
in our hearts, εἰς τὸ συναποθανεῖν καὶ συζῆν, to die and live together.[39]
And hereupon is that exhortation in the 13. to the Hebrews grounded:
"Remember them that are in bonds, as bound with them, and them which
suffer adversity, as being yourselves also in the body";[40] it being a perilous
sign that we be no lively members of that body, if we be not sensible of the
calamities that lie upon our afflicted brethren. We know the woe that is
pronounced against such as are at ease in Sion, and "are not grieved for the
affliction of Joseph," with the judgment following. "Therefore now shall
they go captive, with the first that go captive."[41] We know the angel's bitter
curse against the inhabitants of Meroz. "Curse ye Meroz," said the angel of
the Lord, "curse ye bitterly the inhabitants thereof: because they came not
to help the Lord, to help the Lord against the mighty."[42] Not as if the Lord
did stand in need of our help, or were not able, without our assistance, to
maintain his own cause; but that hereby he would make trial of our readi-
ness to do him service, and prove the sincerity of our love. If we hold our
peace and sit still at this time, deliverance shall arise to God's Church from
another place.[43] But let us look that the destruction do not light upon us
and ours.

---

[37] 1 Cor. 12:25.

[38] Eph. 3:6.

[39] 2 Cor. 7:3.

[40] Heb. 13:3.

[41] Amos 6:1, 6–7.

[42] Judg. 5:23.

[43] Esth. 4:14.

I need not make any application of that which I have spoken. The face of Christendom, so miserably rent and torn as it is at this day, cannot but present itself as a rueful spectacle unto all our eyes, and, if there be any bowels in us, stir up compassion in our hearts. Neither need I to be earnest in exciting you to put your helping hands to the making up of these breaches. Your forwardness herein hath prevented[44] me, and instead of petitioning (for which I had prepared myself) hath ministered unto me matter of thanksgiving.[45] A good work is at all times commendable, but the doing of it in fit time addeth much to the lustre thereof, and maketh it yet more goodly. The season of the year is approaching, wherein "kings go forth to battle."[46] The present supply and offer of your subsidy was done in a time most seasonable, being so much also the more acceptable, as it was granted "not grudgingly, or of necessity," but freely, and with a willing mind. "God loveth a cheerful giver," and he "is able to make all grace abound towards you; that ye always having all sufficiency in all things, may abound to every good work."[47]

And thus, being by your goodness so happily abridged of that which I intended further to have urged from the conjunction which we have with the body, I pass now unto the second part of the communion of saints, which consisteth in the union which we all have with one head. For Christ our head is the main foundation of this heavenly union. Out of him there is nothing but confusion. Without him we are nothing but disordered heaps of rubbish, but "in him all the building, fitly framed together, groweth unto an holy temple in the Lord"; and "in him are we builded together for an habitation of God through the Spirit," Ephesians 2. 21, 22. Of ourselves we are but lost sheep, scattered and wandering upon every mountain. From him it is, that there is "one fold, and one shepherd,"[48] God having purposed in himself to "gather together in one all things in Christ, both which are in heaven, and which are on earth, even in him," Ephesians 1.10. This is

---

[44] ["gone before, preceded."]

[45] [King James had instructed Ussher to encourage the Commons to grant subsidies to the crown, but they had already done so two days previously.]

[46] 2 Sam. 11:1.

[47] 2 Cor. 9:7–8. [Supply was granted without conditions: "They meddled not with the Palatinate; but a free Gift to the King, of Two Subsidies, without any Question made." *Journal of the House of Commons: Volume 1, 1547–1629* (London, 1802), 523.]

[48] John 10:16.

the effect of our Saviour's prayer, John 17. 21. "That they all may be one, as thou Father art in me, and I in thee, that they also may be one in us, etc. I in them, and thou in me, that they may be made perfect in one." And this is it which we find so oft repeated by Saint Paul: "We being many, are one body in Christ," Romans 12. 5. "Ye are all one in Christ Jesus," Galatians 3. 28. And in the text we have in hand: "we being many, are one bread and one body." Why? Because "we are all partakers of that one bread"; namely, of that bread, whereof he had said in the words immediately going before, "the bread which we break, is it not the communion of the body of Christ?"[49]

Under the name of bread therefore here is comprehended both *panis Domini*, and *panis Dominus*;[50] not only the bread of the Lord, but also the Lord himself, who is that "living bread which came down from heaven," John 6. 51. For, as Saint Peter, saying that "baptism doth save us,"[51] understandeth thereby both the outward part of that sacrament (for he expressly calleth it a figure), and more than that too (as appeareth by the explication presently adjoined: "not the putting away of the filth of the flesh"), even the inward purging of our consciences by virtue of the death and resurrection of Jesus Christ; so Saint Paul here, making the reason of our union to be our "partaking all of this one bread," hath not so much respect unto the external bread in the sacrament (though he exclude not that neither) as unto the true and heavenly bread figured thereby. Whereof the Lord himself pronounceth in the sixth of John: "The bread that I will give is my flesh, which I will give for the life of the world";[52] and, to show that by partaking of this bread, that wonderful union we speak of is effected: "He that eateth my flesh, and drinketh my blood, dwelleth in me, and I in him."[53]

It is a lamentable thing to behold, how this holy sacrament, which was ordained by Christ to be a bond whereby we should be knit together in

---

[49] 1 Cor. 10:16.

[50] ["the bread of Lord" and "the bread [which was] the Lord." This distinction, used in scholastic theology, has its origin in Augustine who wished to make a distinction between the way that Judas and the other disciples received the bread. Judas ate the bread of the Lord against the Lord unto punishment, whilst the other disciples received his body and life. Augustine, *In Joannis Evangelium Tractatus CXXIV* 59.1 (*PL* 35:1796; *NPNF1* 7:308).]

[51] 1 Pet. 3:21.

[52] John 6:32, 51.

[53] John 6:56.

unity, is, by Satan's malice and the corruption of man's disposition, so strangely perverted the contrary way; that it is made the principal occasion of that woeful distraction which we see amongst Christians at this day, and the very fuel of endless strifes, and implacable contentions. And forasmuch as these mischiefs have proceeded from the inconsiderate confounding of those things, which in their own nature are as different as may be; for the clearer distinguishing of matters, we are in the first place to consider that a sacrament, taken in its full extent, comprehendeth two things in it: that which is outward and visible, which the schools call properly *sacramentum*, in a more strict acceptation of the word, and that which is inward and invisible, which they term *rem sacramenti*, the principal thing exhibited in the sacrament.[54] Thus in the Lord's Supper, the outward thing, which we see with our eyes, is bread and wine; the inward thing, which we apprehend by faith, is the body and blood of Christ. In the outward part of this mystical action, which reacheth to that which is *sacramentum* only, we receive this body and blood but sacramentally; in the inward, which containeth *rem*, the thing itself in it, we receive them really: and consequently the presence of these in the one is relative and symbolical, in the other, real and substantial.

To begin then with that which is symbolical and relative, we may observe out of the Scripture, which saith, that "Abraham received the sign of circumcision, a seal of the righteousness of the faith which he had being uncircumcised,"[55] that sacraments have a twofold relation to the things whereof they be sacraments: the one of a sign, the other of a seal. Signs, we know, are relatively united unto the things which they do signify, and in this respect are so nearly conjoined together, that the name of the one is usually communicated unto the other. "This cup is the new testament," or, the new covenant, saith our Saviour in the institution of the holy Supper, Luke 22. 20. "This is my covenant," saith God in the institution of circumcision in the Old Testament, Genesis 17. 10. but how it was his covenant, he explaineth in the verse immediately following: "Ye shall circumcise the flesh

---

[54] [These references first appear in the 1631 edition.] Peter Lombard, *Sententiarum Libri Quatuor* 4.10.2 [*PL* 192:860; *The Sentences: Book 4: On the Doctrine of Signs*, trans. Giulio Silano, 4th ed. (Toronto: Pontifical Institute of Mediaeval Studies, 2010), 51 (here 4.10.1.6)]; Gratian, *De Consecratione* 2.48, *ex Augustino* [*Corpus Iuris Canonici*, ed. Aemilius Ludovicus Richter, revised by Aemilius Friedberg, 2 vols (Leipzig: Tauchnitz, 1879–81), 1:1131–32. Ussher notes the traditional ascription of this passage to Augustine].

[55] Rom. 4:11.

of your foreskin; and it shall be a sign of the covenant betwixt me and you." So words being the signs of things, no sooner is the sound of the word conveyed to our ears, but the notion of the thing signified thereby is presented unto our mind; and thereupon in the speech of the Scripture nothing is more ordinary, than by the term of "word" to note a thing.[56] We read in the fourth of the first of Samuel, that the Philistines were afraid and said, "God is come into the camp," verse 7. when the Israelites brought thither "the Ark of the Covenant of the Lord of hosts, which dwelleth between the Cherubims," vers. 4. and yet was that no other but this relative kind of presence whereof now we speak; in respect whereof also the show-bread is in the Hebrew named, לחם הפנים "the bread of faces," or, "the presence bread." We see with us, the room, wherein the King's chair and other ensigns of state are placed, is called "the Chamber of Presence," although the King himself be not there personally present. And as the rude and undutiful behaviour of any in that place, or the offering of any disrespect to the King's portraiture, or to the arms royal, or to any other thing that hath relation to his Majesty, is taken as a dishonour done unto the King himself, so here, he that eateth the bread and drinketh the cup of the Lord unworthily, is accounted guilty of offering indignity to the "body and blood of the Lord."[57]

In this sort we acknowledge sacraments to be signs, but bare signs we deny them to be; seals they are, as well as signs of the covenant of grace. As it was therefore said of John the Baptist, that he was "a prophet and more than a prophet,"[58] so must we say of sacraments, that they be signs, and more than signs, even pledges and assurances of the interest which we have in the heavenly things that are represented by them. He that hath in his chamber the picture of the French King, hath but a bare sign; which possibly may make him think of that King when he looketh on it, but showeth not that he hath any manner of interest in him. It is otherwise with him that hath the King's great seal for the confirmation of the title that he hath unto all the lands and livelihood which he doth enjoy. And as here, the wax that is affixed to those letters patent, howsoever for substance it be the very same with that which is to be found everywhere, yet, being applied to this

---

56 So the ten commandments are called ten words, Exod. 34:28. With God no word shall be impossible, that is no thing. Luke 1:37, etc.

57 1 Cor. 11:27.

58 Matt. 11:9.

use, is of more worth to the patentee, than all the wax in the country beside: so standeth it with the outward elements in the matter of the sacrament. The bread and wine are not changed in substance, from being the same with that which is served at ordinary tables, but in respect of the sacred use whereunto they are consecrated, such a change is made, that now they differ as much from common bread and wine, as heaven from earth. Neither are they to be accounted barely significative but truly exhibitive also, of those heavenly things whereto they have relation, as being appointed by God to be a means of conveying the same unto us, and putting us in actual possession thereof. So that in the use of this holy ordinance, as verily as a man with his bodily hand and mouth receiveth the earthly creatures, so verily doth he with his spiritual hand and mouth, if any such he have, receive the body and blood of Christ.

And this is that real and substantial presence, which we affirmed to be in the inward part of this sacred action. For the better conceiving of which mystery, we are to inquire, first, what the thing is which we do here receive; secondly, how and in what manner we are made partakers of it. Touching the first, the truth which must be held is this: that we do not here receive only the benefits that flow from Christ, but the very body and blood of Christ, that is, Christ himself crucified. For as none can be made partaker of the virtue of the bread and wine to his bodily sustenance, unless he first do receive the substance of those creatures, so neither can any participate in the benefits arising from Christ to his spiritual relief, except he first have communion with Christ himself. We must "have the Son," before we "have life";[59] and therefore "eat" him we must, as himself speaketh, that is, as truly be made partakers of him, as we are of our ordinary food, if we will "live" by him.[60] As there is a giving of him on God's part, for "unto us a Son is given,"[61] so there must be a receiving of him on our part: for "as many as received him, to them gave he power to become the sons of God."[62] And as we are "called by God unto the communion of his Son Jesus Christ our Lord,"[63] so, if we do hear his voice, and not harden our

[59] 1 John 5:12.

[60] John 6:57.

[61] Isa. 9:6.

[62] John 1:12.

[63] 1 Cor. 1:9.

hearts by unbelief, we are indeed made "partakers of Christ."[64] This is that "great mystery," for so the Apostle termeth it, of our union with Christ, whereby we are made "members of his body, of his flesh, and of his bones,"[65] and this is that "eating of the flesh of the Son of man, and drinking of his blood," which our Saviour insisteth so much upon, in the sixth of John.

Where if any man shall demand, that I may now come unto the second point of our inquiry, "How can this man give us his flesh to eat?,"[66] he must beware that he come not preoccupied with such dull conceits as they were possessed withal, who moved that question there. He must not think that we cannot truly feed on Christ, unless we receive him within our jaws, for that is as gross an imagination as that of Nicodemus, who could not conceive how a man could be "born again," unless he should "enter the second time into his mother's womb";[67] but must consider that the "eating and drinking," which our Saviour speaketh of, must be answerable to the "hungering and thirsting," for the quenching whereof this heavenly banquet is provided. Mark well the words which he useth, toward the beginning of his discourse concerning this argument. "I am the bread of life: he that cometh to me, shall never hunger; and he that believeth on me, shall never thirst. But I said unto you, that ye also have seen me, and believe not."[68] And compare them with those in the end: "It is the Spirit that quickeneth, the flesh profiteth nothing: the words that I speak unto you, they are spirit, and they are life. But there are some of you that believe not."[69] Now observe, that such as our hungering is, such is our eating. But everyone will confess, that the hunger here spoken of is not corporal, but spiritual. Why then should any man dream here of a corporal eating? Again, the corporal eating, if a man might have it, would not avail anything to the slaking of this hunger. Nay, we are expressly told that the flesh thus taken, for so we must understand it, profiteth nothing; a man should never be the better, nor one jot the holier, nor any whit further from the second death, if he had filled his belly with it. But that manner of feeding on this flesh, which Christ him-

---

[64] Heb. 3:14.

[65] Eph. 5:30, 32.

[66] John 6:52.

[67] John 3:4.

[68] John 6:35–36.

[69] John 6:63–64.

self commendeth unto us, is of such profit, that it preserveth the eater from death, and maketh him to live for ever.[70] It is not therefore such an eating, that every man who bringeth a bodily mouth with him may attain unto, but it is of a far higher nature; namely, a spiritual uniting of us unto Christ, whereby he dwelleth in us, and we live by him.

If any do further inquire, how it is possible that any such union should be, seeing the body of Christ is in heaven, and we are upon earth, I answer, that if the manner of this conjunction were carnal and corporal, it would be indeed necessary that the things conjoined should be admitted to be in the same place; but it being altogether spiritual and supernatural, no local presence, no physical nor mathematical continuity or contiguity is any way requisite thereunto. It is sufficient for the making of a real union in this kind, that Christ and we, though never so far distant in place each from other, be knit together by those spiritual ligatures, which are intimated unto us in the words alleged out of the sixth of John: to wit, the "quickening Spirit" descending downward from the head, to be in us a fountain of supernatural life, and a "lively faith," wrought by the same Spirit, ascending from us upward to lay fast hold upon him, who "having by himself purged our sins, sitteth on the right hand of the Majesty on high."[71]

First therefore, for the communion of the Spirit, which is the ground and foundation of this spiritual union; let us call to mind what we have read in God's book: that Christ, the second Adam, was made "a quickening spirit,"[72] and that he "quickeneth whom he will";[73] that unto him "God hath given the Spirit without measure,"[74] and "of his fullness have all we received";[75] that "he that is joined unto the Lord, is one spirit,"[76] and that "hereby we know that we dwell in him, and he in us, because he hath given us of his Spirit."[77] By all which it doth appear, that the mystery of our union with Christ consisteth mainly in this: that the selfsame Spirit which is in him, as in the head, is so derived from him into every one of his true mem-

---

[70] John 6:50–51, 54, 58.

[71] Heb. 1:3.

[72] 1 Cor. 15:45.

[73] John 5:21.

[74] John 3:34.

[75] John 1:16.

[76] 1 Cor. 6:17.

[77] 1 John 3:24; 4:13.

bers, that thereby they are animated and quickened to a spiritual life. We read in the first of Ezekiel, of four living creatures, and of four wheels standing by them: "when those went," saith the text, "these went; and when those stood, these stood; and when those were lifted up from the earth, the wheels were lifted up over against them." He that should behold such a vision as this, would easily conclude by that which he saw, that some invisible bands there were, by which these wheels and living creatures were joined together, howsoever none did outwardly appear unto the eye; and the Holy Ghost, to give us satisfaction herein, discovereth the secret, by yielding this for the reason of this strange connexion: that "the spirit of the living creature was in the wheels," Ezekiel 1. 21. From whence we may infer, that things may truly be conjoined together, though the manner of the conjunction be not corporal, and that things distant in place may be united together, by having the spirit of the one communicated unto the other.

Nay, if we mark it well, we shall find it to be thus in every of our own bodies, that the formal reason of the union of the members consisteth not in the continuity of the parts (though that also be requisite to the unity of a natural body), but in the animation thereof by one and the same spirit. If we should suppose a body to be as high as the heavens, that the head thereof should be where Christ our head is, and the feet where we his members are, no sooner could that head think of moving one of the toes, but instantly the thing would be done, without any impediment given by that huge distance of the one from the other. And why? Because the same soul that is in the head, as in the fountain of sense and motion, is present likewise in the lowest member of the body. But if it should so fall out, that this or any other member proved to be mortified, it presently would cease to be a member of that body; the corporal conjunction and continuity with the other parts notwithstanding. And even thus is it in Christ; although, in regard of his corporal presence, "the heaven must receive him, until the times of the restitution of all things,"[78] yet is he here with us "always, even unto the end of the world,"[79] in respect of the presence of his Spirit; by the vital influence whereof from him, as from the head, "the whole body is fitly joined together, and compacted by that which every joint supplieth, according to the effectual working in the measure of every part."[80] Which quickening Spirit if

---

[78] Acts 3:21.

[79] Matt. 28:20.

[80] Eph. 4:16.

it be wanting in any, no external communion with Christ or his Church can make him a true member of this mystical body; this being a most sure principle, that "he which hath not the Spirit of Christ, is none of his," Romans 8. 9.

Now, among all the graces that are wrought in us by the Spirit of Christ, the soul, as it were, of all the rest, and that whereby "the just doth live," is faith.[81] "For we through the Spirit wait for the hope of righteousness by faith," saith St. Paul to the Galatians.[82] And again: "I live, yet not I, but Christ liveth in me; and the life which I now live in the flesh, I live by the faith of the Son of God, who loved me, and gave himself for me."[83] By faith it is, that we do "receive" Christ;[84] and so likewise Christ "dwelleth in our hearts by faith."[85] Faith therefore is that spiritual mouth in us, whereby we "eat the flesh of the Son of man, and drink his blood,"[86] that is, as the Apostle expresseth it without the trope, "are made partakers of Christ";[87] he being by this means as truly, and every ways as effectually made ours, as the meat and drink which we receive into our natural bodies.

But you will say, if this be all the matter, what do we get by coming to the sacrament? seeing we have faith, and the quickening Spirit of Christ, before we come thither. To this I answer that the Spirit is received in divers measures, and faith bestowed upon us in different degrees; by reason whereof our conjunction with Christ may every day be made straighter, and the hold which we take of him firmer.[88] To receive the Spirit "not by measure,"[89] is the privilege of our head. We that "receive out of his fullness,"[90] have not our portion of grace delivered unto us all at once, but must daily

---

[81] Hab. 2:4; Rom. 1:17; Gal. 3:11; Heb. 10:38.

[82] Gal. 5:5.

[83] Gal. 2:20.

[84] John 1:12.

[85] Eph. 3:17.

[86] [John 6:53.]

[87] Heb. 3:14.

[88] [This note first appears in 1631.] *Aliud est nasci de Spiritu, aliud pasci de Spiritu* ["It is one thing to be born of the Spirit, another to be nourished by the Spirit"], saith St. Augustine. By the one we have life; by the other we have it more abundantly. John 10:10 [Augustine, *Sermones de Scripturis* 71.19 (*PL* 38:454; *NPNF1* 6:324)].

[89] John 3:34.

[90] John 1:16.

look for "supply of the Spirit of Jesus Christ."[91] So also, while we are in this world, "the righteousness of God is revealed" unto us "from faith to faith,"[92] that is, from one degree and measure of it to another, and consequently, we must still labour to "perfect that which is lacking in our faith,"[93] and evermore pray, with the apostles, "Lord, increase our faith."[94] As we have therefore "received Christ Jesus the Lord," so must we "walk in him; rooted and built up in him, and stablished in the faith,"[95] that we "may grow up into him in all things, which is the head."[96] And to this end God hath ordained public officers in his Church, "for the perfecting of the saints for the work of the ministry, for the edifying of the body of Christ, till we all come in the unity of the faith, and of the knowledge of the Son of God, unto a perfect man, unto the measure of the stature of the fullness of Christ,"[97] and hath accordingly "made them able ministers of the Spirit that quickeneth,"[98] and "ministers by whom we should believe, even as the Lord shall give to every man."[99] When we have therefore received the Spirit and faith,[100] and so spiritual life, by their ministry, we are not there to rest, but "as newborn babes we must desire the sincere milk of the word, that we may grow thereby."[101] And as grown men too, we must desire to be fed at the Lord's table, that by the strength of that spiritual repast we may be enabled to do the Lord's work; and may continually be nourished up thereby in the life of grace, unto the life of glory.

Neither must we here with a fleshly eye look upon the meanness of the outward elements, and have this faithless thought in our hearts, that there is no likelihood a bit of bread, and a draught of wine, should be able to produce such heavenly effects as these. For so we should prove ourselves to be no wiser than Naaman the Syrian was, who, having received

---

[91] Phil. 1:19.

[92] Rom. 1:17.

[93] 1 Thess. 3:10.

[94] Luke 17:5.

[95] Col. 2:6–7.

[96] Eph. 4:15.

[97] Eph. 4:12–13.

[98] 2 Cor. 3:6.

[99] 1 Cor. 3:5.

[100] Gal. 3:2; John 17:20.

[101] 1 Pet. 2:2.

direction from the man of God, that he should wash in Jordan seven times, to be cleansed of his leprosy, replied with indignation, "Are not Abana and Pharpar, rivers of Damascus, better than all the waters of Israel? May I not wash in them, and be clean?" But, as his servants did soberly advise him then, "if the Prophet had bid thee do some great thing, wouldst thou not have done it? How much rather then, when he saith to thee, 'Wash and be clean'?"[102] So give me leave to say unto you now: if the Lord had commanded us to do some great thing, for the attaining of so high a good, should not we willingly have done it? How much rather then, when he biddeth us to eat the bread, and drink the wine, that he hath provided for us at his own table, that by his blessing thereupon we may grow in grace, and be preserved both in body and soul unto everlasting life?

True it is indeed, these outward creatures have no natural power in them to effect so great a work as this is, no more than the water of Jordan had to recover the leper, but the work wrought by these means is supernatural, and God hath been pleased in the dispensation both of the word and of the sacraments so to ordain it, that these heavenly treasures should be presented unto us "in earthen vessels, that the excellency of the power might be of God."[103] As therefore in the preaching of the Gospel, the minister doth not *dare verba*,[104] and beat the air with a fruitless sound, but the words that he speaketh unto us are Spirit and life, "God being pleased by the foolishness of preaching to save them that believe,"[105] so likewise in the administration of the Lord's Supper, he doth not feed us with bare bread and wine, but, if we have the life of faith in us (for still we must remember that this table is provided not for the dead, but for the living), and come worthily, "the cup of blessing which he blesseth" will be unto us "the communion of the blood of Christ," and "the bread which he breaketh, the communion of the body of Christ";[106] of which precious body and blood we being really

made partakers (that is, in truth and indeed, and not in imagination only), although in a spiritual and not a corporal manner, the Lord doth "grant us, according to the riches of his glory, to be strengthened with might by his

---

[102] 2 Kgs 5:12–13.

[103] 2 Cor. 4:7.

[104] ["pour out words," lit. "to give words."]

[105] 1 Cor. 1:21.

[106] 1 Cor. 10:16.

Spirit in the inner man," that we may "be filled with all the fullness of God."[107] For the sacraments, as well as the word, be a part of that "ministration of the Spirit," which is committed to the "ministers of the New Testament,"[108] forasmuch as "by one Spirit," as before we have heard from the Apostle, "we have been all baptized into one body, and have been all made to drink into one Spirit."[109]

And thus have I finished the first part of my task, my *congregatio homogeneorum*, as I call it, the knitting together of those that appertain to the same body, both with their fellow-members, and with their head, which is the thing laid down in the express words of my text. It remaineth now that I proceed to the Apostle's application hereof unto the argument he hath in hand, which is *segregatio heterogeneorum*, a dissevering of those that be not of the same communion, that the faithful may not partake with idolaters, by countenancing, or any way joining with them in their ungodly courses. For that this is the main scope at which St. Paul aimeth, in his treating here of the sacrament, is evident both by that which goeth before in the 19 verse, "Wherefore my dearly beloved, flee from idolatry," and that which followeth in the 21. "Ye cannot drink the cup of the Lord, and the cup of devils; ye cannot be partakers of the Lord's table, and of the table of devils."

Whereby we may collect thus much, that as the Lord's Supper is a seal of our conjunction one with another, and with Christ our head, so is it an evidence of our disjunction from idolaters, binding us to disavow all communion with them in their false worship. And indeed, the one must necessarily follow upon the other, considering the nature of this heinous sin of idolatry is such, that it can no ways stand with the fellowship which a Christian man ought to have, both with the head, and with the body of the Church. To this purpose, in the sixth of the second to the Corinthians we read thus: "What agreement hath the temple of God with idols? For ye are the temple of the living God; as God hath said, I will dwell in them, and walk in them, and I will be their God, and they shall be my people. Wherefore come out from among them, and be ye separate, saith the Lord, and touch not the unclean thing; and I will receive you."[110] And in the second chapter of the Epistle to the Colossians: "Let no man beguile you of your

---

[107] Eph. 3:16, 19.

[108] 2 Cor. 3:6, 8.

[109] 1 Cor. 12:13.

[110] 2 Cor. 6:16–17.

reward, in a voluntary humility, and worshipping of angels, intruding into those things which he hath not seen, vainly puffed up by his fleshly mind: and not holding the head, from which all the body, by joints and bands having nourishment ministered and knit together, increaseth with the increase of God."[111] In which words the Apostle sheweth unto us, that such as under pretence of humility were drawn to the worshipping of angels, did "not hold the head," and consequently could not retain communion with the body, which receiveth his whole growth from thence. Answerably whereunto the fathers assembled out of divers provinces of Asia in the synod held at Laodicea, not far from the Colossians, did solemnly conclude, that "Christians ought not to forsake the Church of God, and go and invocate angels,"[112] and pronounced an anathema against any that should be found to do so, "because," say they, "he hath forsaken our Lord Jesus Christ, the Son of God, and given himself to idolatry,"[113] declaring plainly, that by this idolatrous invocation of angels, a discession[114] was made both from the Church of God, as they note in the beginning, and from Christ the head of the Church, as they observe in the end of their canon.

For the further understanding of this particular, it will not be amiss to consider what Theodoret, a famous bishop of the ancient Church, hath written of this matter in his commentary upon the 2d to the Colossians: that is, "They that defended the law," saith he, "induced them also to worship the angels, saying that the law was given by them. And this vice continued in Phrygia and Pisidia for a long time: for which cause also the synod assembled in Laodicea, the chief city of Phrygia, forbad them by a law to pray unto angels. And even to this day among them and their borderers,

---

[111] Col. 2:18–19.

[112] Council of Laodicea, Canon 35. ὅτι οὐ δεῖ χριστιανοὺς ἐγκαταλείπειν τὴν ἐκκλεσίαν τοῦ θεοῦ, καὶ ἀπίεναι, καὶ ἀγγέλους ὀνομάζειν [Giovanni Domenico Mansi, *Sacrorum Conciliorum Nova et Amplissima Collectio*, repr. ed., 53 vols in 60 (Paris: Welter, 1901–27), 2:570; NPNF2 14:150], that is, τοῖς ἀγγέλοις προσεύχεσθαι, or, εὔχεσθαι ἀγγέλοις, as Theodoret expoundeth these words of the canon in *Epist. ad. Colossenses*, 2 et 3 [PG 82:613B, 620D; *Theodoret of Cyrus: Commentaries on the Letters of St. Paul*, ed. Robert C. Hill, 2 vols (Brookline, MA: Holy Cross Orthodox Press, 2001), 2:95].

[113] ὅτι ἐγκατέλιπε τὸν κύριον ἡμῶν Ἰησοῦν χριστὸν, τὸν υἱὸν τοῦ θεοῦ, καὶ εἰδωλολατρεία προσῆλθεν [Council of Laodicea, Canon 35; *Mansi, Sacrorum Conciliorum ... Collectio*, 2:570; NPNF2 14:150].

[114] ["departure."]

there are oratories of Saint Michael to be seen. This therefore did they counsel should be done, using humility, and saying, that the God of all was invisible, and inaccessible, and incomprehensible; and that it was fit men should get God's favour by the means of angels. And this is it which the Apostle saith; in humility, and worshipping of angels."[115] Thus far Theodoret, whom Cardinal Baronius discerning to come somewhat close unto him, and to touch the idolatry of the popish crew a little to the quick, leaveth the poor shifts wherewith his companions labour to obscure the light of this testimony, and telleth us plainly, that "Theodoret, by his leave, did not well understand the meaning of Paul's words,"[116] and that those oratories of Saint Michael were erected anciently by catholics, and not by those heretics which were condemned in the Council of Laodicea, as he mistook the matter.[117] As if any wise man would be persuaded upon his bare word, that the memory of things done in Asia so long since, should be more fresh in Rome at this day, than in the time of Theodoret, who lived twelve hundred years ago.

Yet must I needs confess, that he showeth a little more modesty herein than Bellarmine his fellow Cardinal doth; who would make us believe, that the place in the nineteenth of the Revelation, where the angel saith to Saint John that would have worshipped him, "See thou do it not: I am thy fellow-servant: worship God,"[118] maketh for them, and demandeth very soberly, "Why they should be reprehended, who do the same thing that John did," and, "whether the Calvinists knew better than John, whether angels were to be adored or no."[119] And as for invocation of them, he telleth us, that Saint Jacob plainly prayed unto an angel, in the 48 of Genesis, when in blessing the sons of Joseph he said, "the angel which delivered

---

[115] [Theodoret, *Epist. ad. Colossenses* 2 (*PG* 82:613A–B; *Theodoret of Cyrus: Commentaries on the Letters of St. Paul*, 2:95).]

[116] *Ex his videas (quod necessario dicendum est) Theodoretum haud feliciter (ejus pace sit dictum) assecutum esse Pauli verborum sensum.* Caesar Baronius, *Annales Ecclesiastici*, 12 vols (Rome, 1588–1607), 1:573 (ann. 60).

[117] *Incaute nimis, quae a catholicis essent antiquitus instituta, haereticis, quorum nulla esset memoria, tribuens.* Baronius, *Annales Ecclesiastici*, 1:573 (ann. 60).

[118] [Rev. 19:10.]

[119] *Cur nos reprehendimur, qui facimus quod Joannes fecit? num melius Joanne norunt calvinistae, sintne angeli adorandi?* Robert Bellarmine, *De Sanctorum Beatitudine* 1.14 [*Opera Omnia*, 6 vols (Naples: Giuliano, 1856–1862), 2:446].

me from all evil, bless those children."[120] Whom for answer we remit to Saint Cyril, in the first chapter of the third book of his *Thesaurus*, and entreat him to tell us, how near of kin he is here to those heretics of whom Saint Cyril there speaketh. His words be these: "that he doth not mean (in that place, Genesis 48. 16.) an angel, as the heretics understand it, but the Son of God, is manifest by this: that when he had said, 'the angel', he presently addeth, 'who delivered me from all evils'." Which Saint Cyril presupposeth, no good Christian will ascribe to any but to God alone.[121]

But to come more near yet unto that which is idolatry most properly, an idol, we must understand, in the exact propriety of the term, doth signify any image; but according to the ecclesiastical use of the word, it noteth such an image as is set up for religious adoration. And in this latter sense we charge the adherents of the Church of Rome with gross idolatry, because that contrary to God's express commandment they are found to be worshippers of images.[122] Neither will it avail them here to say, that the idolatry forbidden in the Scripture is that only which was used by Jews and pagans. The Apostle indeed in this place, dehorting[123] Christians from idolatry, propoundeth the fall of the Jews in this kind before their eyes: "Neither be ye idolaters," saith he, "as some of them were." And so doth he also add concerning another sin, in the verse following: "Neither let us commit fornication, as some of them committed."[124] As well then might one plead, that Jewish or heathenish fornication were here only reprehended, as Jewish or heathenish idolatry. But as the one is a foul sin, whether it be committed by Jew, pagan, or Christian, so, if such as profess the name of Christ, shall practise that which the word of God condemneth in Jews and pagans for idolatry, their profession is so far from diminishing, that it augmenteth rather the heinousness of the crime. "The idols of the heathen are silver and

---

[120] *Hic aperte S. Jacob angelum invocavit.* Bellarmine, *De Sanctorum Beatitudine*, 1.19 [*Opera*, 2:451].

[121] [Cyril of Alexandria, *Thesaurus de Sancta et Consubstantiali Trinitate* 12 (*PG* 75:193A–196A).]

[122] See for this the excellent homily "Of the peril of idolatry" [*The Two Books of Homilies Appointed to be Read in Churches*, ed. John Griffiths (Oxford: Oxford University Press, 1859), 167–272].

[123] ["dissuading," "urging to refrain from."]

[124] 1 Cor. 10:7–8.

gold, the work of men's hands," saith the Psalmist,[125] and so the idols (of Christians, in all likelihood) mentioned in the Revelation, are said to be "of gold, and silver, and brass, and stone, and of wood; which neither can see, nor hear, nor walk."[126] The description of these idols, we see, agreeth in all points with popish images. Where is any difference?

The heathen, say they, held the images themselves to be gods, which is far from our thought. Admit, some of the simpler sort of the heathen did so. What shall we say of the Jewish idolaters, of whom the Apostle here speaketh, who erected the golden calf in the wilderness? Can we think that they were all so senseless, as to imagine that the calf, which they knew was not at all *in rerum natura*,[127] and had no being at that time when they came out of Egypt, should yet be that "God which brought them up out of the land of Egypt"?[128] And for the heathen: did the Romans and Grecians, when they dedicated in several places an hundred images, for example, to the honour of Jupiter, the king of all their gods, think that thereby they had made an hundred Jupiters? Or, when their blocks were so old, that they had need to have new placed in their stead, did they think by this change of their images, that they made change also of their gods? Without question they must so have thought, if they did take the very images themselves to be their gods, and yet the prophet bids us consider diligently, and we shall find that the heathen nations "did not change their gods."[129] Nay, what do we meet with more usually in the writings of the fathers, than these answers of the heathens for themselves? "We worship the gods by the images."[130] "We fear not them, but those to whose image they are made, and to whose names they are consecrated."[131] "I do not worship that stone, nor that im-

---

[125] Ps. 135:15.

[126] Rev. 9:20.

[127] [Lit. "in the nature of things" but understood as "in existence," "in the realm of actuality."]

[128] Exod. 32:4.

[129] Jer. 2:10–11.

[130] *Deos per simulcra veneramur.* Arnobius, *Adversus Gentes* 6.9 [*PL* 5:1180A; *ANF* 6:509].

[131] *Non ipsa, inquiunt, timemus; sed eos, ad quorum imaginem ficta, et quorum nominibus consecrata sunt.* Lactantius, *Divinarum Institutionum* 2.2 [*PL* 6:258B; *ANF* 7:41].

age which is without sense."[132] "I neither worship the image, nor a spirit in it: but by the bodily portraiture, I do behold the sign of that thing which I ought to worship."[133]

But admit they did not account the image itself to be God, will the papist further say: yet were those images set up to represent either things that had no being, or devils, or false gods, and in that respect were idols; whereas we erect images only to the honour of the true God, and of his servants the saints and angels. To this I might oppose that answer of the heathen to the Christians: "We do not worship evil spirits: such as you call angels, those do we also worship, the powers of the great God, and the ministers of the great God,"[134] and put them in mind of St. Augustine's reply: "I would you did worship them; you should easily learn of them not to worship them."[135] But I will grant unto them, that many of the idolatrous Jews' and heathens' images were such as they say they were, yet I deny that all of them were such, and confidently do avouch, that idolatry is committed by yielding adoration to an image of the true God himself. For proof whereof (omitting the idols of Micah,[136] and Jeroboam,[137] which were erected to the memory of Jehovah the God of Israel; as also the Athenians' superstitious worship of the unknown[138] god, Acts 17. 23. if, as the common

---

[132] *Non ego illum lapidem colo, nec illud simulacrum quod est sine sensu.* Augustine, *Enarrationes in Psalmos* 96.11 [*PL* 37:1244; *NPNF1* 8:477, where numbered 97.9].

[133] *Nec simulacrum nec daemonium colo; sed per effigiem corporalem ejus rei signum intueor, quam colere debeo.* Augustine, *Enarrationes in Psalmos* 113, sermo 2, 4 [*PL* 37:1483; *LF* 37:286, where numbered 115.4].

[134] *Non colimus mala daemonia: angelos quos dicitis, ipsos et nos colimus, virtutes Dei magni, et ministeria Dei magni.* Augustine, *Enarrationes in Psalmos* 96.12 [*PL* 37:1246; *NPNF1* 8:477, where numbered 97.10].

[135] *Utinam ipsos colere velletis; facile ab ipsis disceretis non illos colere.* Augustine, *Enarrationes in Psalmos* 96.12.

[136] Judg. 17:3, 13.

[137] 2 Kgs 10:16, 29, 31.

[138] Trebellius Pollio, in *The Life of Claudius* [*Divus Claudius* 2.4; *LCL* 263:154–55], calleth the God of Moses, *Incertum Numen* ["an unknown divinity"]; so doth Lucan the God of the Jews, *Pharsalia* 2: *et dedita sacris incerti Judaea Dei* ["and Judea given over to the worship of an unknown god"; *LCL* 220:100–101]. As therefore the Jews, by the relation of Tacitus, *Historiae* 2.78, worshipped their God in mount Carmel, *non simulacro aut templo, sed ara tantum* ["not with an image or temple; there is only an altar"; *LCL* 111:286–87]; so it might be that the Athenians also did the like: especially if we consider that their *ara misericordiae* ["altar of mercy"] (which might possibly be the same with this) is thus described by Statius, *Thebaidos* 12:

use of idolaters was, they added an image to their altar), I will content myself with these two places of Scripture; the one whereof concerneth the
Jews, the other the heathen. That which toucheth the heathen, is in the first
chapter of the Epistle to the Romans where, the Apostle having said that
God had showed unto them that which might be known of him and that
"the invisible things of him," that is, "his eternal power and Godhead,"[139]
was manifested unto them by the creation of the world and the contempla-
tion of the creatures, he addeth presently that God was sorely displeased
with them, and therefore gave them up unto vile affections, because "they
changed the glory of that incorruptible God, into an image made like to
corruptible men, and to birds, and four-footed beasts, and creeping
things."[140] Whereby it is evident, that the idolatry condemned in the wisest
of the heathen, was the adoring of the invisible God, whom they acknowledged to be the Creator of all things, in visible images fashioned to the similitude of men and beasts.

The other place of Scripture is the fourth of Deuteronomy, where
Moses useth this speech unto the children of Israel: "The Lord spake unto
you out of the midst of the fire: ye heard the voice of the words, but saw no
similitude, only ye heard a voice," verse 12. And what doth he infer upon
this? "Take ye therefore good heed unto yourselves," saith he in the 15.
verse, "for ye saw no manner of similitude on the day that the Lord spake
unto you in Horeb, out of the midst of the fire. Lest ye corrupt yourselves,
and make you a graven image, the similitude of any figure, the likeness of
male or female, the likeness of any beast that is on the earth, the likeness of
any winged fowl that flieth in the air, the likeness of any thing that creepeth
on the ground, the likeness of any fish that is in the waters beneath the
earth." Where we may observe: first, that God in the delivery of the law did
purposely use a voice only; because that such a creature as that was not to
be expressed by visible lineaments, as if that voice should have said unto
the painter, as Echo is feigned to do in the poet.

Nulla autem effigies, nulli commissa metallo
Forma Dei; mentes habitare et pectora gaudet.

["No image is there, no shape of deity committed to metal; she joys to dwell in
minds and hearts; *LCL* 498:284–85].

[139] [Rom. 1:20.]

[140] [Rom. 1:23. Elrington corrects "men" to the KJV's "man" in *WJU*, 2:443.]

Vane, quid affectas faciem mihi ponere, pictor?
Si mihi vis similem pingere, pinge sonum.[141]

Secondly, that when He uttered the words of the second commandment in Mount Sinai, and forbad the making of the likeness of any thing
"that is in heaven above, or in the earth beneath, or in the waters under the
earth," he did at that time forbear to show himself in any visible shape, either of man or woman, either of beast in the earth, fowl in the air, or fish in
the waters beneath the earth; to the end it might be the better made known,
that it was his pleasure not to be adored at all in any such forms, and that
the worshipping of images, not only as they have reference to the creatures
whom they do immediately represent, or to false gods, but also as they have
relation to himself (the true God, who was then speaking unto them in the
mount), did come within the compass of the idolatry, which was condemned in that commandment.

In vain therefore do the Romanists go about to persuade us that their
images be no idols, and as vainly also do they spend time in curiously distinguishing the several degrees of worship; the highest point whereof, which
they call *Latreia*, and acknowledge to be due only unto God, they would be
loathe we should think that they did communicate to any of their images.
But here we are to understand, first of all, that idolatry may be committed
by giving not the highest only, but also the lowest degree of religious adoration unto images, and therefore, in the words of the commandment, the
very "bowing down unto them," which is one of the meanest degrees of
worship, is expressly forbidden. Secondly, that it is the received doctrine of
popish divines, that the image should be honoured with the same worship,
wherewith that thing is worshipped, whose image it is, and therefore what
adoration is due to Christ and the Trinity, the same by this ground they are
to give unto their images.[142] Thirdly, that in the Roman pontifical published
by the authority of Clement the VIII (to omit other testimonies in this kind)
it is concluded, that the cross of the pope's legate shall have the right hand,
upon this very reason, *quia debetur ei latria,* because the worship proper to

---

[141] Ausonius, *Epigrammata* 32 ["Fond painter, why dost thou essay to limn my face?
... if thou wouldst paint my likeness, paint sound"; *LCL* 115:174–75].

[142] *Constans est theologorum sententia, imaginem eodem honore et cultu honorari et coli, quo coli-
tur id cujus est imago.* Juan Azor, *Institutiones Morales,* 3 vols (Cologne, 1613–18), 1:588
(1.9.6).

God is due to it.[143] Now whether they commit idolatry, who communicate unto a senseless thing that worship which they themselves confess to be due unto God alone, let all the world judge.

They were best therefore from henceforth confess themselves to be idolaters, and stand to it, that every kind of idolatry is not unlawful. Their Jesuit Gregorius de Valentia will tell them for their comfort, that it is no absurdity to think that St. Peter, when he deterreth the faithful by name *ab illicitis Idolorum cultibus* (ἀθεμίτους εἰδωλολατρείας St. Peter calleth them, that is, abominable idolatries), doth insinuate thereby, that some worship[144] of images is lawful.[145] John Monceye, the Frenchman, in his *Aaron Purgatus* (dedicated to the late pope Paul the fifth),[146] and in his twenty questions propounded to Visorius,[147] stretcheth yet a strain higher. For howsoever he cannot away with the name of idols and idolatry, yet he liketh the thing itself so well, that he undertaketh to clear Aaron from committing any error in setting up the golden calf, and laboureth to purge Laban, and Micah, and Jeroboam too from the imputation of idolatry, having found indeed, that nothing had been done by them in this kind, which is not agreeable to the practice of the Roman church at this day.

And lest the poor people, whom they have so miserably abused, should find how far they have been misled; we see that the masters of that church do in the service books and catechisms, which come unto the hands of the vulgar, generally leave out the words of the 2. commandment that make against the adoration of images, fearing lest by the light thereof, the mystery of their iniquity should be discovered. They pretend indeed that

---

[143] *Crux legati, quia debetur ei latria, erit a dextris. Pontificale Romanum Clementis VIII Pont. Max. Iussu restitutum atque editum* (Rome, 1595), 672. [Available in facsimile edition: *Pontificale Romanum: Editio Princeps* (1595–1596), ed. Manlio Sodi and Achille Maria Triacca (Vatican: Libreria Editrice Vaticana, 1997).]

[144] Some idolatry he should say: for that is St. Peter's word. 1 Pet. 4:3.

[145] Gregory of Valencia, *De Idololatria Contra Sectariorum Contumelias Disputatio; una cum Apologetico adversus Iacobum Heerbrandum Lutheranum* (Ingolstadt, 1580), 241–42.

[146] [Franciscus Moncaeus (Monceaux), *Aaron Purgatus, sive De Vitulo Aureo* (Arras, 1606). It is only fair to note that the dedicatee banned the book three years later and that it would have the dubious honour of appearing first in the alphabetical list of *Index Librorum Prohibitorum Alexandri VII Pontificis Maximi: Iussu editus* (Rome, 1664), 1.]

[147] [For the twenty questions and Robert Viseur's response, see Visorius, *Aaronis Purgati, seu Pseudo-Cherubi ex aureo vitulo recens conflati destructio* (Paris, 1609), 59r–99r.]

this commandment is not excluded by them, but included only in the first, whereas in truth they do but craftily conceal it from the people's eyes, because they would not have them to be ruled by it. Nay, Vasquez the Jesuit doth boldly acknowledge, that it plainly appeareth, by comparing the words of this commandment with the place which hath been alleged out of the 4. of Deuteronomy, that the Scripture did not only forbid the worshipping of an image for God, but also the adoration of the true God himself in an image. He confesseth further, that he and his fellow Catholics do otherwise.[148] What saith he then to the commandment, think you? Because it will not be obeyed, it must be repealed, and not admitted to have any place among the moral precepts of God. It was, saith he, a positive and ceremonial law, and therefore ought to cease in the time of the Gospel.[149] And as if it had not been enough for him to match the Scribes and Pharisees in impiety, who "made the commandment of God of none effect, that they might keep their own tradition,"[150] that he might fulfill the measure of his fathers, and show himself to be a true child of her, who beareth the name of being "the mother of harlots and abominations of the earth,"[151] he is yet more mad, and sticketh not to maintain, that not only a painted image, but any other thing of the world, whether it be without life and reason, or whether it be a reasonable creature, may, in the nature of the thing, and if the matter be discreetly handled, be adored with God, as his image; yea, and counteth it no absurdity at all, that a very wisp of straw should be thus worshipped.[152]

---

[148] Gabriel Vásquez, *De Cultu Adorationis* (Mainz, 1601), 196–97 (lib. 2, disput. 4, cap. 3, sec. 74–75).

[149] *Cum fuerit juris positivi et caeremonialis illa legis Mosaicae prohibito, tempore legis evangelicae debuit cessare; atque id, quod alias jure naturali licitum et honestum est, ut imagines depingere, et illis etiam uti ad adorationem, in lege evangelica locum habere debet* ["Since that prohibition of the Mosaic law was a positive and ceremonial law, it ought to cease in the time of the gospel; and that, which otherwise was lawful and honest by natural law, that we should depict images, and even use them for adoration, ought to have a place in the law of the gospel"]. Vásquez, *De Cultu Adorationis*, 203 (lib. 2, disput. 4, cap. 4, sec. 84).

[150] Matt. 15:6; Mark 7:9.

[151] Rev. 17:5.

[152] Vásquez, *De Cultu Adorationis*, 453, 455–56, 457–58 (lib. 3, disput. 1, cap. 2, sec. 5, 8, 10).

But let us turn yet again, and we shall see greater abominations than these.[153] We heard how this blessed sacrament which is here propounded by the Apostle as a bond to unite Christians together in one body, hath been made the apple of strife, and the occasion of most bitter breaches in the Church. We may now observe again, that the same holy sacrament, which by the same Apostle is here brought in as a principal inducement to make men "flee from idolatry,"[154] is by our adversaries made the object of the grossest idolatry that ever hath been practised by any. For their constant doctrine is, that in worshipping the sacrament they should give unto it *latriae cultum qui vero Deo debetur*, as the Council of Trent hath determined, "that kind of service which is due to the true God," determining their worship in that very thing which the priest doth hold betwixt his hands.[155] Their practice also runs accordingly, for an instance whereof we need go no further than to Sanders' book of the Lord's Supper, before which he hath prefixed an epistle dedicatory, superscribed in this manner: "To the body and blood of our Saviour Jesus Christ, under the forms of bread and wine, all honour, praise, and thanks, be given for ever," adding further in the process of that blockish epistle, "Howsoever it be with other men, I adore thee my God and Lord really present under the forms of bread and wine, after consecration duly made: beseeching thee of pardon for my sins, &c."[156]

Now if the conceit which these men have concerning the sacrament should prove to be false, as indeed we know it to be most absurd and monstrous, their own Jesuit Coster doth freely confess that they should be in such an "error and idolatry, *qualis in orbe terrarum nunquam vel visus vel auditus fuit*, as never was seen or heard of in this world. For the error of them is more tolerable," saith he, "who worship for God a statue of gold or silver, or an image of any other matter, as the Gentiles adored their gods; or a red cloth lifted up upon a spear, as it is reported of the Lappians; or living creatures, as did sometime the Egyptians; than of those that worship a piece of

---

[153] Ezek. 8:15.

[154] [1 Cor. 10:14.]

[155] *Council of Trent*, Session 13, chap. 5 [*Decrees of the Ecumenical Councils*, ed. Norman P. Tanner, 2 vols (London: Sheed and Ward, 1990), 2:695].

[156] [Nicholas Sanders, *The Supper of Our Lord, Set Foorth According to the Truth of the Gospell and the Catholicke Faith* (Louvain, 1566), sig. Aii r, v.]

bread."[157] We therefore, who are verily persuaded that the papists do thus, must of force, if we follow their Jesuit's direction, judge them to be the most intolerable idolaters that ever were.

Nay, according to their own principles, how is it possible that any of themselves should certainly know, that the host which they worship should be any other thing but bread? seeing the change doth wholly depend upon "consecration duly made," as Sanders speaketh, and that dependeth upon the intention of the priest, which no man but himself can have notice of. Bellarmine, disputing against Ambrosius Catharinus, one of his own brethren, that a man hath no certain knowledge of his own justification, can take advantage of this, and allege for himself, that one "cannot be certain by the certainty of faith, that he doth receive a true sacrament; forasmuch as the sacrament cannot be made without the intention of the minister, and none can see another man's intention."[158] Apply this now to the matter we have in hand and see into what intricate labyrinths these men have brought themselves. Admit the priest's intention stood right at the time of consecration, yet if he that baptized him failed in his intention when he administered that sacrament, he remaineth still unbaptized, and so becometh incapable of priesthood, and consequently, whatsoever he consecrateth is but bread still. Yea, admit he were rightly baptized too: if either the bishop that conferred upon him the sacrament of orders, for so they hold it to be, or those that baptized or ordained that bishop, missed their right intention, neither will the one prove bishop, nor the other priest, and so with what intention soever either the one or the other doth consecrate, there remaineth but bread still. Neither doth the inconvenience stay here, but ascendeth upward to all their predecessors, in any one of whom if there fall out to be a nullity of priesthood, for want of intention either in the baptizer or in the ordainer, all

---

[157] *Tolerabilior est enim error eorum, qui pro Deo colunt statuam auream aut argenteam, aut alterius materiae imaginem, quo modo gentiles deos suos venerabantur; vel pannum rubrum in hastam elevatum, quod narratur de Lappis; vel viva animalia, ut quondam Aegyptii: quam eorum qui frustum panis.* Francis Coster, *Enchiridion Controversiarum Praecipuarum Nostri Temporis de Religione* (Cologne, 1608), 419 (cap. 12). [Ussher appears to have been intrigued by the idea of the Lapps worshipping their red cloth. This example can be found in *A Bodie of Divinitie, or Summe and Substance of Christian Religion* (1645), 3, and in a sermon on Rom. 1:20 preached in 1651 (Cambridge University Library, MS Mm.6.55, fol. 207r).]

[158] *Neque potest certus esse certitudine fidei, se percipere verum sacramentum cum sacramentum sine intentione ministri non conficiatur, et intentionem alterius nemo videre possit.* Bellarmine, *De Justificatione* 3.8 [*Opera*, 4/1:543].

the generation following, according to their principles, go without their priesthood too, and so deliver but bread to the people, instead of the body of Christ. The papists themselves therefore, if they stand unto their own grounds must needs confess, that they are in no better case here than the Samaritans were in, of whom our Saviour saith, "Ye worship ye know not what."[159] But we know that what they worship, be the condition or intention of their priest what it will be, is bread indeed; which while they take to be their God, we must still account them guilty of spiritual fornication, "and such fornication, as is not so much as named amongst the Gentiles."[160]

These then being the idolaters with whom we have to deal, let us learn first how dangerous a thing it is to communicate with them in their false worship. For if we will be partakers of Babylon's sins, we must look to receive of her plagues.[161] Secondly, we are to be admonished, that it is not sufficient that in our own persons we refrain worshipping of idols, but it is further required that we restrain, as much as in us lieth, the practice thereof in others, lest by suffering God to be dishonoured in so high a manner, when we may by our calling hinder it, we make ourselves partakers of other men's sins. Eli the high priest was a good man, and gave excellent counsel unto his lewd sons, yet we know what judgment fell upon him, "because his sons made themselves vile, and he frowned not upon them,"[162] that is, restrained them not; which God doth interpret to be a kind of idolatry, in "honouring of his sons above him."[163] The church of Pergamum did for her own part hold fast Christ's name, and denied not his faith, yet had the Lord something against her, "because she had there, them that held the doctrine of Balaam, who taught Balak to cast a stumbling-block before the children of Israel, to eat things sacrificed unto idols, and to commit fornication."[164] So we see what special notice our Saviour taketh of the works, and charity, and service, and faith, and patience of the church of Thyatira, yet for all this he addeth, "Notwithstanding, I have a few things against thee, because thou sufferest that woman Jezebel, which calleth herself a prophet-

---

[159] John 4:22.

[160] [1 Cor. 5:1.]

[161] Rev. 18:4.

[162] 1 Sam. 3:13.

[163] 1 Sam. 2:29.

[164] Rev. 2:14.

ess, to teach and to seduce my servants to commit fornication, and to eat things sacrificed unto idols."[165]

In the second of Judges God telleth the children of Israel what mischief should come unto them by tolerating the Canaanitish idolaters in their land. "They shall be thorns in your sides," saith he, "and their gods shall be a snare unto you."[166] Which words contain in them the intimation of a double danger: the one respecting the soul, the other the body. That which concerneth the soul is, that their idols should be "a snare unto them." For God well knew that man's nature is as prone to spiritual fornication, as it is to corporal. As therefore for the preventing of the one, he would not have a common harlot tolerated in Israel, "lest the land should fall to whoredom, and become full of wickedness,"[167] so for the keeping out of the other, he would have provocations taken away, and all occasions whereby a man might be tempted to commit so vile a sin. The bodily danger that followeth upon the toleration of idolaters is that "they should be in their sides," that is, as in another place it is more fully expressed, "they should be pricks in their eyes, and thorns in their sides, and should vex them in the land wherein they dwelled."[168] Now in both these respects it is certain that the toleration of the idolaters with whom we have to do, is far more perilous than of any other. In regard of the spiritual danger, wherewith simple souls are more like to be ensnared: because this kind of idolatry is not brought in with an open show of impiety, as that of the pagans, but is "a mystery of iniquity,"[169] a wickedness covered with the veil of piety, and the harlot, which maketh the inhabitants of the earth drunk with the wine of this fornication, is both gilded herself, and presenteth also her abominations unto her followers in "a cup of gold."[170] If we look to outward peril, we are like to find these men, not thorns in our sides to vex us, but daggers in our hearts to destroy us. Not that I take all of them to be of this furious disposition (mistake me not, I know a number myself of a far different temper), but because there are never wanting among them some turbulent humours, so inflamed with the spirit of fornication, that they run mad with it, and are

---

[165] Rev. 2:20.

[166] Judg. 2:3.

[167] Lev. 19:29.

[168] Num. 33:55.

[169] [2 Thess. 2:7.]

[170] Rev. 17:2, 4.

transported so far, that no tolerable terms can content them, until they have attained to the utmost pitch of their unbridled desires. For compassing whereof, there is no treachery, nor rebellion, nor murder, nor desperate course whatsoever, that, without all remorse of conscience, they dare not adventure upon.

Neither *do* they thus only, but they *teach* men also so to do, arming both pope, and bishops, and people, and private persons, with power to cast down even kings themselves from their thrones if they stand in their way, and give any impediment to their designs. Touching the pope's power herein, there is no disputing. One of them telleth us, that "there is no doubt, but the pope may depose all kings, when there is a reasonable cause so to do."[171] For bishops, cardinal Baronius informeth us by the example of Dacius the bishop of Milan's dealing against the Arians, that "those bishops deserve no blame, and ought to suffer no envy, who roll every stone" (yea and rather than fail, would blow up stones too), "that they may not live under an heretical prince."[172] For the people, Dominicus Bannes, a Dominican friar, resolves that they need not, in this case, expect any sentencing of the matter by pope or other, but "when the knowledge of the fault is evident, subjects may lawfully (if so be they have sufficient strength) exempt themselves from subjection to their princes, before any declaratory sentence of a judge."[173] And that we may understand that the proviso which he inserteth, "of having strength sufficient," is very material, he putteth us in mind, that "the faithful," the papists he meaneth, "of England are to be excused hereby, who do not exempt themselves from the power of their superiors, nor make war against them. Because that generally they have not power suffi-

---

[171] *Dubium non est, quin papa possit omnes reges, cum subest causa rationabilis, deponere.* Augustinus Triumphus [Augustine of Ancona], *Summa de Potestate Ecclesiastica* (Rome, 1584), 250 (quaest. 46, art. 2).

[172] *Quo exemplo satis intelligas, non mereri calumniam, neque invidiam episcopos illos pati debere, qui, ne sub haeretico principe degant, omnem lapidem volvunt.* Baronius, *Annales Ecclesiastici* 7:294–95 (ann. 538). [Ussher, warming to his theme, anticipates the discussion of the Powder Treason which follows below.]

[173] *Quando adest evidens notitia criminis, licite possunt subditi (si modo eis vires suppetant) eximere se a potestate suorum principum ante judicis sententiam declaratoriam.* Domingo Báñez, *De Fide, Spe & Charitate ... Commentaria in Secundam Secundae Angelici Doctoris* (Salamanca, 1584), 686E–687A (quaest. 12, art. 2).

cient to make such wars against princes, and great dangers are imminent over them."[174]

Lastly, for private persons, we may read in Suarez that an heretical king, "after sentence given against him, is absolutely deprived of his kingdom, so that he cannot possess it by any just title: and therefore from thenceforth may be handled altogether as a tyrant; and consequently he may be killed by any private person."[175] Only the Jesuit addeth this limitation: that, "if the pope do depose the king he may be expelled or killed by them only to whom he shall commit that business. But if he enjoin the execution thereof to nobody, then it shall appertain to the lawful successor in the kingdom; or if none such be to be found, it shall belong to the kingdom itself."[176] But let him once be declared to be a tyrant; Mariana, Suarez's countryman and fellow Jesuit, will tell you better how he should be handled. "That a tyrant," saith he, "may be killed by open force and arms, whether by violent breaking in into the court, or by joining of battle, is a matter confessed: yea, and by deceit and ambushes too, as Ehud did in killing Eglon the king of the Moabites. Indeed it would argue a braver mind to profess open enmity, and publicly to rush in upon the enemy of the commonwealth: but it is no less prudence to take advantage by fraud and ambushes, because it is done without stir, and with less danger surely, both public and private."[177] His conclusion is, that "it is lawful to take away his life, by any art whatsoever: with this proviso only, that he be not constrained either

---

[174] *Ex hac conclusione sequitur esse excusandos Anglicanos et Saxonios fideles, qui non se eximunt a potestate superiorum, nec bellum contra illos gerunt. Quoniam communiter non habent facultatem ad haec bella gerenda contra principes, et imminent illis gravia pericula.* Báñez, *De Fide*, 685E.

[175] *Post sententiam latam omnino privatur regno, ita ut non possit justo titulo illud possidere: ergo extunc poterit tanquam omnino tyrannus tractari; et consequenter a quocunque privato poterit interfici.* Francisco Suárez, *Defensio Fidei Catholicae et Apostolicae adversus Anglicanae Sectae Errores* (Cologne, 1614), 819B (6.4.14).

[176] *Si papa regem deponat, ab illis tantum poterit expelli, vel interfici, quibus ipse id commiserit. Quod si nulli executionem imperet, pertinebit ad legitimum in regno successorem; vel, si nullus inventus fuerit, ad regnum ipsum spectabit.* Suárez, *Defensio Fidei*, 820F (6.4.18).

[177] *Itaque aperta vi et armis posse occidi tyrannum, sive impetu in regiam facto, sive commissa pugna, in confessio est. Sed et dolo atque insidiis exceptum quod fecit Aiod, &c. Est quidem majoris virtutis et animi simultatem aperte exercere, palam in hostem reipublicae irruere: sed non minoris prudentiae, fraudi et insidiis locum captare, quod sine motu contingat, minori certe periculo publico atque privato.* Juan de Mariana, *De Rege et Regis Institutione* (Hanau, 1611), 64–65 (1.7).

wittingly or unwittingly to be the cause of his own death."[178] Where the tenderness of a Jesuit's conscience is well worth the observing. He maketh no scruple at all to take away the man's life; only he would advise that he be not made away, by having poison conveyed into his meat or drink, lest in taking hereof, forsooth, he which is to be killed, should by this means have some hand in procuring his own death. Yet poison him you may, if you list, so that the venom be "externally applied by some other, he that is to be killed helping nothing thereunto: namely, when the force of the poison is so great, that a seat or garment being infected therewith, it may have strength to kill."[179] And that such means of poisoning hath been used, he proveth by divers practices of the Moors, which we leave to be considered of by Fitzherbert, who (to prove that Squire's intention of poisoning Queen Elizabeth in this manner, was but a mere fiction) would persuade us that it is not agreeable to the grounds of nature and reason, that any such thing should be.[180]

Thus we see what pestilent doctrine is daily broached by these incendiaries of the world: which, what pernicious effects it hath produced, I need not go far to exemplify. This assembly and this place cannot but call to mind the memory of that barbarous plot of the Powder-treason. Which being most justly charged to have exceeded "all measure of cruelty," as involving not the king alone, but also his children, and the states of the kingdom, and many thousands of innocent people, in the same ruin; a wicked

---

[178] *In ejus vitam grassari quacunque arte concessum; ne cogatur tantum, sciens aut imprudens, sibi conscire mortem.* Juan de Mariana, *De Rege*, 68.

[179] *Hoc tamen temperamento uti in hac quidem disputatione licebit, si non ipse qui perimitur venenum haurire cogitur, quo intimis medullis concepto pereat; sed exterius ab alio adhibeatur, nihil adjuvante eo qui perimendus est: nimirum cum tanta vis est veneni, ut, sella eo aut veste delibuta, vim interficiendi habeat.* Juan de Mariana, *De Rege*, 67.

[180] [This is a reference to one of the more bizarre plots to assassinate Queen Elizabeth, one which was thought to implicate both the Jesuits and the King of Spain. Edward Squier was alleged to have plotted to apply poison to the queen's saddle. Thomas Fitzherbert, English secretary to Philip II at the time of the plot, wrote in Squire's defence, arguing that "the force also of that poison (if any such had been) is declared by reasons and authority both of physic and philosophy that it could not work any such effect as was imagined, or pretended," in *An Apology of T.F. in Defence of Himself and Other Catholics, falsly charged with a fayned conspiracy against her Majesties person, for the which one Edward Squyre was wrongfully condemned and executed in the yeare of our Lorde 1598*, "Advertisement to the Reader," sig. A2v, appended to *A Defence of the Catholyck Cause* (Antwerp, 1602).]

varlet, with whose name I will not defile this place, steppeth forth some four years after, and with a brazen forehead biddeth us not to wonder at the matter. "For of an evil and pernicious herb, both the seeds are to be crushed, and all the roots to be pulled up, that they grow not again. And otherwise also, for a few wicked persons it falleth out oftentimes that many perish in shipwreck."[181] In the latter of which reasons we may note these men's insolent impiety toward God, in arrogating unto themselves such an absolute power for the murdering of innocents, as he that is Lord of all hath over his own creatures, the best of whom, if he do enter into judgment with them, will not be found righteous in his sight.[182] In the former, we may observe their deadly malice toward God's anointed, which they sufficiently declare will not be satisfied, but by the utter extirpation of him and all his royal progeny.

And whereas, for the discovery of such wicked spirits, his majesty in his princely wisdom did cause an Oath of Allegiance to be framed, by the tendering whereof he might be the better able to distinguish betwixt his loyal and disloyal subjects, and to put a difference betwixt a seditious and a quiet-minded Romanist, this companion derideth his simplicity, in imagining that that will serve the turn, and supposing that a papist will think himself any whit bound by taking such an oath. "See," saith he, "in so great craft, how great simplicity doth bewray[183] itself. When he had placed all his security in that oath, he thought he had found such a manner of oath, knit with so many circumstances, that it could not, with safety of conscience, by any means be dissolved by any man. But he could not see, that, if the pope

---

[181] *At, inquies, omnem modum crudelitatis excessit ea conjurato; cum et prolem, et regni ordines simul implicuisset. Id velim ne mireris. Nam malae et perniciosae herbae et semina conterenda, et radices omnes evellendae sunt, ne recrescant. Alias etiam, propter paucos sceleratos, multi saepe naufragio pereunt.* B. P., ἐξετασ. epistolae, I. R. impress. anno 1609. [Ussher's refusal to speak the name from the pulpit is paralleled by this reference which gives only the author's initials. Bartholus Pacenius, Ἐξετασις, *Epistola Nomine Regis Magnae Britanniae, Ad Omnes Christianos Monarchos, Principes, & Ordines, scriptae: quae, praefationis monitoriae loco, ipsius Apologiae pro iuramento fidelitatis, praefixa est* (Mons [Mainz?], 1609), sig. A4r. This work is usually attributed to Robert Abercomby, the Scottish Jesuit who claimed to have received Anne of Denmark, James's queen, into the Roman church. It is a libellous attack on James's *Apology for the Oath of Allegiance* and Abercromby strenuously denied that he was the author. See *ODNB*, "Abercromby, Robert (1536–1613)."]

[182] [Possible allusion to Job 4:18; 15:15, etc.]

[183] ["reveal" or "expose" unintentionally.]

did dissolve that oath, all the tyings of it, whether of performing fidelity to the king, or of admitting no dispensation, would be dissolved together. Yea, I will say another thing that is more admirable. You know, I believe, that an unjust oath, if it be evidently known or openly declared to be such, bindeth no man, but is void *ipso facto*.[184] That the king's oath is unjust, hath been sufficiently declared by the pastor of the Church himself. You see therefore that the obligation of it is vanished into smoke: so that the bond, which by so many wise men was thought to be of iron, is become less than of straw."[185]

If matters now be come unto this pass, that such as are addicted to the pope will account the Oath of Allegiance to have less force to bind them than a rope of straw, judge ye whether that be not true which hath been said, that in respect not of spiritual infection only, but of outward danger also to our state, any idolaters may be more safely permitted than papists. Which I do not speak, to exasperate you against their persons, or to stir you up to make new laws for shedding of their blood. Their blindness I do much pity, and my heart's desire and prayer to God for them is, that they might be saved. Only this I must say, that, things standing as they do, I cannot preach peace unto them. For as Jehu said to Joram, "What peace, so long as the whoredoms of thy mother Jezebel, and her witchcrafts are so many?"[186] So must I say unto them: What peace can there be, so long as you suffer yourselves to be led by the mother of harlots and abominations of the earth, who by her sorceries hath deceived all nations, and made them drunk with the wine of her fornication?[187] Let her put away her whoredoms

---

[184] ["By the fact (or act) itself."]

[185] *Sed vide in tanta astutia, quanta sit simplicitas. Cum omnem securitatem in eo juramento sibi statuisset, talem se modum juramenti tot circumstantiis connexuisse existimabat, qui, salva conscientia, nulla ratione a quoquam dissolvi posset. Sed videre non potuit, si pontifex juramentum dissolverit, omnes illius nexus, sive de fidelitate regi praestanda, sive de dispensatione non admittenda, pariter dissolutos fore* [*foro* in 2nd edition of 1610]. *Immo aliud dicam admirabilius. Nosti, credo, juramentum injustum, si tale esse evidenter sciatur vel aperte declaretur, neminem obligare; sed ipso facto nullum esse. Regis juramentum injustum esse, ab ipso Ecclesiae pastore sufficienter declaratum est. Vides igitur jam, in summum abiisse illius obligationem; ut vinculum, quod a tot sapientibus ferreum putabatur, minus sit, quam stramineum.* [Pacenius, Ἐξέτασις, sig. B2v.]

[186] 2 Kgs 9:22.

[187] Rev. 17:2, 5; 18:23.

out of her sight, and her adulteries from between her breasts;[188] let her repent of her murders, and her sorceries, and her idolatries: or rather, because she is past all hope, let those that are seduced by her, cease to communicate with her in these abominable iniquities; and we shall be all ready to meet them, and rejoice with the angels in heaven for their conversion. In the meantime, they who sit at the helm, and have the charge of our church and common-wealth committed to them, must provide by all good means, that God be not dishonoured by their open idolatries, nor our king and state endangered by their secret treacheries. Good laws there are already enacted to this purpose, which if they were duly put in execution, we should have less need to think of making new. But it is not my part to press this point. I will therefore conclude as I did begin: "I speak as to wise men; judge ye what I say."[189]

2 Timothy 2. 7.

"Consider what I say; and the Lord give you understanding in all things."

---

[188] Hos. 2:2.

[189] 1 Cor. 10:15.

A BRIEF DECLARATION OF THE UNIVERSALITY OF THE CHURCH (1624)

A Brief Declaration of the Universality of the Church of Christ, and the Unity of the Catholic Faith Professed Therein: Delivered in a Sermon Before the King's Majesty, the 20th of June, 1624, at Wanstead.[1]

Ephesians 4.13.

"Till we all come in the unity of the faith, and of the knowledge of the Son of God, unto a perfect man, unto the measure of the stature of the fullness of Christ."

WHEN THE LORD'S ark was to set forward, the form of prayer used by Moses was, "Rise up, Lord, and let thine enemies be scattered, and let them that hate thee, flee before thee."[2] The sweet psalmist of Israel, framing his descant to this ground, beginneth the psalm, which he prepared to be sung at the removing of the ark, after the same manner: "Let God arise, let his

---

[1] [The text followed here is that of 1631. The sermon was first published in 1624, with a second impression in 1625 (appended to the first London printing of *An Answer to a Challenge Made by a Iesuite in Ireland*), and a third in 1629. 'The third impression, corrected and amended' appeared in 1631 and can be found in *The Workes of the Most Reverend Father in God, Iames Vssher, Archbishop of Armagh, and Primate of Ireland* (1631), with its own frontispiece and separate pagination. This early collection of Ussher's works was a composite of pieces produced on several presses. A fourth impression was published in 1687. The sermon can be found in *WJU*, 2:469–506. There are a number of manuscript witnesses. Ussher's own preparatory notes can be consulted in Bodleian, MS Rawlinson D1290, fols 59r–62r. Fragmentary notes are included in *CUL*, MS Add. 69, fols 130v–129v (reversed pagination). The account found in Balliol College, Oxford, MS 259, fols 420r–39r appears to be copied from one of the printed editions of the 1620s.]

[2] Num. 10:35.

enemies be scattered: let them also that hate him, flee before him," and then goeth on, till at length he hath raised his note unto his full height: "Thou hast ascended up on high; thou hast led captivity captive; thou hast received gifts for men."[3] Which being by our Apostle, in this chapter, interpreted of the ascension of our Saviour Christ into heaven,[4] and made the very spring from whence the matter of my present text is derived, leadeth us to the just application of the type to the truth, and putteth us in mind that the removing of the ark, which gave occasion to the penning of this psalm, was an adumbration of our Saviour's removal from the earth to heaven; and that by this absence of his we are no losers, but gainers, seeing he is ascended up on high, both to triumph over his and our foes ("he led captivity captive"), and to confer benefits upon his friends ("he gave gifts unto men").

The ark of the covenant,[5] we know, was appointed to be a figure of Jesus, "the mediator of the new covenant,"[6] the great king, prophet, and priest of his Church. Therefore was it ordered, that the ark should have "a crown of gold" about it;[7] than which, what could be more fit to set forth the state of our king? For thus "we see Jesus crowned with glory and honour."[8] Upon the ark stood the propitiatory or mercy-seat, whence God did use to deliver his oracles from betwixt the cherubim; than which, what more lively representation could there be of the prophetical office of our Saviour? Of whom it is written, "God hath in these last days spoken unto us by his Son."[9] The ark had both the rod and the tables of the law, by God's appointment placed within it; than which, what could be more apt to express the satisfaction, which our high priest was to make unto his Father's justice, as well by his passive as by his active obedience?[10] For, as he

---

[3] Ps. 68:1, 18.

[4] Eph. 4:8, 10.

[5] Heb. 9:4.

[6] Heb. 12:24.

[7] Ex. 37:2.

[8] Heb. 2:9.

[9] Heb. 1:2.

[10] [Christ's passive obedience (from the Latin *patior, pati, passus sum* – to suffer) was his bearing the penalty for our sin in our place. His active obedience is his fulfillment of the law and, for Ussher, satisfies the Father's demand for perfect obedience, rather than merely qualifying him to stand as our mediator, a spotless

felt the stroke of the rod for us, that, "the chastisement of our peace being laid upon him, with his stripes we might be healed,"[11] so "it behoved" him also "to fulfil the law and all righteousness,"[12] that so he might be "the end of the law for righteousness to everyone that believeth."[13] The letter of the law being not more certainly to be found within the ark, than the accomplishment thereof within him, according to that which he spake by his holy prophet, "In the volume of the book it is written of me, that I should do your will, O God: yea, thy law is within my heart."[14]

The ark had many removes from place to place, whilst it sojourned in the tabernacle, but was brought up at last into the temple, there to dwell upon God's holy hill, the place of which he himself had said, "This is my rest for ever; here will I dwell, for I have a delight therein."[15] Where, at first entry, King Solomon stood ready to entertain him with this welcome: "Arise, O Lord God, into thy resting place, thou, and the ark of thy strength: let thy priests, O Lord God, be clothed with salvation, and let thy saints rejoice in goodness."[16] Our blessed Saviour, in the days of his flesh had no resting place, but continually went about doing good,[17] until at length he was received up into heaven, and sat on the right hand of God.[18] For when he had ended his progress upon earth, and finished there that work which his Father had given him to do,[19] he left the world, and went to his Father,[20] making his last remove unto the high court of heaven, where he is to reside until the time of the restitution of all things.[21] "The temple of

---

sacrifice. These are to be considered as two aspects of Christ's whole vicarious obedience rather than as two distinct phases of his life. See Richard Snoddy, *The Soteriology of James Ussher: The Act and Object of Saving Faith* (New York: Oxford University Press, 2014), 45, 47, 116–20.]

[11] Isa. 53:5.

[12] Matt. 3:15; 5:17.

[13] Rom. 10:4.

[14] Ps. 40:7–8; Heb. 10:7.

[15] Pss. 132:14; 68:16.

[16] 2 Chr. 6:41.

[17] Acts 10:38.

[18] Mark 19:19.

[19] John 17:4.

[20] John 16:28; 19:30.

[21] Acts 3:21.

God was opened in heaven, and there was seen in his temple the ark of his testament," saith St. John in the Apocalypse.[22] If we look to the corporal presence of our Saviour, in the temple of heaven must this ark be sought for. In no other place is it to be found. But if we look to the virtue coming from him, by the operation of his word and Spirit, so we shall find him in his temple upon earth, present with us always, even unto the end of the world.[23] For these were the gifts that, when he ascended into heaven, he did bestow upon men.

This the prophet layeth down thus: "Thou hast ascended up on high: thou hast received gifts for men."[24] The Apostle citeth it thus: "When he ascended up on high, he gave gifts unto men."[25] The reconciliation is easy: he received those gifts, not to retain them with himself, but to distribute them for the behoof[26] of his Church. So for the Spirit, St. Peter teacheth us, Acts 2. 33: "Therefore being by the right hand of God exalted (there is his ascending up on high), and having received of the Father the promise of the Holy Ghost (there is his receiving), he hath shed forth this which ye now see and hear (there is his giving of this gift unto men)." And for the ministry of the word, he himself intimateth as much in his commission given to the Apostles. Matthew 28. 18, 19: "All power is given unto me in heaven and in earth (there he receiveth). Go ye therefore, and teach all nations (there he giveth this gift unto men)." "He gave some apostles, and some prophets, and some evangelists, and some pastors and teachers, for the perfecting of the saints," saith our Apostle here,[27] that herein also that might be fulfilled, which we heard to have been uttered, when the ark was brought to his resting place: "Let thy priests, O Lord God, be clothed with salvation, and let thy saints rejoice in goodness."[28]

The work of the ministry, how meanly soever it be esteemed in the world, yet, in the estimation of our Saviour Christ, was one of the choicest gifts, that in this solemnity of his triumphant ascending up far above all

---

[22] Rev. 11:19.

[23] Matt. 28:20.

[24] Ps. 68:18.

[25] Eph. 4:8.

[26] ["use" or "advantage."]

[27] Eph. 4:11–12.

[28] 2 Chr. 6:41 [given as 16:41 in all editions from 1631]; Ps. 132:9, 16.

heavens,[29] he thought fit to bestow upon his Church here upon earth, as that which tended both to the "perfecting of the saints,"[30] and to "the edifying" of his own "body." For as it hath pleased the Father, "that in him all fullness should dwell,"[31] so the Son is also pleased not to hold it any disparagement, that "his body," the Church, should be accounted "the fullness of him that filleth all in all."[32] That, howsoever in himself he be most absolutely and perfectly complete, yet is his Church so nearly conjoined unto him, that he holdeth not himself full without it, but as long as any one member remaineth yet ungathered and unknit unto this mystical body of his, he accounteth, in the meantime, somewhat to be deficient in himself. And therefore our Apostle having, in the words immediately going before this text, declared, that the ministry was instituted "for the edifying of the body of Christ," addeth presently, "till we all come, in the unity of the faith, and of the knowledge of the Son of God, unto a perfect man, unto the measure of the stature of the fullness of Christ."[33]

In which words we may observe as well the matter of this building ("we all"), as the structure of it; and further also consider in the structure, first, the laying of the foundation ("in the unity of the faith, and of the knowledge of the Son of God"); secondly, the bringing of the work to perfection, and the raising of it to his just height ("unto a perfect man, unto the measure of the stature of the fullness of Christ").

The matter then of this spiritual edifice, that we may begin with that, are we ourselves. "Ye also, as lively stones, are built up a spiritual house," saith St. Peter.[34] To this St. Paul doth here add a note of universality ("we all") as suiting best with the nature of the catholic or universal Church, which is that body of Christ, of the edifying whereof he here treateth; of which therefore he telleth us more plainly in another place, that "by one Spirit we are all baptized into one body, whether we be Jews or Gentiles, whether we be bond or free."[35] For the catholic Church is not to be sought

---

[29] Eph. 4:10.

[30] Eph. 4:12.

[31] Col. 1:19.

[32] Eph. 1:23.

[33] Eph. 4:12–13.

[34] 1 Pet. 2:5.

[35] 1 Cor. 12:13.

for in any one angle[36] or quarter of the world, but among "all that in every place call upon the name of Jesus Christ our Lord, both theirs and ours."[37] Therefore to their Lord and ours was it said, "Ask of me, and I will give thee the heathen for thine inheritance, and the uttermost parts of the earth for thy possession."[38] And to his[39] mystical body, the catholic Church, accordingly, "I will bring thy seed from the east, and gather thee from the west; I will say to the north, give up; and to the south, keep not back: bring my sons from far, and my daughters from the ends of the earth; even every one that is called by my name."[40]

Thus must we conceive of the catholic Church, as of one entire body, made up by the collection and aggregation of all the faithful unto the unity thereof, from which union there ariseth unto every one of them such a relation to, and a dependence upon the Church catholic, as parts use to have in respect of their whole. Whereupon it followeth, that neither particular persons, nor particular churches, are to work as several divided bodies by themselves (which is the ground of all schism), but are to teach, and to be taught, and to do all other Christian duties, as parts conjoined unto the whole, and members of the same commonwealth or corporation; and therefore the bishops of the ancient Church, though they had the government of particular congregations only committed unto them, yet in regard of this communion which they held with the universal, did usually take to themselves the title of bishops of the catholic Church. Which maketh strongly as well against the new separatists, as the old Donatists, who either hold it a thing not much material, so they profess the faith of Christ, whether they do it in the catholic communion, or out of it;[41] or else (which is worse) dote

---

[36] ["corner."]

[37] 1 Cor. 1:2.

[38] Psa. 2:8.

[39] [Emended: "this" from 1631, but "his" in earlier editions.]

[40] Isa. 43:5–7.

[41] *Quam multi nihil interesse credentes in qua quisque parte Christianus sit; ideo permanebant in parte Donati, quia ibi nati erant, et eos inde discedere, atque ad Catholicam nemo transire cogebat. Et paulo post. Putabamus quidem nihil interesse ubi fidem Christi teneremus; sed gratias Domino, qui nos a divisione collegit, et hoc uni Deo congruere, ut in unitate colatur, ostendit.* ["How many, believing that it mattered not to which party a Christian might belong, remained in the schism of Donatus only because they had been born in it, and no one was compelling them to forsake it and pass over into the Catholic Church." And a little later, "We thought, indeed, that it mattered not in what communion we

so much upon the perfection of their own part, that they refuse to join in fellowship with the rest of the body of Christians, as if they themselves were the only people of God, and all wisdom must live and die with them and their generation.

And herein, of all others, do our Romanists most fearfully offend, as being the authors of the most cruel schism that ever hath been seen in the Church of God. Those infamous schisms of the Novatians and Donatists were but petty rents, in comparison of this huge rupture, which hath pulled asunder east and west, north and south, and grown to such a head at home, that in our western parts, where this faction was so prevalent, it hath for divers ages past been esteemed catholic. In the seventeenth of the Revelation we have a "woman" described unto us, sitting upon "seven mountains," and upon "many waters." The woman is there expounded to be "that great city which reigneth over the kings of the earth."[42] The seven mountains, upon which that city sat, needed not to be expounded. Every child knew what was meant thereby. The waters are interpreted "peoples, and multitudes, and nations, and tongues,"[43] which is that very universality and catholicism, that the Romanists are wont so much to brag of. For this "woman" is the particular church of Rome, the city church; [that] which they call the mother-church, the Holy Ghost styleth the "mother of harlots and abominations of the earth."[44] Those "peoples, and multitudes, and nations, and tongues," are such as this proud city reigneth over: the Catholic-Roman Church they are commonly called by themselves, but by the Holy Ghost, the "beast" upon which the woman sits.[45]

This "woman" is the head of the faction, and the very mother of this schism. The "beast," that is to say, they that suffer themselves to be thus ridden by her, are her abettors and supporters in it. For the particular church of Rome, not being content to be a fellow-member with the rest of the churches of Christ, and to have a joint dependence with them upon the

---

held the faith of Christ; but thanks to the Lord, who has gathered us from a state of schism, and has taught us that it is fitting that the one God be worshipped in unity."] Augustine, *Epist. 93, Ad Vincentius* 17, 18 [PL 33:330; NPNF1 1:388–89].

[42] Rev. 17:18.

[43] Rev. 17:15.

[44] Rev. 17:5.

[45] Rev. 17:3, 7.

whole body of the Church catholic, "which is the mother of us all,"[46] will needs go out of her rank, and, scorning any longer to be accounted one of the branches of the catholic Church, would fain be acknowledged to be the root of it; so that now all other churches must hold their dependence upon it, or otherwise be cast forth as withered branches, which are fit only to be thrown into the fire, and burned. The wisdom of God foresaw this insolence long beforehand, and therefore caused a caveat to be entered against it, even in that epistle which was specially directed to the church of Rome itself. The words are plain enough, Rom. 11. 18: "If thou boast, thou bearest not the root, but the root thee." The church of Rome therefore must know that she is no more a root to bear up other churches, than other churches are to bear up her: she may not go beyond her line, and boast herself to be the root of the catholic Church, but be contented to be borne herself by the root, as well as other particular churches are. For a stream to sever itself from the common fountain, that it may be counted a fountain itself, without dependence upon any other, is the next way to make an end of it, and dry it up. The church of Rome may do well to think of this, and leave off her vain boasting. "I sit a Queen, and am no widow, and shall see no sorrow."[47] Other churches may fail, and the gates of hell may prevail against them, but it cannot fall out so with me. Whereas she might remember, that they were Romans, unto whom the Apostle so long since gave this admonition: "Be not high-minded, but fear. For if God spared not the natural branches, take heed lest he also spare not thee. Behold therefore the goodness and severity of God: on them which fell, severity, but towards thee, goodness, if thou continue in his goodness; otherwise thou also shall be cut off."[48]

The Romans therefore by their pride may get a fall,[49] as well as others, and the church of Rome by infidelity may be cut off, as well as any other congregation, and yet the catholic Church subsist for all that, as having for her foundation neither Rome, nor Rome's bishop, but Jesus Christ, the Son of the living God. And yet this proud dame and her daughters, the particular church of Rome I mean, and that which they call the "Catholic Roman" (or the faction rather that prevaileth in them both), have in these

---

[46] Gal. 4:26.

[47] Rev. 18:7.

[48] Rom. 11:20–22.

[49] [see Prov. 16:18.]

latter ages confined the whole Church of Christ within themselves, and excluded all others that were not under the Roman obedience, as aliens from the commonwealth of Israel, and strangers from the covenants of promise.[50] The Donatists were cried out against by our forefathers, for shutting up the Church within the parts of the south, and rejecting all others that held not correspondency[51] with that patch of theirs; and could they think well then of them, that should conclude the Church within the western parts of the world, and exclude all other Christians from the body of Christ, that held not by the same root there that they did? It is a strange thing to me, that wise men should make such large discourses of the *catholic* Church, and bring so many testimonies to prove the universality of it, and not discern, that, while by this means they think they have gotten a great victory over us, they have in very truth overthrown themselves. For when it cometh to the point, instead of the catholic Church which consisteth of the communion of all nations, they obtrude[52] their own piece unto us, circumscribing the Church of Christ within the precincts of the Romish jurisdiction, and leaving all the world beside to the power of Satan. For with them it is a resolved case, that "to every creature it is altogether of necessity to salvation, to be subject to the Roman bishop."[53]

What must then become of the poor Muscovites and Grecians, to say nothing of the reformed churches, in Europe? What of the Egyptian and Ethiopian churches in Africa? What of the great companies of Christians scattered over all Asia, even from Constantinople unto the East Indies, which have and still do endure more afflictions and pressures for the name of Christ than they have ever done that would be accounted the only friends of Christ? Must these, because they are not the pope's subjects, be therefore denied to be Christ's subjects? Because they are not under the obedience of the Roman Church, do they thereupon forfeit the estate which they claim in the catholic Church, out of which there is no salvation?

---

[50] [cf. Eph. 2:12.]

[51] ["correspondence" or "agreement."]

[52] ["thrust or force upon."]

[53] *Subesse Romano pontifici omni humanae creaturae declaramus, dicimus, definimus, et pronunciamus, omnino esse de neccesitate salutis.* ["We declare, we proclaim, we define, and we announce, that to every human creature it is absolutely necessary for salvation to be subject to the Roman pontiff."] Boniface VIII, in *Extravagantes Communes* 1.8.1 (*Unum sanctam*) [*Corpus Iuris Canonici*, ed. Aemilius Ludovicus Richter, revised by Aemilius Friedberg, 2 vols (Leipzig: Tauchnitz, 1879–81), 2:1246].

Must we give all these for gone, and conclude that they are certainly damned? They who talk so much of the *catholic* Church, but indeed stand for their own *particular*, must of force sink as low in uncharitableness, as they have thrust themselves deep in schism. We who talk less of the universality of the Church, but hold the truth of it, cannot find in our hearts to pass such a bloody sentence upon so many poor souls that have given their names to Christ. He, whose pleasure it was to spread the Church's seed so far, said to east, west, north, and south, "Give"; it is not for us then to say, "Keep back."[54] He hath given to his Son "the heathen for his inheritance, and the uttermost parts of the earth for his possession."[55] We for our parts dare not abridge this grant, and limit this great lordship, as we conceive it may best fit our own turns, but leave it to his own latitude, and seek for the catholic Church neither in this part, nor in that piece, but, as it hath been before said in the words of the Apostle, among "all that in every place call upon the name of Jesus Christ our Lord, both theirs and ours."[56]

Yea, but how can this be, will some say, seeing the *catholic* Church is but *one*, and the principal reason, for which it is accounted one, is the "unity of the faith" professed therein?[57] How then can this unity of faith be preserved in all places, if one special church be not set as a mistress over all the rest, and one chief bishop appointed for a master over all others, by whom in matters of faith every one must be ruled? And out of such different professions, as are to be found among the divided Christians in those several parts of the world, how can there be fit matter drawn for the making up of one universal Church? To this I answer, and so pass from the *matter* of the building to the *structure*, that it is most true indeed, that in the Church there is "one Lord, one faith, one baptism,"[58] for so we are taught by the Apostle in this chapter. But yet, in the first place, it is to be considered, that this "unity of the faith" must be compassed by such means as God hath or-

---

[54] [cf. Ps. 43:5–6.]

[55] [Ps. 2:8.]

[56] 1 Cor. 1:2.

[57] *Ecclesia ex pluribus personis congregatur: et tamen una dicitur, propter unitatem fidei.* ["The church is gathered from many persons: and yet it is said to be one, on account of the unity of the faith."] [Pseudo-]Jerome, *Breviarum in Psalmos,* 23 [PL 26:887A; Ussher rightly expressed doubt about Jerome's authorship: *si modo is horum commentariorum author*].

[58] Eph. 4:5.

dained for the procuring of it, and not by any politic tricks of man's devising. Now for the bringing of us all to this "unity of the faith," the Apostle here telleth us, that Christ "gave some apostles, and some prophets, and some evangelists, and some pastors and teachers."[59] If he had thought that the maintenance of this unity did depend upon the singularity of any one Apostle, or pastor, or teacher, is it to be imagined, that he would have overslipped[60] such a singular person (even in that very place where, of all others, his presence was most requisite) and run altogether, as he does, upon the plural number?

That the multitude of teachers dispersed over the world, without any such dependency or correspondency, should agree together in laying the foundations of the same faith, is a special work of God's Spirit. And it is "the unity of the Spirit" which the Apostle here speaketh of, and exhorteth us to "keep in the bond of peace."[61] Whereas the unity of which our adversaries boast so much (which is nothing else but a wilful suffering of themselves to be led blindfold by one man, who commonly is more blind than many of themselves), is no fruit of the Spirit, but of mere carnal policy, and may serve peradventure for a bond of peace betwixt themselves and their own party (such as the priests of Antichrist were to have, and as many as would be content to yield themselves to the conduct of such a commander),[62] but hath proved the greatest block that ever stood in the way for giving impediment to the peace and unity of the universal Church, which here we look after. And therefore Nilus, Archbishop of Thessalonica, entering into the consideration of the original ground of that long continued schism, whereby the west stands as yet divided from the east, and the Latin churches from the Greek, wrote a whole book purposely of this argument, wherein he showeth "that there is no other cause to be assigned of this distraction, but that the pope will not permit the cognizance of the controversy unto a general council, but will needs sit himself as the alone teacher of the point in question, and have others hearken unto him as if they were

---

[59] Eph. 4:11.

[60] ["omitted" or "neglected."]

[61] Eph. 4:3.

[62] *Pace sua, id est, impietatis suae unitate se jactant; agentes se non ut Christi episcopos, sed ut antichristi sacerdotes.* ["They boast of their harmony, that is, their oneness in impiety, bearing themselves not as bishops of Christ, but as priests of Antichrist."] Hilary of Poitiers, *Contra Arianos, vel Auxentium Mediolanensem* 1 [PL 10:609C–D].

his scholars: and that this is contrary both to the ordinances and the practice of the Apostles and the fathers."[63] Neither indeed is there any hope that ever we shall see a general peace for matters of religion settled in the Christian world as long as this supercilious master shall be suffered to keep this rule in God's house, how much soever he be magnified by his own disciples, and made the only foundation upon which the unity of the catholic Church dependeth.

Now in the next place, for the further opening of the "unity of the faith," we are to call unto mind the distinction which the Apostle maketh betwixt "the foundation,"[64] and that which is "builded thereupon," betwixt the "principles of the doctrine Christ," and that which he calleth "perfection."[65] The "unity of the faith and of the knowledge of the Son of God" here spoken of, hath reference, as we heard, to the foundation; as that which followeth of "a perfect man," and "the measure of the stature of the fullness of Christ," to the superstruction[66] and perfection. In the former there is a general unity among all true believers; in the latter, a great deal of variety, there being several degrees of perfection to be found in several persons, "according to the measure of the gift of Christ."[67] So we see in a material building, that still there is but one foundation, though great disparity be observed in sundry parts of the superstruction. Some rooms are high, some low, some dark, some lightsome, some more substantially, some more slightly builded, and in tract of time some prove more ruinous than others. Yet all of them belong to one building, as long as they hold together, and stand upon the same foundation. And even thus is it in the spiritual building also, whether we respect the *practical* part of Christianity, or the *intellectual*.

---

[63] Λόγος ἀποδεικνὺς μὴ ἄλλο τὶ τὸ τῆς διαστάσεως τῆς Λατίνων ἐκκλησίας καὶ ἡμῶν μέχρι τοῦ παρόντος, αἴτιον εἶναι ἢ τὸ μὴ βούλεσθαι τὸν Πάπον οἰκουμενίκῳ [PG: Πάππον οἰκουμενικῇ] συνόδῳ τὴν τοῦ ἀμφισβητημένου διάγνωσιν ἐπιτρέψαι. ἀλλ᾽ αὐτὸν μόνον διδάσκαλον ἐθέλειν τοῦ ζητουμένου καθέζεσθαι, τοὺς δὲ ἄλλους, ἐν μαθητῶν μοίρᾳ ὑπακούοντας ἔχειν, καὶ ὅτι τὸ τοιοῦτον ἀλλότριον τῶν ἀποστολικῶν καὶ πατρικῶν νόμων καὶ πράξεων. Neilos Kabasilas, *De Causis Dissensionum in Ecclesia* 1 [PG 149:684A].

[64] 1 Cor. 3:10–12.

[65] Heb. 6:1.

[66] ["superstructure" or the act of building up a superstructure on some foundation.]

[67] Eph. 4:7.

In the practical we see wonderful great difference betwixt Christian and Christian. Some by God's mercy attain to a higher measure of perfection, and keep themselves unspotted from the common corruptions of the world; others watch not so carefully over their ways, and lead not such strict lives, but are oftentimes overtaken and fall foully; that he, who looketh upon the one and the other, would hardly think that one heaven should receive them both. But although the one doth so far outstrip the other in the practice of new obedience, which is the Christian man's race, yet are there certain fundamental principles, in which they both concur, as a desire to fear God's name,[68] repentance for sins past,[69] and a sincere purpose of heart for the time to come to cleave unto the Lord.[70] Which whosoever hath, is under mercy, and may not be excluded from the communion of saints. In like manner for the intellectual part: the "first principles of the oracles of God," as the Apostle calleth them, hold the place of the common foundation, in which all Christians must be grounded.[71] Although some be "babes," and for further knowledge are "unskilful in the word of righteousness," othersome[72] are of "perfect age, who by reason of use have their senses exercised to discern both good and evil."[73]

The oracles of God contain abundance of matter in them, and whatsoever is found in them is a fit object for faith to apprehend, but that all Christians should uniformly agree, in the profession of all those truths that are revealed there, is a thing that rather may be wished, than ever hoped for. Yet the variety of men's judgements, in those many points that belong to theological faith, doth not dissolve the unity which they hold together in the fundamental principles of the catholic faith. The "unity of the faith" commended here is a catholic unity, and such as every true Christian attaineth unto. "Till we *all* come in the unity of the faith," saith the Apostle. As there is a "common salvation,"[74] so is there a "common faith,"[75] which is "alike

---

[68] Neh. 1:11.

[69] Luke 13:3, 5; Heb. 6:1.

[70] Acts 11:23.

[71] Heb. 5:12.

[72] ["some others."]

[73] Heb. 5:13–14.

[74] Jude 3.

[75] Tit. 1:4.

precious" in the highest Apostle and the meanest believer.[76] For we may not think that heaven was prepared for deep clerks only, and therefore, beside that larger measure of knowledge, whereof all are not capable, there must be "a rule of faith common to small and great,"[77] which as it must consist but of few propositions (for simple men cannot bear away many), so is it also requisite, that those articles should be of so much weight and moment, that they may be sufficient to make a man wise unto salvation; that, howsoever in other points learned men may go beyond common Christians, and exceed one another likewise by many degrees, yet, in respect of these radical truths, which is the necessary and common food of all the children of the Church, there is not an unity only, but such a kind of equality also, brought in among all sorts of Christians,[78] as was heretofore among the congregation of the Israelites in the collection of their manna, where "he that gathered much had nothing over, and he that gathered little had no lack."[79]

If then salvation by believing these common principles may be had, and to salvation none can come that is not first a member of the catholic Church of Christ, it followeth thereupon, that the unity of the faith, generally requisite for the incorporating of Christians into that blessed society, is not to be extended beyond those common principles. Which may further be made manifest unto us by the continual practice of the catholic Church herself, in the matriculation[80] of her children, and the first admittance of them into her communion. For when she prepared her *catechumen*[81] for baptism, and by that door received them into the congregation of Christ's flock, we may not think her judgment to have been so weak, that she should omit any thing herein, that was essentially necessary for the making of one a member of the Church. Now the profession which she required of

---

[76] 2 Pet. 1:1.

[77] *Regula fidei, pusillis magnisque communis.* Augustine, *Epist. 187* 29 [PL 33:843].

[78] Μιᾶς γὰρ καὶ τῆς αὐτῆς πίστεως οὔσης οὔτε ὁ πολὺ περὶ αὐτῆς δυνάμενος εἰπεῖν ἐπλεόνασεν, οὔτε ὁ τὸ ὀλίγον ἠλαττόνησε ["For the faith being ever one and the same, neither does one who is able at great length to discourse regarding it, make any addition to it, nor does one, who can say but little, diminish it"]. Irenaeus, *Adversus Haereses* 1.10.2 [PG 7:553A; *ANF* 1:331].

[79] Exod. 16:18 [earlier editions also cite 2 Cor. 8:15].

[80] [An act of formal admission, generally with reference to a university or college.]

[81] [A catechumen was a convert under instruction before baptism.]

all that were to receive baptism, was, for the *agenda*[82] or practical part, an abrenunciation[83] of the devil, the world, and the flesh, with all their sinful works and lusts; and for the *credenda*, the things to be believed, an acknowledgment of the articles of the creed; which being solemnly done, she then baptized them *in this faith*, intimating thereby sufficiently that this was that one faith, commended unto her by the Apostles, as the other that one baptism, which was appointed to be the sacrament of it.[84]

This creed, though for substance it was the same everywhere, yet for form was somewhat different, and in some places received more enlargements than in others. The western churches herein applied themselves to the capacity of the meaner sort, more than the eastern did, using in their baptism that shorter form of confession, commonly called the Apostles' Creed, which in the more ancient times was briefer also than now it is. As we may easily perceive, by comparing the symbol recited by Marcellus Ancyranus (in the profession of the faith which he delivered to Pope Julius), with the expositions of the Apostles' Creed written by the Latin doctors, wherein the mention of the Father's being "maker of heaven and earth," the Son's death and descending into hell, and "the communion of saints," is wholly omitted.[85] All which, though they were of undoubted verity, yet, for brevity's sake seem at first to have been omitted in this short sum; because some of them perhaps were not thought to be altogether so necessary for all men (which is Suarez's judgement touching the point of the descent into hell);[86] and some, that were most necessary, either thought to be sufficiently implied in other articles (as that of Christ's death in those of his crucifixion and burial), or thought to be sufficiently manifested by the light of reason, as that of the creation of heaven and earth. For howsoever this, as it is a truth revealed by God's word, becometh an object for faith to apprehend,[87] yet it is otherwise also clearly to be understood by the discourse of reason,[88]

---

[82] ["the things to be done."]

[83] ["absolute renunciation" or "repudiation."]

[84] *Sacramentum fidei* ["sacrament of faith"]. Augustine, *Epist. 98* 9–10 [*PL* 33:363–64; *NPNF1* 1:410].

[85] Epiphanius, *Panarion* 72.3 [*PG* 42:385D–388A].

[86] Francisco Suárez, *Commentariorum ac Disputationum in Tertiam Partem Divi Thomae*, 5 vols (Venice, 1604–1606), 2:478–81 (Disp. 43.2).

[87] Heb. 11:3.

[88] Rom. 1:20.

even as the unity and all the other attributes of the Godhead likewise are. Which therefore may be well referred unto those *praecognita*, or common principles, which nature may possess the mind withal, before that grace enlighteneth it, and need not necessarily to be inserted into that symbol, which is the badge and cognizance whereby the believer is to be differenced and distinguished from the unbeliever.

The creed which the eastern churches used in baptism was larger than this, being either the same or very little different from that which we commonly call the Nicene Creed, because the greatest part of it was repeated and confirmed in the first general council held at Nicea, where the first draught thereof was presented to the synod by Eusebius, Bishop of Caesarea, with this preamble: "As we have received from the bishops that were before us, both at our first catechizing, and when we received baptism; and as we have learned from the holy Scriptures; and as we have both believed and taught, when we entered into the ministry, and in our bishopric itself; so believing at this present also, we declare this our faith unto you." To this the Nicene fathers added a more clear explication of the deity of the Son, against the Arian heresy, wherewith the Church was then troubled, professing him to be "begotten, not made," and to be "of one substance with the Father."[89] The second general council, which was assembled fifty-six years after at Constantinople, approving this confession of the faith as "most ancient and agreeable to baptism,"[90] enlarged it somewhat; in the article that concerned the Holy Ghost especially, which at that time was most oppugned by the Macedonian heretics. And whereas the Nicene confession proceeded no further than to the belief which we have in the holy Trinity, the fathers of Constantinople made it up, by adding that which was commonly professed touching the catholic Church and the privileges belonging thereunto. Epiphanius, repeating this creed at large, affirmeth it to have

---

[89] Καθὼς παρελάβομεν παρὰ τῶν πρὸ ἡμῶν ἐπισκόπων, καὶ ἐν τῇ πρώτῃ κατηχήσει, καὶ ὅτε τὸ λουτρὸν ἐλαμβάνομεν, καὶ καθὼς ἀπὸ τῶν θείων γραφῶν μεμαθήκαμεν, καὶ ὡς ἐν τῷ πρεσβυτερίῳ, καὶ ἐν αὐτῇ τῇ ἐπισκόπῇ ἐπιστεύομεν τε καὶ ἐδιδάσκομεν, οὕτω καὶ νῦν πιστεύοντες, τὴν ἡμετέραν πίστιν ὑμῖν προσαναφέρομεν. Socrates Scholasticus, *Historia Ecclesiastica* 1.8 [*PG* 67:69C; *NPNF2* 2:10]. Cf. Theodoret, *Ecclesiastica Historia* 1.12 [*PG* 82:945D, 948A–B; *NPNF2* 3:51].

[90] Πρεσβυτάτην τε οὖσαν καὶ ἀκόλουθον τῷ βαπτίσματι. Synodical epistle of the Council of Constantinople, in Theodoret, *Ecclesiastica Historia* 5.9 [*PG* 82:1216B; *NPNF2* 3:138].

been delivered unto the Church by the Apostles.[91] Cassian avoucheth as much, where he urgeth this against Nestorius, as the creed anciently received in the church of Antioch, from whence he came.[92] The Roman church, after the days of Charles the Great,[93] added the article of the procession of the Holy Ghost from the Son unto this symbol, and the Council of Trent hath now recommended it unto us, "as that principle in which all that profess the faith of Christ do necessarily agree; and the firm and only foundation, against which the gates of hell shall never prevail."[94]

It is a matter confessed therefore by the fathers of Trent themselves, that in the Constantinopolitan Creed, or in the Roman Creed at the farthest (which differeth nothing from the other, but that it hath added *filioque*[95] to the procession of the Holy Ghost, and out of the Nicene Creed, *Deum de Deo*,[96] to the articles that concern the Son), that only foundation and principle of faith is to be found, in the unity whereof all Christians must necessarily agree. Which is otherwise cleared sufficiently by the constant practice of the Apostles and their successors, in the first receiving of men into the society of the Church. For in one of the Apostles' ordinary sermons, we see, there was so much matter delivered, as was sufficient to convert men unto the faith, and to make them capable of baptism; and those sermons treated only of the first principles of the doctrine of Christ, upon the receiving whereof, the Church, following the example of the Apostles, never did deny baptism unto her *catechumeni*. In these first principles therefore must

---

[91] Epiphanius, *Ancoratus* 119 [*PG* 43:232B–233A; *FoC* 128:222–24, here numbered 118].

[92] John Cassian, *De Incarnatione Christi* 6.3–4 [*PL* 50:140A–150A; *NPNF2* 11:592–593].

[93] [Charlemagne.]

[94] Council of Trent, Session 3. *Symbolum fidei, quo sancta Romana Ecclesia utitur, tanquam principium illud, in quo omnes, qui fidem Christi profitentur, necessario conveniunt, ac fundamentum firmum et unicum, contra quod portae inferi numquam praevalebunt, totidem verbis, quibus in omnibus ecclesiis legitur, exprimendum esse censuit.* ["The council voted that the creed which the holy Roman church uses as that basic principle on which all who profess the faith of Christ necessarily agree as the firm and sole foundation against which the powers of death shall never prevail, should be expressed in the words in which it is read in all the churches." *Decrees of the Ecumenical Councils*, ed. Norman P. Tanner, 2 vols (London: Sheed and Ward, 1990), 2:662.]

[95] ["and from the Son."]

[96] ["God from God."]

the foundation be contained, and that common unity of faith which is required in all the members of the Church.

The foundation then being thus cleared, concerning the superstruction, we learn from the Apostle, that some "build upon this foundation gold, silver, precious stones, wood, hay, stubble."[97] Some proceed from one degree of wholesome knowledge unto another, increasing their main stock by the addition of those other sacred truths that are revealed in the word of God, and these build upon the foundation "gold," and "silver," and "precious stones." Others retain the precious foundation, but lay base matter upon it: "wood," "hay," "stubble," and such other either unprofitable or more dangerous stuff. And others go so far, that they overthrow the very foundation itself. The first of these be wise, the second foolish, the third mad builders. When the day of trial cometh, the first man's "work shall abide," and he himself shall "receive a reward";[98] the second shall lose his work, but not himself ("he shall suffer loss," saith the Apostle, "but he himself shall be saved");[99] the third shall lose both himself and his work together. And as, in this spiritual structure, very different kinds of materials may be laid upon the same foundation, some sound and some unsound, so, in either of them, there is a great difference to be made betwixt such as are more contiguous[100] to the foundation, and such as be remoter off. The fuller explication of the first principles of faith, and the conclusions deduced from thence, are in the rank of those verities that be more nearly conjoined to the foundation; to which those falsities are answerable on the other side, that grate upon the foundation, and any way endanger it.

For that there be divers degrees both of truths and errors in religion, which necessarily must be distinguished, is a thing acknowledged, not by us alone, but by the learnedest also of our adversaries. "There be some catholic verities," say they, "which do so pertain to faith, that these being taken away, the faith itself must be taken away also. And these by common use we call not only catholic, but verities of faith also. There are other verities which be catholic also and universal, namely, such as the whole Church holdeth, which yet being overthrown, the faith is shaken indeed, but not overturned. And in the errors that are contrary to such truths as these, the

---

[97] 1 Cor. 3:12.

[98] 1 Cor. 3:14.

[99] 1 Cor. 3:15.

[100] [Touching or bordering.]

faith is obscured, not extinguished; weakened, not perished."[101] Neverthe-less, "though the faith be not altogether destroyed by them, yet is it evil at ease, and shaken, and, as it were, disposed to corruption. For, as there be certain hurts of the body, which do not take away the life, but yet a man is the worse for them, and disposed to corruption either in whole or in part; as there be other mortal hurts, which take away the life: so likewise are there certain degrees of propositions, which contain unsound doctrine, although they have not manifest heresy."[102] In a word, the general rule concerning all these superstructions is, that the more near they are to the foundation, of so much greater importance be the truths, and so much more perilous be the errors; as again, the farther they are removed off, the less necessary doth the knowledge of such verities prove to be, and the swerving from the truth less dangerous.

Now from all that hath been said, two great questions may be re-solved, which trouble many. The first is, what we may judge of our forefa-thers, who lived in the communion of the church of Rome? Whereunto I answer, that we have no reason to think otherwise, but that they lived and died under the mercy of God. For we must distinguish the *papacy* from the *church* wherein it is, as the Apostle doth *Antichrist* from the *temple of God*, wherein he sitteth.[103] The foundation upon which the Church standeth is that common faith, as we have heard, in the unity whereof all Christians do

---

[101] *Quaedam sunt catholicae veritates, quae ita ad fidem pertinent, ut his sublatis, fides quoque ipsa tollatur. Quas nos usu frequenti non solum catholicas, sed fidei veritates appellavimus. Aliae veritates sunt etiam ipsae catholicae et universales; nempe quas universa Ecclesia tenet, quibus licet eversis, fides quatitur, sed non evertitur tamen. Atque in hujusmodi veritatum contrariis erroribus, dixi fidem obscurari, non extingui; infirmari, non perire. Has ergo numquam fidei veritates censui vocandas, quamvis doctrinae Christianae veritates sint.* Melchior Cano, *De Locis Theologicis libri duodecim* (Louvain, 1564), 765 (lib. 12, cap. 11, '*De propositione erronea, sapiente haeresim, piarum aurium offensiva, temeraria, scandalosa*', numbered cap. 10 in some edi-tions).

[102] *Necessario oportet distinguere alios gradus propositionum, per quas etiamsi fides destruatur omnino, tamen male habet, et quatitur, et quasi disponitur ad corruptionem. Sicut sunt quaedam corporum laesiones, quae non auferunt vitam, sed male habet homo per eas, et disponitur ad cor-ruptionem aut in toto aut in parte; aliae vero sunt laesiones mortales, quae vitam eripiunt: ita sunt quidam gradus propositionum, continentes doctrinam non sanam, etiamsi non habeant haeresim manifestam.* Domingo Báñez, *De Fide, Spe & Charitate ... Commentaria in Secundam Secundae Angelici Doctoris* (Salamanca, 1584), 643C (quaest. 11, artic. 2).

[103] 2 Thess. 2:4.

generally accord. Upon this old[104] foundation Antichrist raiseth up his new buildings, and layeth upon it not hay and stubble only, but far more vile and pernicious matter, which wrencheth and disturbeth the very foundation itself. For example, it is a ground of the catholic faith that Christ was born of the virgin Mary, which in the Scripture is thus explained: "God sent forth his Son, made of a woman."[105] This the papacy admitteth for a certain truth, but insinuateth withal, that upon the altar God sendeth forth his Son made of bread. For the transubstantiation which these men would have us believe, is not an annihilation of the bread, and a substitution of the body of Christ in the stead thereof, but a real conversion of the one into the other, such as they themselves would have esteemed to be a bringing forth of Christ, and a kind of generation of him. For, to omit the wild conceits of Postellus in his book *De nativitate mediatoris ultima*,[106] this is the doctrine of their graver divines, as Cornelius à Lapide the Jesuit doth acknowledge in his Roman lectures, that "by the words of consecration truly and really as the bread is transubstantiated, so Christ is produced and, as it were, generated upon the altar, in such a powerful and effectual manner that, if Christ as yet had not been incarnate, by these words, *Hoc est corpus meum* ["this is my body"], he should be incarnated, and assume an human body."[107] And doth not this new divinity, think you, shrewdly threaten the ancient foundation of the catholic belief of the incarnation?

Yet such as in the days of our forefathers, opposed the popish doctrine of transubstantiation, could allege for themselves, that the faith which they maintained was then "preserved among the laity, and so had anciently

---

[104] [Emended. The earliest editions read "old," but the 1631 and 1687 editions read "new." Elrington omits this word in *WJU*, 2:490.]

[105] Gal. 4:4.

[106] [Guillaume Postel, *De nativitate mediatoris ultima, nunc futura, et toti orbi terrarum in singulis ratione praeditis manifestanda* (Basel, 1547). Postel's thought was rather eclectic, being heavily influenced by Kabbalah, and he claimed to have received revelations from spiritual beings. His eucharistic views are discussed in Yvonne Petry, *Gender, Kabbalah and the Reformation: The Mystical Theology of Guillaume Postel* (Leiden: Brill, 2004), 127–30.]

[107] *Per verba consecrationis vere et realiter uti transubstantiatur panis, ita producitur et quasi generatur Christus in altari; adeo potenter et efficaciter ut, si Christus necdum esset incarnatus, per haec verba, Hoc est corpus meum, incarnaretur, corpusque humanum assumeret: uti graves theologi docent.* Cornelius à Lapide, *Commentaria in Quatuor Prophetas Maiores* (Paris, 1622), 131A (on Isa. 7:14).

been preserved."[108] And of mine own knowledge I can testify, that when I have dealt with some of the common people that would be counted members of the Roman church, and demanded of them what they thought of that which I knew to be the common tenet of their doctors in this point, they not only rejected it with indignation, but wondered also that I should imagine any of their side to be so foolish, as to give credit to such a senseless thing. Neither may we account it to have been a small blessing of God unto our ancestors, who lived in that kingdom of darkness, that the ignorance wherein they were bred, freed them from the understanding of those things, which being known might prove so prejudicial to their souls' health. "For there be some things, which it is better for a man to be ignorant of, than to know,"[109] and the not knowing of those profundities, which are indeed "the depths of Satan,"[110] is to those, that have not the skill to dive into the bottom of such mysteries of iniquity, a good and an happy ignorance.

The ignorance of those principles of the catholic faith, that are absolutely necessary to salvation, is as dangerous a gulf on the other side, but the light of those common truths of Christianity was so great, and so firmly fixed in the minds of those that professed the name of Christ, that it was not possible for the power of darkness to extinguish it, nor the gates of hell to prevail against it. Nay, the very solemn days, which by the ancient institution of the Church were celebrated for the commemoration of the blessed Trinity, the nativity, passion, resurrection, and ascension of our Saviour Christ, did so preserve the memory of these things among the common

---

[108] *Confitentur alii, quod fides sua, qua astruunt quod panis et vinum remanent post consecrationem in naturis suis, adhuc servatur laicis, et antiquitus servabatur* ["Others confess that their faith, by which they maintain that the bread and the wine remained in their natural state after consecration, is still preserved among the laity and so was preserved from antiquity"]. "Confession" of John Tissington against John Wyclif. [Here Ussher is citing a manuscript in his possession (*quam MS. habeo*), almost certainly that collection which is now denoted Bodleian, MS e Mus. 86 (in which see fol. 42v), and part of which carries annotations in Ussher's hand. This had earlier passed through the hands of John Bale and John Foxe. The documents are reproduced in *Fasciculi Zizaniorum Magistri Johannis Wyclif cum tritico*, ed. Rev. Walter W. Shirley, Rolls Series (London: Longman, Brown, Green, Longmans, and Roberts, 1858), in which see p.145.]

[109] *Sunt enim quaedam, quae nescire, quam scire sit melius.* Augustine, *Enchiridion de Fide, Spe et Charitate*, 17 [*PL* 40:239; *NPNF1* 3:242].

[110] Rev. 2:24.

people, that by the popish doctors themselves it is made an argument of gross and supine ignorance, that any should not have explicit knowledge of those mysteries of Christ, which were thus publicly solemnized in the Church.[111] And, which is the principal point of all, the ordinary instruction appointed to be given unto men upon their death-beds was, that they should look "to come to glory, not by their own merits, but by the virtue and merit of the passion of our Lord Jesus Christ"; that they should "place their whole confidence in his death only, and in no other thing"; and that they should "interpose his death between God and their sins, betwixt them and God's anger."[112]

So that where these things did thus concur in any, as we doubt not but they did in many thousands, the knowledge of the common principles of the faith, the ignorance of such main errors as did endanger the foundation, a godly life, and a faithful death, there we have no cause to make any question, but that God had fitted a subject for his mercy to work upon. And yet, in saying thus, we do nothing less than say that such as these were *papists*, either in their life or in their death. Members the Roman Church perhaps they were, but such as by God's goodness were preserved from the mortality of *popery* that reigned there. For popery itself is nothing else but the botch or the plague of that church, which hazardeth the souls of those it seizeth upon, as much as any infection can do the body. And therefore, if anyone will needs be so foolhardy as to take up his lodging in such a pesthouse,[113] after warning given of the present danger, we in our charity may

---

[111] Silvestro Mazzolini [Prierias], *Sylvestrinae Summae, Quae Summa Summarum Merito Nuncupatur*, 2 vols (Lyon, 1553), 2:440 ("*Fides*," 6); Cf. Aquinas, *Summa Theologiae*, ed. Thomas Gilby, Blackfriars edition, 61 vols (London: Eyre & Spottiswoode, 1964–1981), 31:90–91 (IIa-IIae, q. 2, a. 7, co.).

[112] See James Ussher, *De Christianarum Ecclesiarum ... Successione & Statu* (London, 1613), 193–95 (7.21–22) [*WJU*, 2:212–13]; idem, *An Answer to a Challenge Made by a Jesuit in Ireland* (Dublin, 1624), 514–15 [*WJU*, 3:568–69]. [The quotations are derived from George Cassander, "Pio Lectori," appended to John Fisher, *Opusculum de fiducia & misericordia Dei* (Cologne, 1556), sigs N3v–N4v; Kaspar Ulenberg, *Graves et Iustae Causae, cur Catholicis in communione veteris, eiusque veri Christianismi, constanter usque ad vitae finem permanendum sit; Cur item omnibus iis, qui se vocant Evangelicos, relictis erroribus, ad eiusdem Christianismi consortium, vel postliminio sit redeundum* (Cologne, 1589), 462–63; Stanisław Hozjusz (Hosius), *Confessio Catholicae Fidei Christiana: vel potius explicatio quaedam confessionis a patribus factae in synodo provinciali, quae habita est Petrikoviae* (Mainz, 1557), fol. 224r (cap. 73).]

[113] [A hospital for persons with an infectious disease such as plague.]

well say, "Lord have mercy upon him"; but he, in the meantime, hath great cause to fear, that God in his justice will inflict that judgment upon him, which in this case he hath threatened against such as will "not believe the truth, but take pleasure in unrighteousness."[114] And so much may suffice for that question.

The second question, so rife in the mouths of our adversaries, is: "Where was your church before Luther?" Whereunto an answer may be returned from the grounds of the solution of the former question; that our church was even there where now it is. In all places of the world, where the ancient foundations were retained, and these common principles of faith, upon the profession whereof men have ever been wont to be admitted, by baptism, into the Church of Christ: there we doubt not but our Lord had his subjects, and we our fellow-servants. For we bring in no new faith, nor no new church. That which in the time of the ancient fathers was accounted to be "truly and properly Catholic," namely, "that which was believed everywhere, always, and by all";[115] that in the succeeding ages hath evermore been preserved, and is at this day entirely professed in our Church. And it is well observed by a learned man, who hath written a full discourse of this argument, that, "whatsoever the father of lies either hath attempted or shall attempt, yet neither hath he hitherto effected, nor shall ever bring it to pass hereafter, that this catholic doctrine, ratified by the common consent of Christians always and everywhere, should be abolished; but that in the thickest mist rather of the most perplexed troubles, it still obtained victory, both in the minds and in the open confession of all Christians, no ways overturned in the foundation thereof: and that in this verity that one Church of Christ was preserved in the midst of the tempests of the most cruel winter, or in the thickest darkness of her wanings."[116]

---

[114] 2 Thess. 2:12.

[115] *In ipsa catholica Ecclesia magnopere curandum est, ut id teneamus quod ubique, quod semper, quod ab omnibus creditum est: hoc est etenim vere proprieque catholicum.* Vincent of Lérins, *Commonitorium* 2 [PL 50:640; NPNF2 11:132, here numbered 6].

[116] *Quicquid vel molitus sit vel moliturus sit mendacii pater, non tamen vel effecisse hactenus vel effecturum posthac, ut haec doctrina catholica, omnium Christianorum consensu semper et ubique rata, aboleatur: quin potius illam in densissima maxime involutarum perturbationum caligine victricem extitisse, et in animis et in aperta confessione Christianorum omnium; in suis fundamentis nullo modo labefactatam. In illa quoque veritate unam illam Ecclesiam fuisse conservatam in mediis saevissimae hyemis tempestatibus, vel densissimis tenebris suorum interluniorum.* Jean de

Thus if at this day we should take a survey of the several professions of Christianity that have any large spread in any part of the world, as of the religion of the Roman and the Reformed churches in our quarters, of the Egyptians and Ethiopians in the south, of the Grecians and other Christians in the eastern parts, and should put by the points wherein they did differ one from another, and gather into one body the rest of the articles wherein they all did generally agree, we should find, that in those propositions which without all controversy are universally received in the whole Christian world, so much truth is contained, as, being joined with holy obedience, may be sufficient to bring a man unto everlasting salvation. Neither have we cause to doubt, but that "as many as do walk according to this rule,"[117] neither overthrowing that which they have builded by superinducing[118] any damnable heresies thereupon, nor otherwise vitiating their holy faith with a lewd and wicked conversation, "peace shall be upon them, and mercy, and upon the Israel of God."

Now these common principles of the Christian faith, which we call κοινόπιστα, or things generally believed of all, as they have universality, and antiquity, and consent concurring with them, which by Vincent's rule are the special characters of that which is truly and properly catholic;[119] so, for their duration, we are sure that they have still held out, and been kept as the seminary of the catholic Church in the darkest and difficultest times that ever have been; where, if the Lord of Hosts had not in his mercy reserved this seed unto us, we should long since "have been as Sodom, and should have been like unto Gomorrah."[120] It cannot be denied indeed, that Satan and his instruments have used their utmost endeavour, either to hide this light from men's eyes by keeping them in gross ignorance, or to deprave it by bringing in pernicious heresies, and that in these latter ages they have much prevailed both ways, as well in the west and north, as in the east and south. Yet far be it, for all this, from any man to think, that "God should so

---

Serres [Serranus], *De Fide Catholica, sive Principiis Religionis Christianae* (Paris, 1607), 172.

[117] Gal. 6:16.

[118] ["bringing in as an addition to something."]

[119] *Universitatem, antiquitatem, consensionem.* Vincent of Lérins, *Commonitorium*, 2 [*PL* 50:640; *NPNF2* 11:132, here numbered 6].

[120] Isa. 1:9.

cast away his people," that in those times there should not be left "a remnant according to the election of grace."[121]

The Christian Church was never brought unto a lower ebb, than was the Jewish synagogue in the days of our Saviour Christ, when "the interpreters of the law" had taken away the key of knowledge,[122] and that little knowledge that remained was miserably corrupted, not only with the leaven of the Pharisees, but also with the damnable heresy of the Sadducees. And yet a man at that time might have seen the true servants of God standing together with these men in the selfsame temple, which might well be accounted, as the house of the saints in regard of the one, so a den of thieves in respect of the other. When the pestilent heresy of the Arians had polluted the whole world, the people of Christ were not to be found among them only who made an open secession from that wicked company, but among those also who held external communion with them, and lived under their ministry. Where they so learned the other truths of God from them, that they were yet ignorant of their main error, God in his providence so ordering matters that, as it is noted by St. Hilary, "the people of Christ should not perish under the priests of Antichrist."[123]

If you demand then, "Where was God's temple all this while?" the answer is at hand: there where Antichrist sat. Where was Christ's people? Even under Antichrist's priests, and yet this is no justification at all, either of Antichrist, or of his priests, but a manifestation of God's great power, who is able to uphold his Church, even there "where Satan's throne is."[124] Babylon was an infectious place, and the infection thereof was mortal, and yet God had his people there, whom he preserved from the mortality of that infection. Else, how should he have said, "Come out of her, my people; that ye be not partakers of her sins, and that ye receive not of her

---

[121] Rom. 11:2, 5.

[122] Luke 11:52.

[123] *Et hujus quidem usque adhuc impietatis fraude perficitur;* ["and all this impiety was carried out by deceit";] *ut jam sub Antichristi sacerdotibus Christi populus non occidat.* Hilary of Poitiers, *Contra Arianos, vel Auxentium Mediolanensem* 1 [*PL* 10:613A; the "deceit" Hilary speaks of is the tendency of Arians such as Auxentius to use orthodox language in such a way that the common people would not always perceive their fundamental errors. The people thus imbibed much catholic truth, not the error of the heretics].

[124] Rev. 2:13.

plagues."[125] If the place had not been infectious, he should not have needed to forewarn them of the danger wherein they stood, of partaking in her sins; and if the infection had not been mortal, he would not have put them in mind of the plagues that were to follow; and if, in the place thus mortally infected, God had not preserved a people alive unto himself, he could not have said, "Come out of her, my people."

The enemy indeed had there sown his tares, but sown them in the Lord's field, and among the Lord's wheat.[126] And a field, we know, may so be overgrown with such evil weeds as these, that at the first sight a man would hardly think that any corn were there at all;[127] even as in the barn itself, the mixture of the chaff with the wheat is sometime such, as a far off man would imagine that he did see but a heap of chaff, and nothing else.[128] Those worthy husbandmen that in these last six hundred years have taken pains in plucking up those pernicious weeds out of the Lord's field, and severing the chaff from his grain, cannot be rightly said, in doing this, either to have brought in another field, or to have changed the ancient grain. The field is the same, but weeded now, unweeded then; the grain the same, but winnowed now, unwinnowed then. We preach no new faith, but the same catholic faith that ever hath been preached; neither was it any part of our meaning to begin a new church in these latter days of the world, but to re-form the old. A tree that hath the luxurious branches lopped off, and the noxious things that cleave unto it taken away, is not by this pruning and purging of it made another tree than it was before; neither is the Church *reformed* in our days another Church than that which was *deformed* in the days of our forefathers, though it hath no agreement, for all that, with popery,

---

[125] Rev. 18:4.

[126] Matt. 13:24–25.

[127] *Infelix lolium, et steriles dominantur avenae* ["the luckless darnel and barren oats hold sway"; Virgil, *Georgics* 1.154; *LCL* 63:108–109 (1999 rev. ed.)].

[128] *Grana cum coeperint trituari, inter paleas jam se non tangunt, ita quasi non se noverunt, quia intercedit palea. Et quicunque longius attendit aream, paleam solummodo putat: nisi diligentius intueatur, nisi manum porrigat, nisi spiritu oris, id est, flatu purgante, discernat, difficile pervenit ad discretionem granorum.* ["In the early stages of threshing, the grains of corn do not touch one another amid the chaff; they are so to say strangers, by reason of the chaff which separates them. Someone looking at the threshing floor from a distance may perceive nothing but chaff. Unless he looks more carefully, unless he puts out his hand and separates the mixture by blowing it apart with breath from his mouth, he will hardly succeed in distinguishing the grain."] Augustine, *Enarrationes in Psalmos, In Psalmum XXV* 2.5 [*PL* 36:191; *ACW* 29:245].

which is the pestilence that walked in those times of darkness, and the destruction that now wasteth at noonday.[129]

And thus have I finished that which I had to speak concerning the unity of the faith, for the further explication whereof the Apostle addeth, "and of the knowledge of the Son of God." Wherein we may observe both the nature of this grace, and the object of it. For the former, we see that faith is here described unto us by knowledge, to show unto us, that knowledge is that thing that is necessarily required in true believing; whereof this may be an argument sufficient, that in matters of faith the Scripture doth use indifferently the terms of knowing and believing. So Job 19. 25, "I know that my Redeemer liveth." John 17. 3, "This is life eternal, that they know thee the only true God, and Jesus Christ whom thou hast sent." Isaiah 53. 11, "By his knowledge shall my righteous servant justify many." As therefore in the fundamental truths of the Christian religion unity of faith is required among all those that belong to the catholic Church, so in those main grounds likewise there is unity of knowledge generally required among all that profess the name of Christ.

For some things there be, the knowledge whereof is absolutely necessary, *necessitate medii vel finis*,[130] as the schoolmen speak, without which no man may expect, by God's ordinary law, to attain unto the end of his faith, the salvation of his soul. And in these a man may lose himself, not by heresy only, which is a flat denying, but by ignorance also, which is a bare not knowing of them; these things being acknowledged to be so necessary, that, although it lay not in our power to attain thereunto, yet this invincible ignorance should not excuse us from everlasting death.[131] Even as, if there were

---

[129] [see Ps. 91:6.]

[130] ["Necessity of means or (to obtain an) end"].

[131] *Necessarium necessitate medii appellant theologi illud, quod, ex lege ordinaria Dei, sic ad salutem necessarium est, ut quicunque etiam ob ignorantiam invincibilem, vel quacunque alia de causa, id non fuerit assecutus, is nequeat etiam consequi salutem.* Gregory of Valencia, *Commentariorum Theologicorum*, 4 vols (Lyon, 1609), 3:289 (quaest. 2, punct. 2). *Illa quae sunt necessaria necessitate finis, si desint nobis etiam sine culpa nostra, non excusabunt nos ab aeterna morte; quamvis non fuerit in nostra potestate illa assequi. Quemadmodum etiam, si non sit nisi unicum remedium, ut aliquis fugiat mortem corporalem, et tale remedium ignoretur et ab infirmo et medico; sine dubio peribit homo ille.* ["If those things that are necessary by the necessity of the end should be lacking for us, even if it is not our fault, [they] will not excuse us from everlasting death; although it was not within our power to attain them—just as, also, if there should be only one remedy for someone to escape the death of the body, and such a remedy should be ignored by patient and doctor,

---

one only remedy, whereby a sick man could be recovered, and freed from corporal death; suppose the patient and the physician both were ignorant of it, the man must perish, as well not knowing it, as if being brought unto him he had refused it. And therefore in this case it is resolved, that from the explicit faith, and actual knowledge of these things, nothing can excuse but only such an incapacity as is found in infants, naturals,[132] and distracted persons, and that in all others which have the use of reason, although they want the means of instruction, this ignorance is not only perilous, but also damnable.[133]

The danger then of this ignorance being, by the confession of the most judicious divines of both sides, acknowledged to be so great, the woeful estate of the poor country wherein I live is much to be lamented, where the people generally are suffered to perish for want of knowledge; the vulgar superstitions of popery not doing them half that hurt that the ignorance of those common principles of the faith doth, which all true Christians are bound to learn. The consideration whereof hath sometime drawn me to treat with those of the opposite party, and to move them; that, howsoever in other things we did differ one from another, yet we should join together in teaching those main points, the knowledge whereof was so necessary unto salvation, and of the truth whereof there was no controversy betwixt us. But what for the jealousies, which these distractions in matters of religion have bred among us, and what for other respects, the motion took small effect; and so betwixt us both, the poor people are kept still in miserable ignorance, neither knowing the grounds of the one religion nor of the other.

Here the case, God be thanked, is far otherwise, where your Majesty's care can never be sufficiently commended, in taking order, that the

---

without doubt that man will perish."] Domingo Báñez, *De Fide, Spe & Charitate* ... *Commentaria in Secundam Secundae Angelici Doctoris* (Salamanca, 1584), 413C–D (quaest. 2, artic. 8).

[132] [Those without the normal powers of reason or understanding.]

[133] *Sicut ad legis Christi habitualem fidem omnis viator obligatur sine ulla exceptione: sic ab ejus actuali fide nullus excusatur nisi sola incapacitate, &c. Parvulos autem et furiosos, caeterisque passionibus mente captos, seu alia naturali impossibilitate prohibitos, incapaces voco: etsi non simpliciter, tamen secundum quid; sc[ilicet] dum his defectibus laborant.* Pierre d'Ailly, *Quaestio Vesperiarum,* in *Quaestiones super I, III et IV libros Sententiarum. Recommendatio Sacrae Scripturae. Principium in cursum Bibliae, praesertim in Evangelium Marci. Quaestio insuis vesperis. Quaestio de resumpta. Recommendatio doctrinae evangelicae* (Strasbourg, 1490).

chief heads of the catechism should, in the ordinary ministry, be diligently propounded and explained unto the people throughout the land. Which I wish were as duly executed everywhere, as it was piously by you intended. Great scholars possibly may think, that it standeth not so well with their credit, to stoop thus low, and to spend so much of their time in teaching these rudiments and first principles of the doctrine of Christ. But they should consider, that the laying of the foundation skilfully, as it is the matter of greatest importance in the whole building, so is it the very masterpiece of the wisest builder. "According to the grace of God which is given unto me, as a wise master-builder, I have laid the foundation," saith the great Apostle.[134] And let the learnedest of us all try it whenever we please; we shall find, that to lay this groundwork rightly, that is, to apply ourselves unto the capacity of the common auditory, and to make an ignorant man to understand these mysteries in some good measure, will put us to the trial of our skill, and trouble us a great deal more, than if we were to discuss a controversy, or handle a subtle point of learning in the schools. Yet Christ did give as well his Apostles, and prophets, and evangelists, as his ordinary pastors and teachers, to bring us all, both learned and unlearned, unto "the unity of this faith and knowledge," and the neglecting of this is the frustrating of the whole "work of the ministry."[135] For let us preach never so many sermons unto the people, our labour is but lost, as long as the foundation is unlaid, and the first principles untaught, upon which all other doctrine must be builded.

He therefore that will "study to show himself approved unto God, a workman that needeth not to be ashamed, dividing the word of God aright,"[136] must have a special care to plant this kingdom both in the minds and in the hearts of them that hear him. I say, in the hearts as well as in the minds, because we may not content ourselves with a bare *theoretical* knowledge, which is an information only of the understanding, and goeth no further than the brain, but we must labour to attain unto a further degree both of *experimental* and of *practical* knowledge, in the things that we have learned. A young man may talk much of the troubles of the world, and a scholar in the university may show a great deal of wit in making a large declaration upon that argument, but when the same men have afterwards

---

[134] 1 Cor. 3:10.

[135] Eph. 4:11[–12].

[136] 2 Tim. 2:15.

been beaten in the world, they will confess that they spake before they knew not what, and count their former apprehension of these things to be but mere ignorance, in respect of that new learning which now they have bought by dear experience. The tree in Paradise, of which our first parents were forbidden to eat, was called "the tree of knowledge of good and evil" because it signified unto them, that as now, while they stood upon terms of obedience with their Creator, they knew nothing but good, so at what time soever they did transgress his commandment, they should begin to know evil also, whereof before they had no knowledge.[137] Not but that they had an *intellectual* knowledge of it before (for he that knoweth good cannot be ignorant of that which is contrary unto it, *rectum* being always *index sui et obliqui*),[138] but that till then they never had felt any evil, they never had any *experimental* knowledge of it. So our Apostle in this epistle boweth his knees unto the Father of our Lord Jesus Christ, that he would grant unto these Ephesians "to know the love of Christ which passeth knowledge,"[139] showing that there is a further degree of knowledge in this kind, that may be felt by the heart, though not comprehended by the brain; and in the Epistle to the Philippians, he counteth all things but loss "for the excellent knowledge sake of Christ Jesus his Lord."[140] Meaning hereby a knowledge grounded upon deep experience of the virtue of Christ's death and resurrection in his own soul, as he expoundeth it himself in the words following: "That I may know him, and the power of his resurrection, and the fellowship of his sufferings, and be made conformable unto his death."[141]

There is an experimental knowledge then to be looked after, beside the mental; and so is there a *practical* knowledge likewise, as well as an intellectual. When Christ is said to have known no sin, we cannot understand this of intellectual knowledge (for had he not thus known sin, he could not have reproved it as he did), but of practical. So that, "he knew no sin," in St. Paul,[142] must be conceived to be the very same with "he did no sin," in

---

[137] Gen. 2:9, 17.

[138] ["Right (straightness, as in a line) being always a measure of itself, and of an oblique (which crosses it)." See Aristotle, *De Anima* 1.5 (*LCL* 288:60–61; 411a, 5); cf. Aquinas, *Summa Theologiae* 32:34–37 (IIa-IIae, q. 9, a. 4)].

[139] Eph. 3:19.

[140] Phil. 3:8.

[141] Phil. 3:10.

[142] 2 Cor. 5:21.

St. Peter.[143] In the first to the Romans, they that "knew God,"[144] because "they glorified him not as God," are therefore said, "not to have God in their knowledge."[145] God made his ways and his laws known to the children of Israel in the desert, and yet he said of them, "It is a people that do err in their heart, and they have not known my ways."[146] For there is an error in the heart, as well as in the brain; and a kind of ignorance arising from the will, as well as from the mind. And therefore in the Epistle to the Hebrews, all sins are termed ἀγνοήματα, ignorances,[147] and sinners ἀγνοοῦντες καὶ πλανώμενοι, ignorant and erring persons.[148] Because, however in the general the understanding may be informed rightly, yet, when particular actions come to be resolved upon, men's perverse wills and inordinate affections cloud their minds, and lead them out of the way. That therefore is to be accounted sound knowledge, which sinketh from the brain into the heart, and from thence breaketh forth into action, setting head, heart, hand, and all awork; and so much only must thou reckon thyself to know in Christianity, as thou art able to make use of in practice. For, as St. James saith of faith, "Show me thy faith by thy works,"[149] so doth he in like manner of knowledge, "Who is a wise man, and endued with knowledge amongst you? Let him show out of a good conversation his works with meekness of wisdom."[150] And St. John, much to the same purpose, "Hereby do we know that we know him, if we keep his commandments. He that saith, I know him, and keepeth not his commandments, is a liar, and the truth is not in him."[151]

He speaketh there of Jesus Christ the righteous, the Son of God, who is here in my text likewise made the object of this knowledge. "Thou art Christ the Son of the living God," is by Christ himself made the rock upon

---

[143] 1 Pet. 2:22.

[144] Rom. 1:21.

[145] Rom. 1:28 [given as 18 in editions from 1631].

[146] Ps. 95:10; Heb. 3:10.

[147] Heb. 9:7; cf. Lev. 16:16–17.

[148] Heb. 5:2. Aristotle, *Nicomachean Ethics* 3.1: Ἀγνοεῖ μὲν οὖν πᾶς ὁ μοχθερὸς ἃ δεῖ πράττειν, καὶ ὧν δὴ ἀφεκτέον, καὶ διὰ τὴν τοιαύτην ἁμαρτίαν, ἄδικοι καὶ ὅλως κακοὶ γίνονται [*LCL* 73:122–23].

[149] Jas. 2:18.

[150] Jas. 3:13.

[151] 1 John 2:3–4.

which the whole Church is builded.[152] And "other foundation," saith St. Paul, "can no man lay, than that is laid, which is Jesus Christ."[153] Not that we should think that there were no other fundamental doctrine to be acknowledged but this alone (for the articles of the Holy Ghost, forgiveness of sins, resurrection of the dead, eternal judgment, and such other like, have their place also in the foundation),[154] but because this is the most special object of faith, and the primary foundation of the other. For first, as God is made the coaequate[155] object of the whole body of divinity, notwithstanding it treateth also of men and angels, heaven and hell, sin and obedience, and sundry other particulars, because all these are brought to God reductively, if not as explications of his nature, yet of his works and kingdom; so likewise may Christ be made the primary head of other fundamental articles, because they have all reference unto him, being such as concern either his Father, or his Spirit, or his incarnation, or his office of mediation, or his Church, or the special benefits which he hath purchased for it.

Secondly, howsoever this faith and knowledge, being taken in their larger extent, have for their full object whatever is revealed in the word of God, yet as they build us upon the foundation, as they incorporate us into the mystical body, as they are the means of our justification and life, they look upon the Son of God, and him only. The Holy Scriptures, within the bounds whereof the utmost extent of all our faith and knowledge must be contained, "are able to make us wise unto salvation," but yet "through faith which is in Christ Jesus."[156] So, "by his knowledge (or the knowledge of himself) shall my righteous servant justify many," saith the Father of the Son, Isaiah 53. 11. And "the life which I now live in the flesh, I live by the faith of the Son of[157] God, who loved me, and gave himself for me," saith the Apostle, Galatians 2. 20. The children of Israel in the wilderness, being stung with fiery serpents, were directed for their recovery to look upon the brazen serpent, which was a figure of "the Son of Man, lifted up" upon the cross, "that whosoever did believe in him, might not perish, but have eter-

---

[152] Matt. 16:16, 18.

[153] 1 Cor. 3:11.

[154] Augustine, *De Fide et Operibus* 9 [*PL* 40:205–206; *ACW* 48:19–20]; Heb. 6:1–2.

[155] [Made equal or uniform.]

[156] 2 Tim. 3:15.

[157] ['of' omitted from 1631 text but present in all other editions.]

nal life."[158] Now as the Israelites with the same eyes, and with the same visive[159] faculty wherewith they beheld the sands and the mountains in the desert, did look upon the brazen serpent also, but were cured by fastening their sight upon that alone, and not by looking upon any other object, so by the same faith and knowledge whereby we are justified, "we understand that the world was framed by the word of God,"[160] and believe all other truths revealed; and yet *fides qua justificans*, faith as it doth justify us, doth not look upon these, but fixeth itself solely upon the Son of God, not knowing any thing here but Jesus Christ and him crucified. And thus hath our Saviour a special and peculiar place in that larger foundation, according to that of the Apostle, Ephesians 2. 20, "Ye are built upon the foundation of the Apostles and prophets, of which (for so his words in the original may well bear it) Jesus Christ is the chief cornerstone."[161]

It followeth now, that we should proceed from the *foundation* to the *structure*, and so "leaving the principles of the doctrine of Christ, go on unto perfection,"[162] "unto a perfect man, unto the measure of the stature of the fullness of Christ." There is a time wherein Christ is but begun, and as it were a-breeding in us. Galatians 4. 19, "My little children, of whom I travail in birth again until Christ be formed in you." After that he hath been formed in our hearts, he is at first but as a babe there, yet resteth not at that stay, but as in his natural body he "increased in stature,"[163] so in every part of his mystical body he hath set for himself a certain "measure of stature," and a "fullness" of growth; which being attained unto, a Christian is thereby made a "perfect man." And for this end also doth the Apostle here show that the ministry was instituted, "that we henceforth should be no more children," as it is in the words immediately following my text, but that we might "grow up into him in all things, which is the Head, even Christ."[164] For the "perfection," which the Apostle here speaketh of, is not to be taken absolutely, as if any absolute perfection could be found among men in this

---

[158] John 3:14–15.

[159] [Pertaining to the sight; visual.]

[160] Heb. 11:3.

[161] ὄντος ἀκρογωνιαίου λίθου αὐτου (sc. θεμελίου) Ἰησοῦ Χριστοῦ.

[162] Heb. 6:1.

[163] Luke 2:52.

[164] Eph. 4:14–15.

life, but in comparison with childhood; as the opposition is more clearly made by him in 1 Corinthians 14. 20: "Brethren, be not children in under-standing, howbeit in malice be you children, but in understanding be per-fect," that is to say, of man's estate. And in Hebrews 5. 13, 14: "Every one that useth milk, is unskilful in the word of righteousness; for he is a babe: but strong meat belongeth to them that are perfect," that is, "that are of full age," as our interpreters have rightly rendered it.[165]

Now as there is great difference among men in their natural growth, so is there no less variety among them also in respect of their spiritual stat-ure, there being several degrees of this imperfect kind of perfection here spoken of, which, according to the diversity of times, places, and persons, may admit a greater or a lesser measure. For we may not think that the same measure of knowledge, for example, is sufficient for a learned man and an unlearned; for a pastor, and for an ordinary Christian; for those that lived in the time of darkness, and them that enjoy the light of the Gospel; for them that have the means, and them that want it. But according to the measure of the gift of God, we must know notwithstanding, that it is re-quired generally of all men that they "grow in grace, and in the knowledge of our Lord and Saviour Jesus Christ."[166] Not in "knowledge" only, but in "grace"; even "grow up into him in *all* things, which is the head," as our Apostle here admonisheth us.[167] We must proceed "from faith to faith,"[168] that is, from one measure and degree of it unto another; and this being the root, and other graces as it were the branches, if it grow apace, other graces also must hasten and ripen, and grow proportionably with it, else thou may-est justly suspect, that thy growth is not sound, and answerable to that which the Apostle showeth to be in the mystical body of Christ; which, "according to the effectual working in the measure of *every* part, maketh increase of the body, unto the edifying of itself in love."[169] The time will not permit me to proceed any further, and therefore here I end. "Now the God

---

[165] ["our interpreters" being the translators of the KJV.]

[166] 2 Pet. 3:18.

[167] Eph. 4:15.

[168] Rom 1:17.

[169] Eph. 4:16.

of peace, that brought again from the dead our Lord Jesus, that great Shepherd of the sheep, through the blood of his everlasting covenant, make you perfect in every good work to do his will; working in you that which is well-pleasing in his sight, through Jesus Christ: to whom be glory for ever and ever. Amen."[170]

---

[170] Heb. 13:20–21.

A SERMON BEFORE KING CHARLES AT GREENWICH (1626)

Sermon before King Charles at Greenwich, 25 June 1626

1 Corinthians 14. 33.

For God is not the author of confusion, but of peace, as in all the churches of the saints.

THE HOLY APOSTLE in his former words doth set down a course for the ordering and exercise of prophesying in the Church. A thing not being well ordered, liberty of prophesying brings all confusion upon the Church. The delivery of what doctrine a man please without control, is the ground from whence grows sedition in the Church of God.[1] Therefore though the

---

[1] Two manuscript accounts of this sermon which agree very closely can be found in Northamptonshire Record Office, Finch Hatton MS 247, 161–197 and Cambridge University Library, MS Dd.v.31, fols 94r–103r. The version which appears in *WJU*, 13:335–51 is shorter in comparison. There is clearly some organic relationship between the two manuscripts because, whatever their differences in contents, they both also contain the same sermons by the bishops Brian Duppa, Walter Curle, Matthew Wren, and Barnaby Potter, and a number of common errors in references to biblical passages in the text of Ussher's sermon. One could be copied from the other or they could derive from common source material. The NRO manuscript exhibits more archaic words and forms of words, e.g. "twicht" and "cyted" against the Cambridge manuscript's "knit" and "cited." The omission of Apollos from the quotation of 1 Cor. 1:12 in the Cambridge manuscript is easily explained by eyeskip in copying. Elsewhere, "looseness, that is the way to have his heart corrupted," in the Cambridge manuscript becomes "looseness, ~~that~~ which is the way to have his heart corrupted," the strikethrough suggesting that the NRO manuscript's more difficult reading, "that," is earlier. For such reasons the NRO manuscript is here tentatively regarded as the earlier and used as the source text, though the differences are minimal. Elrington's source for the version in *WJU* is not known. It may be a further manuscript witness which is not currently traceable, or he may have

Apostle do commend prophesying, verse 25, yet saith he, "Let it be done in order. Let the prophets speak two or three and let the other[2] judge," verse 29. That is, though they have liberty to deliver that doctrine, which they may learn out of the word of God, yet may they not challenge such a power to themselves, that what doctrine soever they deliver must be without censure. For others must judge. And how? Why, saith the Apostle, "Let the spirit of the prophets be subject unto the prophets." That is to say, let the fewer be content to submit themselves to be ordered by the greater company of their fellow prophets. Then follows the words of my text: "For God is not the author of confusion but of peace," the meaning whereof is this: If every prophet should stand upon his own spirit, and every man teach what he lists,[3] there should be no submitting of one unto another, and so of necessity there must be confusion. But God is not the author of any such, not of confusion but of peace.

There is the proposition. And then the instance with the extent: "as in all the churches of the saints," which words of the Apostle consist of two parts, negative and affirmative. I will begin with the affirmative part. God is the author of peace. It hath its original and its rise from heaven, from above. All true peace comes from God. James 3. 17, "The wisdom from above is first pure, then peaceable." So that you see it comes from God. And thereupon we find he is styled "the God of peace." Philippians 4. 9, "The God of Peace shall be with you." And Romans 15. 33, "Now the God

---

copied from either or both of the extant manuscripts and edited considerably. Elrington's inclusion of short passages unique to one or other of the currently available manuscripts, as indicated in the notes, suggests that he could not have worked from either the NRO manuscript or the CUL manuscript alone. His editorial hand may perhaps be discerned in certain differences, such as the substitution of "flame" in describing the Arminian controversy for the "plague" of both manuscripts, and other softening of language. Only Elrington's more helpful or significant variations draw comment below. In addition to the above, Ussher's preparatory notes survive in Bodleian Library, MS Rawlinson D1290, fols 63v–65v. All footnotes to this sermon are editorial, there being none in the manuscript source. Square brackets around editorial footnotes have been dispensed with. All quotation marks are supplied by the editor. Neither the NRO nor the CUL MSS give the date or the occasion of this sermon. The details are supplied in Ussher's notes in Bodleian Library, MS Rawlinson D1290, fol. 63v: "Before the King, at Greenwich, Jun. 25. 1626." Elrington states 1627 (*WJU*, 13:335) but by this time Ussher had already returned to Ireland. See Ford, *James Ussher*, 144–45.

2 "others" in CUL, MS Dd.v.31, fol. 94r.

3 "wishes" or "desires."

of peace be with you all." And in Romans 16. 20, "And the God of peace shall bruise Satan under your feet shortly." And in the first of Thessalonians 5. 23, "The very God of peace sanctify you throughout." So that he may well be the author of peace, being the God and the very God of peace. As for his Son's name, he is called the "Prince of Peace." Isaiah 9. 6, "His name shall be called wonderful, the mighty God, the everlasting Father, the Prince of Peace." You see it is a part of the name of the Son of God, "the Prince of Peace." So here is God, the God of peace, and his Son, the prince of peace. And therefore they that were types of Christ were sons of peace. Solomon's name did bear the title of peace,[4] and in the seventh to the Hebrews, Melchizedek as he was a just king, so he was a king of Salem, that is king of peace.[5] And in the 1 Hebrews 6, when the Lord did bring his begotten Son into the world, and bid all his angels adore, and worship him, this was one note of that celestial song, Luke 2, "Glory be to God on high, and in earth peace."[6] And as this was the angels' song when he was brought into the world, so it was likewise his own farewell when he departed out of the world as John 14. 17. "Peace I leave with you, my Peace I give unto you." This was the last legacy that Christ bequeathed unto his disciples, when he left the world, even his peace. So likewise his kingdom is a kingdom of peace. Romans 14. 17, "The kingdom of God is righteousness and peace." And they are the basis of God's kingdom. Isaiah 9. 7, "The increase of his government and peace shall have no end." Other kingdoms, the more they increase, the more ado to keep peace. But it is not so in Christ's kingdom. The increase of his government and peace go hand in hand together, the one hinders not the other. "The increase of his government and peace shall have no end." So likewise his way, you know, it is a way of peace. Luke 1. 79, "To guide our feet into the way of peace." Christ's way it is not a troublesome way, contentious and bitter way. It is no such way, but it is a way of peace. So likewise his Gospel, it is a Gospel of peace. Romans 10. 15, "How beautiful are the feet of those that preach the Gospel of peace." What shall I say more? His officers are the ministers of peace, and his subjects are the children of peace. When Christ sent forth his disciples, Luke

---

[4] Solomon or šᵉlōmōh, likely being derived from the verb šlm, to be at peace. *New International Dictionary of Old Testament Theology and Exegesis*, ed. Willem VanGemeren, 5 vols (Carlisle: Paternoster, 1996), 4:1232.

[5] Heb. 7:1–2.

[6] Luke 2:14. Both MSS give as "Luke. 1."

the tenth 5,[7] the first part of their message was this, "into whatsoever house you enter first say, Peace be to this house. And if the children of peace be there, then shall your peace rest upon it." So that Christ's messengers you see are the preachers of peace, and his subjects are the subjects of peace. And how are those subjects joined together the Apostle showeth us Ephesians 4. 3,[8] "Endeavouring to keep the unity of the spirit in the bond of peace." This bond of peace is that which keeps all Christ's subjects in order. Thus you see how God is the God of peace, and the author of peace, and how he knits all his children together by the bond of peace. And if you ask how are these knit together, how doth the Lord this, what cords are there by which Christ's subjects are twicht[9] together, I answer God doth make men children of peace by infusing certain inward gifts and heavenly graces into them, whereby they are disposed into a peaceable temper. There must be some thing within a man to keep him quiet and in good temper, before he can keep good correspondency[10] with those that are without him. As our Saviour saith in Mark 9. 50, "Have salt in your selves, and have peace one with another." The meaning is, a man must have his heart well seasoned with the spiritual graces within, or else it is impossible he should ever keep good quarter and live peaceably with those that are without him. Therefore have this spiritual salt within you, and then have peace with one another. Now there are, beloved, three principal grains of this spiritual salt, and these are the spiritual graces that must season a man's heart before he can live peaceably.

The first is wisdom.

The second is love.

The third is humility and lowliness of mind.

These are the three special grains of that spiritual salt that must season a man's heart whereby he is fitted and disposed for the maintenance of the peace of the Church. I say wisdom first of all. There is the ground as you may see, James 3. 13: "Who is a wise man and endued with knowledge amongst you? Let him show out of a good conversation his works with meekness of wisdom." Beloved, who is a wise man? Who is one endued

---

[7] "15" in both MSS.

[8] "4 . 5." in both MSS.

[9] Archaic form of "twitched," meaning drawn or pulled together. Rendered as "knit" in CUL, MS Dd.v.31, fol. 95r. Elrington gives as "twisted" in *WJU*, 13:339.

[10] "correspondence" or "agreement."

with knowledge amongst you? He that knoweth how to show by a good conversation his works in meekness of wisdom. Why is he a wise man? Because wisdom is always joined with a meek and gentle spirit. Therefore a man is the more humble as you may see in the 3. chapter of James 17 verse before cited,[11] what the Apostle saith of that wisdom which is from above. It is first pure, then peaceable, gentle, and easy to be entreated. Observe the quality of that wisdom which is from above. It is first pure, then peaceable. It is first pure. That is, it is the nature of that wisdom in the first place, not to take things hand over head.[12] But to be able to discern by discretion between that which is pure, and that which is impure. It is a point of wisdom to separate the precious from the vile, and to try all things first, and then to hold fast that which is good: the first of Thessalonians 5. 21. And as wisdom is pure in the first choice, so it is likewise peaceable. As suppose I have made choice of a good thing that I judge to be pure, perhaps another thinks not so, but judges another thing to be pure because he hath not the same strength of judgement that I have.[13] What then? Yet must I be peaceable. And not withstanding another hath not so much wisdom in this case as I have yet the wisdom that I have should make me peaceable. For the wisdom that is from above is first pure, then peaceable. But what if the party that hath made the worst choice, and chose that which is false, and shall oppose himself against me? I answer, see how the Apostle Paul instructeth Timothy, 2 Epistle 2. 24[–25]: "The servant of God must not strive, but be gentle unto all men, apt to teach, patient in meekness, instructing those that oppose themselves, if God peradventure will give them repentance to the acknowledging of the truth." Here is the property of a true minister of God, a true professor and officer of him that is the king of peace. "If any man desire to be contentious, we have no such custom, nor the Churches of God," saith the Apostle, 1 Corinthians 11. 16. But saith the same Apostle, if men oppose yet we must instruct such opposers with meekness, and not fret and fume. We have not so learned Christ. And what is the ground of it? "If God peradventure," saith the Apostle, "will give them repentance to the acknowledging of the truth,"[14] as if he should say, do you think it is an easy

---

[11] Reference is to James 4:17 in both MSS.

[12] "rashly" or "negligently."

[13] Elrington has one who "hath as much wisdom and strength of judgement as I have," *WJU*, 13:340.

[14] 2 Tim. 2:25.

matter, and a thing that grows upon the earth, that a man should discern betwixt truth and falsehood in these spiritual matters? No. For as there must be a conversion of the heart, that must make a man turn from a wicked life to a good life, so there must be likewise the conversion of the mind. And it is the gift of God that one is able to discern more than another. And therefore coming from God, why shouldst thou be so furious unto him to whom it hath not pleased God to reveal so much as he hath done unto thee? So that beloved, this is the first grace that seasoneth us, and fitteth us for this peace, namely spiritual wisdom, which is first pure, then peaceable. The other two are in the heart, love and humility. The Apostle joins them both together in writing to the Ephesians and Philippians, and he layeth the ground thus, in the 4 Ephesians 2[–3]: "With all lowliness and meekness, with long suffering, forbearing one another in love, endeavouring to keep the unity of the Spirit in the bond of peace." But how shall I do this? Why, mark what the Apostle saith in that 2 verse, "with lowliness and meekness, forbearing one another in love." For it is this lowliness and meekness with long suffering in love, that knits this bond so fast. For love, you know the properties of it in the 13 chapter[15] of the first to the Corinthians: "Love suffereth long, and is kind, seeketh not her own, is not easily provoked, thinketh no evil, covereth all things."[16] Love as it is the root of all other graces, so principally of this. It makes a man to be of a quiet temper, and peaceable disposition. So lowliness of mind. 2 Philippians 2, "Fulfill ye my joy, that ye be like minded, having the same love." So that if there be a heart full of love, that heart will not easily be provoked by the dissention of another man. So that the means to keep peace is to have our hearts fraught[17] with love. Well what is the third verse? "Let nothing be done through strife or vainglory, but in lowliness of mind, let each esteem the other better than themselves." So that, get lowliness of mind and a loving heart, and I will warrant thee for ever being the head of a faction and a sower of sedition amongst the brethren.[18] It is pride and a want of love that causeth contention. The Apostle giveth us an excellent pattern in the fifth

---

[15] "verse" in both MSS.

[16] 1 Cor. 13:4–5. The last clause may bring together the idea of 1 Cor. 13:7 with the language of 1 Pet. 4:8.

[17] "filled."

[18] Perhaps "warrant" being used here in the older sense of "guarantee safety" or "protect from harm."

verse. "Let the same mind be in you as was in Christ Jesus." And what doth the prince of peace exhort us unto in the eleventh of Matthew? "Learn of me," saith he, "for I am meek and lowly in heart."[19] And in the 12th of Matthew 19 (which place is taken out of the prophet Isaiah the 42 and 2 and applied to Christ), "He shall not strive nor cry, neither shall his voice be heard in the streets." He it is that was thus humble, and lowly minded, that would have us learn this virtue from him, and if you be like him in the former, ye shall be like him in the latter. So that from all this you see, how that God is the author of peace, and how he doth enable his children to be the sons of peace.

Now what will follow from hence? Surely all those whose hearts can testify unto themselves, that they are inclinable unto peace, it is an argument unto them that God is their father, and they his children, and that he will be with them. Matthew 5. 9, "Blessed are the peacemakers for they shall be called the children of God." If God be the author of peace, then he that studiously follows and labours for peace is God's child, and God will be with him. 2 Corinthians 13. 11, "Be of one mind, live in peace, and the God of love and peace shall be with you." So that unless you will banish God out of your hearts, receive I beseech you this apostolical exhortation. And if he be with you, you see there is a blessing belongs unto you: "Blessed are the peacemakers." The prophet David sets out this virtue and blessedness in the 133 Psalm, a short psalm. "Behold how good and how pleasant a thing it is for brethren to dwell together in unity." You see there is but two parts of this psalm. First, how good a thing it is. Secondly, how pleasant a thing it is. If you would know how pleasant, "it is like the precious ointment upon the head, and runneth down upon the beard, that went down unto the skirts of his garments." No perfume so pleasant. Will you know how good it is? It is "as the dew of Hermon, and as the dew that descendeth upon the mountains of Zion." And in the third of James and the 18, "The fruit of righteousness is sown in peace of them that make peace." And mark the latter end of the 133 Psalm. "There the Lord commandeth blessings, even life for evermore." What? Are they blessed then? Why, wonder not at that. For he that hath all blessings in store hath commanded blessings. Of what nature? "Even life for evermore"; for those brethren that live together in unity. Here fitly then may come in that exhortation in the 34th Psalm, and the 12[–14] verse, and the first Epistle of Peter 3. 10[–11]: "What man is he

---

[19] Matt. 11:29.

that desireth life, and loveth many days, that he may see good? Keep thy tongue from evil and thy lips from speaking guile. Depart from evil, and do good; seek peace and ensue[20] it." As if he should say, dost thou look for life, and good days? Even as it is necessary for the attaining of this to eschew evil and do good, so necessary it is to follow after peace. What if it run so fast from me, that I cannot overtake it? Yet still pursue it. Suppose it run away (that showeth that peace is such a thing as may be gone) and when I think of peace another thinks of war; yet I say, if thou lookest for life, and desirest to be of that company upon whom the Lord commands blessings, thou must not give over the pursuit of it. This is the first thing I intended to speak of concerning the affirmative part: that God is the author of peace, and if we be the children of peace, we are the children of God, and the God of peace will be with us, the Lord will command blessings, even life for evermore.

Aye,[21] but though God fathers peace, he will not own the other. God is not the God of confusion. Confusion is contrary unto peace. The word signifieth a tumult, unquietness or contention, and an unquiet or contentious spirit is not from God. Whence come it then? The Apostle James in his third chapter and 14 verse, tells from whence it is. "If you have," saith he, "bitter envying and strife in your hearts, rejoice not, neither be liars against the truth. This wisdom descendeth not from above, but is earthly, sensual, and devilish." Will you see the pedigree of this contentious wisdom? Put case[22] it is esteemed a high point of wisdom in these days to put men together by the ears.[23] It is "not from above," it is not then heavenly. Whence is it then? It is "earthly, sensual, and devilish." First, it is earthly: there is the world. It is sensual: there is the flesh. And it is devilish: there is the devil. So, you see, God is not the author of it, but the world, the flesh, and the devil. You see the Apostle joins them altogether in one verse. This wisdom, saith he, is not from above, but is earthly, sensual, and devilish. This wisdom that causeth strife and contention is nowadays by some counted zeal. This is no true zeal, but a bitter one. And mark the Apostle, if

---

[20] "pursue" in KJV's rendering of Ps. 34:14 but "ensue" in 1 Pet. 3:11. Earlier translations such as Coverdale's (1535) and Matthew's (1537) gave "ensue" at Ps. 34 [there 33]:14. The meaning is "follow" or "pursue."

[21] "I" in MS.

[22] "suppose."

[23] To put at odds, in close contest.

there be "bitter envying and strife" amongst you, that wisdom is "not from above." Believe it. Such zeal as is bitter, is a counterfeit kind of zeal. It is not that which comes from wisdom which is from above, but it is earthly. But to run this briefly over again—for if we did but seriously consider the pedigree of contention and disorder, it would be a sufficient argument to alienate all men's hearts from it. First, consider it is earthly. That is, it is grounded on worldly respects and considerations, though the pretence be religion. And it is certain when there is dissention either in Church or commonwealth, yet if it be truly examined, it will be found to be grounded upon worldly respects. Those that are causers of dissention either in Church or state, let them pretend the furtherance of religion as long as they list, and how ever they make a fair show in the business, yet if search be made to the quick you shall find that they have strange fetches[24] underneath, their aim being in truth only at carnal and earthly ends. The Apostle in the 16th Romans 17 verse, a place well to be considered, beseecheth the Romans to "mark them" diligently "which cause division, and offences contrary to the doctrine which you have received, and avoid them." As if he should say, you have received the doctrine of peace from us, how comes it to pass that you are disturbed and troubled? Surely some distempered spirits have troubled this calm, or else how should these dissentions come amongst you? Well, saith he, mark those men. And what doth he say in the 18 verse? "For they that are such serve not the Lord Jesus Christ, but their own bellies, and with fair speeches and good words deceive the hearts of the simple." It is worldly. Notwithstanding they pretend the maintenance of the truth, yet some temporal ends and worldly respects is the thing they aim at. So in truth they "serve not the Lord Jesus but their owne bellies." And the same Apostle in the first Epistle to Timothy the 6 and 3[–5][25] shows from what people this contention cometh. "If any man," saith he, "teach otherwise, and consenteth not to the wholesome doctrine of our Lord Jesus Christ, he is puffed up and knoweth nothing but doteth about questions, and strife of words, whereof cometh envy, strife, railings, evil surmisings, vain disputations of men, corrupt minds, and destitute of the truth, supposing gain is godliness." That is, if you go to the original in the 4 verse, there is pride first of all moving of questions,[26] of which there is no good. But "strife, railings,

---

[24] Tricks, artifices.

[25] Both MSS refer to 1 Tim. 3:4.

[26] "moving questions" in MS. "moving of questions" in CUL, MS Dd.v.31, fol. 97v.

evil surmisings, perverse disputings of men of corrupt minds," and, mark the ground, "supposing gain is godliness." That is, so that they may have gain and preferment. That is all they seek after. This wisdom is earthly, and commonly, mark it, the greatest seditions that are, and ever were raised in the Church, have been grounded on worldly respects. And this is one cause of it: part-taking, the holding of some men's persons in admiration for advantage, and what side they are on, that side they will be, and so it goeth along.

We need not go far for a proof of this. If we cast our eyes upon the Netherlands, we shall see that the contentions and divisions that have been brought in amongst them was for earthly and temporal ends,[27] as might be easily instanced. That great schism that was in Israel in the time of Jeroboam had his pretence of devotion, and to save the people a labour from going so far as Jerusalem to worship. But the true end was, as the Holy Ghost discovers, earthly and carnal. It was for fear lest the tribes should cleave to the house of David and the state go thither, and so the king should lose his kingdom.[28] So that, you see, that wisdom which is the cause of division and contention is grounded on worldly respects.

Well, secondly, it is sensual. As the world hath a part in it, so the flesh hath another part in it. What is the Apostle's meaning by that? It is as if he should have said those that are authors of dissention, if you mark them well are very carnal and sensual. As it is in the first of Corinthians 3. 3, "Whereas there is amongst you envying and strife and divisions. Are you not carnal?" Do you not know that these are the fruits of the flesh? As in the 5 to the Galatians [19–]20, "The fruits[29] of the flesh are manifest." What are they? See verse 20. "Strife, emulations, seditions, heresies." These are made manifest to be the fruits of the flesh. And 4 James 1. "From whence comes these broils and wars[30] amongst you? Are they not from hence, even of your lusts that war in your members?" That is, there is some dissention within a man's self. There is a warring of lust within before there be a tumult without, even as it is with the earth. Let the wind blow never so strong

---

[27] In *WJU*, 13:343, Elrington gives this passage as "… whence came those disputes, was it a matter only in the schools that the scholars only had a hand in it, were there not politic respects in it?"

[28] 1 Kgs 12:26–27.

[29] "works" in KJV.

[30] "wars and fightings" in KJV.

without[31] it, it moves it not: but let it but once get into the earth, then presently it makes an earthquake.[32] So let there be a man that hath not his tempest of lust within himself. And the wind and blasts that come from without him will not be able to shake him. Whence cometh wars without, but from wars within. So that, you see, this wisdom as it is worldly, so it is sensual. It is a fruit of the flesh, and they are carnal that follow it. But you will say, let me have this opened a little more, let us see from what part of the corruption of our nature it is from when this doth arise. To note it unto you briefly, first, it is from want of wisdom in the understanding. Secondly, from want of integrity in the heart. And thirdly, by reason of some distemper in the affections. Unto these three heads I refer this corruption of nature that breeds this distemper.

First, this dissention ariseth for want of wisdom in the understanding. For, as Solomon speaketh concerning wrath, that it is a companion of contention,[33] so he saith, wrath "resteth in the bosom of fools."[34] And we shall not see a man given to contention, but you may discern in him much want of wisdom. Therefore we find contention referred unto the foolish, as in many places of Scripture, so in this Book of the Proverbs, contention referred unto the foolish man. 14 chapter 29, "He that is slow to wrath is of great wisdom;[35] but he that is hasty exalteth folly." A hasty man, a troublesome man. The more eager and earnest he is, the more highly he doth exalt his own folly. And in the 18 chapter 6, "A fool's lips enter into contention," but to stop strife, and contention a fool hath not the wit to do it. And in the 20 chapter 3 verse, "It is an honour for a man to cease from strife but every fool will be meddling." A man must not think because he hath engaged himself, therefore he will make the quarrel good. It is an argument of great folly, in a man that is desirous to fish in such troubled waters. But suppose a wise man and a fool meet together, yet a wise man will not contend with a

---

[31] Elrington renders as "upon" and this gives the sense more clearly. *WJU*, 13:344.

[32] This belief, still widespread in the Renaissance, goes back to Aristotle, *Meteorologica* 2.7–8 (*LCL* 397:198). Pent-up wind breaks free, rushing through subterranean chambers and causing movement of the earth's surface above. See David Person, *Varieties: Or, A Surveigh of Rare and Excellent Matters* (1635), 79–80 (2.8); William Shakespeare, *1 Henry IV*, 3.1.27–32.

[33] Likely a reference to Prov. 15:18.

[34] Eccl. 7:9.

[35] "understanding" in KJV and CUL, MS Dd.v.31, fol. 98v.

foolish man. In the 29 chapter 9 see what Solomon saith: "If a wise man contend with a foolish man, whether he rage, or laugh, there is no rest." So that you see where there is dissention there must needs be restless confusion. So that here is the first want of wisdom in the understanding, that is our corruption of nature, from whence this corruption ariseth.

The second is a worse, and more grievous, and that is for want of integrity in the heart. You must understand that when the heart is corrupted and out of order, the whole man is out of order, and corrupted. And as in the natural body the head hath a sympathising with the stomach and the pain of the head ariseth oftentimes from some fumes that arise from the stomach,[36] so it is in spiritual matters. There is a correspondency between the brain and the heart, and if a man give himself to looseness, which[37] is the way to have his heart corrupted, it is a just judgement of God that his head should be infected. The Apostle doth teach it plainly in writing unto Timothy in his 1 Epistle 1 chapter 5[–6] verse. "The end of the commandment is love[38] out of a pure heart, and of a good conscience, and of faith unfeigned, from which some having swerved, have turned aside unto vain janglings." That is, when men take no pains to look to their heart, but forsake the commandments of God, and depart from a good conscience, and become an enemy to all goodness; having "swerved" from this, then they "turn aside unto vain janglings." The same Apostle he sets down the perils of these days. "In the last days," saith he, "shall come perilous times. Men shall be lovers of their own selves, covetous, boasters, lovers of pleasures more than lovers of God."[39] As if he should say in the last days shall be perilous times, men shall be lovers of themselves (that is the ground), they make themselves the idol unto which all bow and bend that shall love themselves more than the peace of the Church, or of the commonwealth, covetous, boasters, proud, despisers of those that are good, lovers of pleasures more than lovers of God. These, saith he, are like Jannes and Jambres that resisted the truth. What were these? They were Pharaoh's logicians, or

---

[36] See Philip Barrough, *The Method of Physick*, 6th ed. (London: Richard Field, 1624), 12–13 (1.9).

[37] NRO's "that" is emended from CUL, MS Dd.v.31, fol. 99r where "that" has been scored through corrected to "which," and this reads better. Perhaps a sign that CUL copies NRO or an earlier MS and emends at this point.

[38] "charity" in KJV.

[39] 2 Tim. 3:1–2, 4.

magicians if you will, men of corrupt minds that would not give place to Moses. Even "as Jannes and Jambres resisted Moses, so do these also resist the truth."[40] Do you not think that Moses was the better scholar of the three? Yes verily, for he was learned in all the learning of the Egyptians. Acts 7 and 22. He could, as we say, outshoot them all in their own bow. Why would they not give place then? They knew they resisted the truth. What was the ground of it? Because they were men of corrupt minds, as the Apostle saith in the 8th verse, "these also resisted the truth, men of corrupt minds." So that you see it is to no end to turn the head before the heart be turned. "But evil men and seducers will wax worse and worse."[41] So there is a second ground: that as there is a want of spiritual wisdom in the mind, so there is want of solid goodness in the heart, which is another cause of this distemper. And as long as that is corrupt all will be nought, and nothing but restless peace within.

Thirdly, there is a distemper in the affections as namely, love, hatred, envy, etc. A number of places of Scripture might be brought for this purpose. We may see it amongst ourselves, that our misplacing of our affections is a great ground of this contention that is amongst us. But you will say, do you think that love, such a virtue, and so good a mother of virtues, should be the ground of contention? Yes, certainly, when it is misplaced. There is a memorable place for this in the 15th of the Acts 36. That betwixt two holy men, Paul and Barnabas, who had agreed to visit the churches, there arose a sharp contention. Everyone knew that Paul was a holy man and a good man, and in the 11 of the Acts and 24 it is said Barnabas "was a good man, and full of the Holy Ghost," yet the contention grew so sharp betwixt them, that they broke company and parted asunder one from another. But what was the reason that these men, so full of the Holy Ghost, should give this scandal? The ground of it was a question arose concerning Mark. Barnabas would fain have Mark go with them in the company to visit the brethren. No, saith Paul, he was a flincher and left us at Pamphylia, and went not with us to the work. Questionless Paul was in the right, yet Barnabas would not yield. The Holy Ghost in that place toucheth not the reason why. But St. Paul doth in the last chapter to the Colossians 10. "Aristarchus my fellow prisoner saluteth you, and Marcus, sister's son to Barnabas." Here was the cause of the contention. It was for his sister's son. Barnabas

---

40 2 Tim. 3:8.

41 2 Tim. 3:13.

would have him go in their company and not to be disgraced. So that here you see natural affection will sway love much, being mistempered and misplaced. Love, though it be an excellent virtue, yet may cause much contention and disorder, if it be misplaced. In the 1 Corinthians 1. 11. 12. and the 3. 4, "It is told me of them of the house of Chloe, that there are dissensions amongst you. Some say I am [of] Paul, and another I am [of] Apollos, and another I am [of] Cephas. Are you not carnal?"[42] Here is love to good men ill placed. Thus many men will addict themselves, and cast their affections upon some one man, and he shall be their only oracle. And what is the issue of this? To have some men's persons in admiration, but perpetual dissention. Now if it be so that love misplaced is the cause of much contention, much more hatred,[43] for Solomon saith of hatred cometh contention.[44] Thus you see this wisdom, this contentious wisdom. Let it be covered with never such fair shows, yet it is earthly: it hath worldly respects. It is sensual: it cometh from the corruption of our carnal nature.

But there is one thing behind: it is devilish. What, a conspiracy betwixt the world, the flesh, and the devil? Yes, you shall see a conspiracy of all your spiritual enemies in it. Thou shalt not only see the world and the flesh to have a hand in it, but the devil also. Lord, bless us, will you say. A man to be the devil's instrument? He's a pressed[45] man to have so base an employment. Yes, look in the ninth of Judges and the 23. The Holy Ghost saith there, "God sent an evil spirit betwixt king Abimelech, and the men of Shechem." There arose a contention betwixt the king and his people. Whence came it? It came from an evil spirit, that, saith the text, went between them. We must not think the devil went in a visible shape from one unto another. No, but he was the cause of it. He had his instruments. He had his oar in that boat. At the beginning it was a devilish evil spirit that put God and man at variance. So that you see that this contentious wisdom, it is not only earthly, and carnal, but also devilish.

Therefore, as you know that it was he at the beginning, that put God and man at variance, even so it is he that now still continues to put brethren

---

[42] "of Paul" and "of Cephas" in CUL, MS Dd.v.31, fol. 100r, though Apollos is omitted.

[43] "much more is hatred" in CUL, MS Dd.v.31, fol. 100r, and this is surely the sense.

[44] Prov. 10:12.

[45] Forced into service.

at variance, whence it is, he that hateth his brother is of that evil one.[46] And know you this, that those that are of a contentious disposition, and nourish faction, they do that service unto a master they are ignorant of, which if they knew, I suppose they would not do. So all this being concluded you see plainly that God is not the author of contention and confusion, but the world, the flesh, and the devil.

Well then, what may we look should come from this dissention that hath such a root and brood? If you would know the issue and fruit of it, see what the Apostle saith of it in the 5th Galatians 15. "If ye bite and devour one another, take heed that ye be not consumed one of another." Desolation must of necessity follow those divisions. What? Do we live amongst Christ's lambs and sheep, or amongst bears and wolves, that one should bite another? That a man shall not see the face of a man, but of a wild beast? Well, bite and devour as long as you will, but take heed you do not consume one another. Take heed that the God of peace do not sever himself from those that know not the way of peace. So in the 12th of Matthew 25, that peremptory speech of our Saviour Christ. "Every kingdom divided against itself is brought to desolation;[47] and every city or house divided against itself shall not stand." It was the speech of the wisest man that ever lived on the face of the earth, beloved. And doth not this nearly[48] concern us now to consider, whether the state should be dissolved or not? Howsoever you think to support it by policy, yet give me leave to believe my Saviour Christ, before the wisest politian[49] of you all. A kingdom divided against itself shall not stand. Take it for certain and as sure as you be here present.[50] Let dissention in kingdom, in city, and in house go forward. All the policy in the world shall never be able to make that kingdom, city, or house to stand, but it shall be dissolved. And those that trust so much to wisdom and policy, shall find in the end, that they have been much deceived. But some will say peradventure if dissention come to the height it might prove so. See the 17 Proverbs 14. What a holy proverb Solomon

---

[46] See 1 John 3:10–15.

[47] "desolation" follows KJV, but "dissolution" in CUL, MS Dd.v.31, fol. 100v.

[48] Emended: "merely" in MS, but "nearly" (as in "closely" or "particularly") in CUL, MS Dd.v.31, fol. 100v. Elrington gives as "nearly" in *WJU*, 13:347, so perhaps he is following CUL, though it is a reasonable inference.

[49] "politician," one dealing in polity.

[50] This sentence is not reproduced in CUL, MS Dd.v.31, fol. 100v.

useth. It is this.[51] "The beginning of strife is as the opening of waters: therefore leave contention, before it be meddled with." The beginning of contention you think is a small matter. Is it a small matter to open a dam think ye? If one should try such a conclusion in the Low Countries, peradventure before he could stop it again, the whole country might be drowned. So that the beginning of contention is no small matter. It is like the opening of waters, which is not easily stopped again. And therefore it is the counsel of wisdom to leave off contention before it be meddled with. Now it lieth in your powers to stop it. This contention, that is but small in the beginning, if it once grow unto a head, it will master the wits of the best to appease and quiet it. A little child, you know, may fire such a house as a thousand men cannot easily quench again.

But, may some say, to what end is all this that you speak? I would to God we had no cause to speak,[52] and pray too that God would be merciful unto us. We see the prognostication of our ruin before our eyes and yet we are not sensible of it. We see distemper in the state and dissension in the Church and yet persuade ourselves all will be well, and that wisdom and policy will hold us out. Beloved, this may not be. I intrude not. Far be it from me to meddle with matters of state. I leave that to my superiors to whom it doth belong. But my text leads me to "all the churches of the saints." Here I am sure I am within my own element. Do we not see a great distemper in the churches of the saints? May we not cast our eyes upon our neighbouring countries, where the self same plague[53] did first begin, where first it begun but with disputations in the schools? Afterward it came to be more openly spoken of, that it troubled the state, and made a breach of peace. At the first they who had disturbed the peace, did supplicate that there might be no breach. But no peace could be had, and when the schism grew to perfection, it came to this pass, that unless they might have congre-

---

[51] These two short sentences are not reproduced in CUL, MS Dd.v.31, fol. 100v. Elrington is quite close to this in *WJU*, 13:347: "But you read of a holy proverb that Solomon maketh use of, and it is this." This suggests that he was not working from CUL alone but had access to NRO or another MS which can no longer be traced.

[52] CUL, MS Dd.v.31, fol. 101r follows this with the addition "We have all cause to speak." Elrington agrees with this in *WJU*, 13:348, adding the conjunction "but."

[53] Elrington renders as "flame" in *WJU*, 13:348. This may reflect Elrington's high church views; not denying that Arminianism was a source of controversy, but avoiding the potentially more value-laden connotations of "plague."

gations of their own, they refused to contribute to the wars. When it was small and at the beginning, it might easily have been stopped, but you see that being not prevented at the first, what a great deal of trouble it hath caused since in those parts, and yet still it grows on. I beseech God that we try not conclusions, to see how far such a thing may go with us before it be stopped.

You may say unto me, how may it be prevented, and what advice can you give to help it before it go further? I answer and protest, I will speak as before God and as one studious of peace, and not of parts, that this I would advise. First, that all odious terms to be laid aside and suppressed. It is come to that pass nowadays that those that will not yield unto that new doctrine, which hath lately almost destroyed[54] the Low Countries, that there is cast upon them that odious and contemptible name of Puritans. It is a pestilent thing tending to the everlasting maintenance of this contention.[55] With what brazen face durst[56] any man ever say that King James, our late dread sovereign of everlasting memory, was a Puritan? Do you not think it a high dishonour to brand him with that reproachful name? And shall there be men found so bold as to brand the foreheads of those men, with that odious name of Puritan, that profess and hold in the same things, no more, nor no less, than our late dread sovereign did profess with his mouth, and maintain with his pen? Do not think that I am hired on either side, but I foresee that the casting of this opprobrious name upon those that have, and do maintain the truth and doctrine they have been bred in, and is maintained in our Church, will prove as desperate and dangerous a thing as those names of Remonstrants and Contraremonstrants hath done in the Netherlands.[57]

The second advice that I intend to give, I will not go far for it. It is in the verse before my text. "Let the spirit of the prophets be subject to the prophets." Whence comes this trouble then? I remember St. Jerome writing upon those words of the Prophet Jeremiah, that both prophets and priests

---

[54] Elrington here gives "hath lately disturbed," *WJU*, 13:348.

[55] Instead of this sentence, Elrington has "..., which is a thing tending to dissension," *WJU*, 13:348.

[56] "dared."

[57] This passage is truncated in Elrington and he has the Puritans maintaining the doctrine "published by the pen of our sovereign," seemingly still referring to King James, but with no reference to the faith of the Church of England. *WJU*, 13:349.

do wickedly, and corruption is gone over the land.[58] Saith he, "I have read and read again, and I could never find contention in the Church, but it did always proceed from them that were appointed priests."[59] It is from the prophets themselves, therefore from whence it doth come. The Apostle Paul in the 20 of the Acts saith, "even of your own selves some shall arise that shall draw a multitude of disciples after them."[60] What shall be done with those prophets? Far be it from me to give counsel, not befitting a man of peace. But let the spirit of the prophets be subject to the prophets. And therefore here let me say that the composing[61] of those controversies and differences of the prophets belongs not to lay men, or any meetings of lay men, who scarcely can understand the state of the question, much less dive into the bowels of it. Yet the spirit of the prophets must be subject to the prophets, or else every prophet will be a pope, but they must be subject and overruled by some others of their own coat, those that are enabled by their study and calling to enter into the deep considerations of those points. Very wisdom telleth us that, that it is fit the prophets should be subject to their censure in such matters as these, and not to others, for the spirit of the prophets must be subject to the prophets. I stand not here to prove whether the points[62] be true, or false, but how the peace of the Church may be preserved. Beloved, let us consider: we were quiet. What is the cause that now our peace is disturbed? What doctrine hath disturbed it? Is it a doctrine broached by some brethren amongst us? See how many of the brethren be of that mind, take a survey of the prophets, and if we see the greater number of the prophets go another way, what can the meaning of the Apostle

---

[58] Jer. 23:15.

[59] There is no corresponding passage in Jerome's comments on Jer. 23:15, nor anywhere else in that commentary (*PL*, 24:679–900). A fairly close match is this comment on Hos. 9:8–9: *Veteres scripturas scrutans, invenire non possum, scidisse Ecclesiam, et de domo Dei populos seduxisse; praeter illos qui sacerdotes a Deo positi fuerant et prophetae* ("On examining the ancient scriptures, I am unable to find the division of the church and the people led away from the house of God; more than those who had been appointed priests and prophets by God"). Jerome, *Commentariorum in Osee Prophetam* (*PL*, 25:895B–C). The slip suggests that Ussher is citing from memory.

[60] Paraphrasing Acts 20:30.

[61] Bringing to order; settling.

[62] Ussher refers below to the "five points," so he has in mind here the matters considered in the five points of the Arminian Remonstrance of 1610 and the five heads of doctrine in the Canons of Dort.

be here, but let the spirit of the fewer prophets be subject to the spirit of the greatest number of their fellow prophets. This is the chief place, on which we build our counsels, yea our general councils on.[63] And it is likewise the opinion of St. Augustine.[64] So that you see here is a means not only in policy but in order that God hath appointed when dissention is in the Church. This I say is God's order and plainly set down, that those that bring in a new doctrine which God hath no hand in,[65] that those fewer, that have been the cause of the breach, that they shall be required to be subject to the greater number of the prophets whose peace they have disturbed. But suppose they have the truth on their side? Why, if they have it, what then? There are certain truths that are not simply necessary, that do not concern the foundation of faith, but are superstructions,[66] in the which though a man hold an error, unless they make it worse by their ill carriage, he may go to heaven for all that. But when there is no danger to profess the contrary, I may doe it then.[67] No, I ought to be silent rather than the peace of the Church should be disturbed. But you will say, the advice that I give comes from a man that is partial. I confess that in these five points that have lately disturbed the peace of the Netherlands, I am fully of the judgement that my late dread sovereign was of before. I do in them all fully agree with him. And should I be ashamed to confess it? And all those points I do confess I have studied long since. But now the thing we look after, as I said before, is not so much the discerning of truth and falsehood (though we be in the right), as the peace of the Church. And this is my profession, as I have said it before in private, so I profess it before God and many witnesses, that if my self were an Arminian, and did hold those five points that have caused that trouble in the Low Countries, the case standing thus as it doth, that the greater number of the prophets blow the horn another way, I hold I were bound in conscience to hold my peace, and keep my judgement

---

[63] MS reads "Councells ... Councells"; and "councels .... counsels" in CUL, MS Dd.v.31, fol. 102r. Elrington renders as "counsels" in *WJU*, 13:349 but omits the reference to "general."

[64] Likely a reference to Augustine, *De Baptismo contra Donatistas*, 2.10 (15) (*PL*, 43:136; *NPNF1*, 4:431, where numbered 2.8 (13)).

[65] Instead of "which God hath no hand in," Elrington has "be it true or false" and omits the final phrase about disturbing the peace. *WJU*, 13:349.

[66] Superstructures, erected upon some foundation.

[67] "may I do it then?" in CUL, MS Dd.v.31, fol. 102r, turning the imagined interlocutor's objection into a question.

to myself, rather than to be unseasonably uttered that it disturb the peace of
the Church.

But, may some say, is not this a prevarication of God's cause? I answer no, but a maintenance[68] of God's order: the spirit of the prophets
must be subject to the prophets. There is a time when a knowledge may be
uttered. Solomon useth this proverb, that "a fool he uttereth all his mind at
once, but a wise man keepeth it till afterwards."[69] It is not possible that all
men in the Church should agree in all things, but it is possible that peace
may be preserved. In the 3 Philippians 15[–16]. "If in any thing ye be otherwise minded, God shall reveal the same unto you. Nevertheless, whereunto we are already come, let us go on in the same rule, and mind the same
thing." As if he should say, there are a number of matters wherein you
agree sufficient to bring you to heaven, and there are some things you agree
not in. Why, if any be otherwise minded than the truth, let them that are on
the truth's side stay till God reveal it unto them, and truth you know is the
daughter of time. It may be darkened. Stay, till the greater number are possessed with the same truth, and then the alteration may be without disturb-
ance of the peace of the Church. And here, I say, it was not so good advice
given as might have been, that both sides should be stopped. It is not an
easy matter to silence a multitude in that they have been born, bred, and
taught in, as to keep in order a few. Those few that move opinions may be
easily made to keep their limits, and not to disturb the peace of the Church,
but to keep their opinions to themselves.[70] It is the peace of the Church we
should all labour for, and that is it I did intend to have pressed. I need not
make an apology for myself, my heart being upright, and it being the last
time perhaps that I may ever speak unto you.[71] And therefore this is my
advice that I have thought good to give, it being that I have done from my
heart, and desire it may be put in practice. And if it be neglected we know
not what danger may come of it: a moderate mind may keep his conclusions

---

[68] "a maintaining" in CUL, MS Dd.v.31, fol. 102v.

[69] Prov. 29:11.

[70] This and the preceding two sentences are omitted in Elrington, *WJU*, 13:350–51,
but at the very end he has these words: "Peradventure it is not so wise counsel as
some do give, who advise that both sides should be silent: but do you think it so
easy a matter to silence all those who have moved the troubles?"

[71] Elrington, perhaps because he knew that Ussher would again preach before
Charles years later, gives this as "This is the last time I shall be called to this place,"
WJU, 13:350–51.

to himself. And thus you see the order and means which the wisdom of God hath thought fit to set down for the maintenance of peace.

So the God of peace be with us, and the Lord give us understanding in all things to live in his peace, that we may depart in his peace, and receive everlasting peace that shall never have end.

THE ORIGINAL OF BISHOPS AND
METROPOLITANS (1644)[1]

THE GROUND of episcopacy is derived partly from the pattern prescribed by God in the Old Testament, and partly from the imitation thereof
brought in by the apostles, and confirmed by Christ himself in the time of
the New. The government of the Church of the Old Testament was committed to the priests and Levites, unto whom the ministers of the New do
now succeed; in like sort as our Lord's Day hath done unto their Sabbath,
that it might be fulfilled which was spoken by the prophet, touching the
vocation of the Gentiles, "I will take of them for priests, and for Levites,
saith the Lord."[2]

That the priests were superior to the Levites, no man doubteth; and
that there was not a parity, either betwixt the priests or betwixt the Levites
themselves, is manifest by the word of God, wherein mention is made of
the heads and rulers both of the one, and of the other.[3]

---

[1] [The text followed here is that of 1644. "The Originall of Bishops and Metropolitans" was first published in *Certain Briefe Treatises Written by Diverse Learned Men, Concerning the Ancient and Moderne Government of the Church* (Oxford, 1641), a collection
probably compiled by Ussher himself. The substance of a separate piece, *The Iudgement of Doctor Rainoldes Touching the Originall of Episcopacy* (London, 1641) was then
folded, largely verbatim, into the argument of "The Original of Bishops and Metropolitans" to form a much expanded edition which was published in *Confessions and
Proofes of Protestant Divines of Reformed Churches, that Episcopacy is in respect of the Office
according to the Word of God, and in respect of the Use the Best* (Oxford, 1644). Ussher
played a central role in assembling and publishing this collection, which was published again after the Restoration in 1662. A Latin translation can be found in *Jacobi
Usserii Archiepiscopi Armachani, Opuscula Duo* (London, 1687; issued again in 1688). In
his edition of Ussher's works, Elrington included the 1641 text of "The Original of
Bishops and Metropolitans" (*WJU*, 7:41–71), followed by the "The Judgement of
Doctor Rainoldes" (*WJU*, 7:73–85).]

[2] Isa. 66:21.

[3] 1 Chr. 24:6, 31; Ezra 8:29.

The Levites were distributed into the three families of the Gershon-ites, Cohathites, and Merarites, and over each of them God appointed one נשיא, ἄρχων, or ruler.[4] The priests were divided by David into four and twenty courses,[5] who likewise had their heads, who in the history of the New Testament are ordinarily called ἀρχιερεῖς, or chief of the priests,[6] and clearly distinguished from that singular one, who was the type of our "great High Priest, that is passed into the heavens, Jesus the Son of God."[7] Yea, in the eleventh chapter of Nehemiah, we find two named bishops, the one of the priests, the other of the Levites that dwelt in Jerusalem. The former so expressly termed by the Greek in the fourteenth, the latter both by the Greek and Latin interpreter in the twenty-second verse,[8] and not without approbation of the Scripture itself, which rendereth the Hebrew word of the same original in the Old,[9] by the Greek ἐπισκοπὴ in the New Testa-ment.[10]

Of Levi it was said by Moses the man of God: "They shall teach Ja-cob thy judgments, and Israel thy law; they shall put incense before thee, and whole burnt sacrifice upon thine altar."[11] Because this latter part of their office hath ceased with them, and the Levitical altar (the truth prefig-ured thereby being now exhibited) is quite taken away, may not we there-fore conclude out of the former part (which hath no such typical relation in it) that our bishops and presbyters should be, as the apostle would have them to be, διδακτικοὶ, "apt to teach,"[12] "able by sound doctrine both to exhort, and to convince the gainsayers"?[13] Nay, and out of the latter part itself, where God had appointed, that "the priests, the Levites, and all the tribe of Levi should eat the offerings of the Lord made by fire,"[14] doth not

---

[4] Num. 3:24, 30, 35.

[5] 1 Chr. 24.

[6] Matt. 2:4; 27:1; Acts 19:14, etc.

[7] Heb. 4:14.

[8] Ἐπίσκοπος Λευιτῶν (LXX). *Episcopus Levitarum* (Jerome [Vulgate]).

[9] פקדה, Ps. 109:8.

[10] Acts 1:20.

[11] Deut. 33:10.

[12] 1 Tim. 3:2.

[13] Titus 1:9.

[14] Deut. 18:1 [given as 28:1 in previous editions].

the apostle by just analogy infer from thence, that forasmuch as "they which waited at the altar, were partaker with the altar; even so had the Lord ordained, that they which preached the Gospel, should live of the Gospel"?[15]

With what show of reason then can any man imagine, that what was instituted by God in the Law, for mere matter of government and preservation of good order, without all respect of type or ceremony, should now be rejected in the Gospel, as a device of Antichrist? that what was by the Lord once "planted a noble vine, wholly a right seed," should now be so "turned into the degenerate plant of a strange vine";[16] that no purging or pruning of it will serve the turn, but it must be cut down root and branch, as "a plant which our heavenly Father had never planted?"[17] But nothing being so familiar nowadays, as to father upon Antichrist, whatsoever in church matters we do not find to suit with our own humours, the safest way will be, to consult with Christ himself herein, and hear what he delivers in the cause.

"These things saith he, that hath the seven stars."[18] He owneth then, we see, these stars, whatsoever they be, and the mystery of them he thus further openeth unto his beloved disciple: "The seven stars, which thou sawest in my right hand, are the angels of the seven churches."[19] From which words a learned man, very much devoted to the now so highly admired discipline, deduceth this conclusion: "How great therefore is the dignity of true pastors, who are both STARS, fixed in no other firmament than in the right hand of Christ, and ANGELS?"[20]

He had considered well, that in the church of Ephesus, one of the seven here pointed at, there were many PRESBYTERS whom "the holy Ghost had made BISHOPS, or overseers, over all that flock; to feed the Church of God, which he had purchased with his own blood."[21] And withal he saw, that by admitting one angel there above the rest (all, as well ex-

---

[15] 1 Cor. 9:13–14.

[16] Jer. 2:21.

[17] Matt. 15:13.

[18] Rev. 3:1.

[19] Rev. 1:20.

[20] *Quanta igitur dignitas verorum Pastorum, qui tum stellae sunt, non in alio firmamento, quam in dextra Christi fixae, tum Angeli?* Thomas Brightman, *Apocalypsis Apocalypseos* (Frankfurt, 1609), 28 [ET: *A Revelation of the Apocalyps* (Amsterdam, 1611), 29].

[21] Acts 20:17, 28.

traordinary prophets,[22] as ordinary pastors,[23] being in their own several stations accounted angels or messengers of the Lord of Hosts) he should be forced also to acknowledge the eminency of one bishop above the other bishops (that name being in those days common unto all the presbyters),[24] and to yield withal, that such a one was to be esteemed as "a star fixed in no other firmament, than in the right hand of Christ."

To salve[25] this therefore, all the stars in every church must be presupposed to be of one magnitude, and though those stars which typified these angels are said to be but seven, yet the angels themselves must be maintained to be far more in number, and in fine, where our Saviour saith, "unto the angel of the church of Ephesus write,"[26] it must by no means be admitted, that any one angel should be meant hereby, but the whole college of pastors rather. And all upon pretence of a poor show of some shallow reasons, that there "was not one angel of Ephesus but many, and among them not any principal."[27]

Which wresting of the plain words of our Saviour is so extreme violent, that M. Beza, though every way as zealously affected to the advancement of the new discipline as was the other, could by no means digest it, but ingenuously acknowledgeth the meaning of our Lord's direction to have been this: "To the angel, that is, to the president, as whom it behoved specially to be admonished touching those matters; and by him, both the rest of his colleagues, and the whole church likewise."[28] And that there was then a standing president over the rest of the pastors of Ephesus, and he the very same (as learned Doctor Rainolds addeth)[29] with him whom afterward

---

[22] Judg. 1:20; Hag. 1:13; Matt. 11:18.

[23] Mal. 2:7.

[24] Phil. 1:1; 1 Tim. 3:2 [given as 1:2 in previous editions in English; correct in Latin versions]; Titus 1:5, 7.

[25] [Elrington renders this as "solve."]

[26] Rev. 2:1.

[27] *Nec uni alicui angelo mittuntur, sed toti (ut ita dicam) collegio pastorum; qui omnes hac communi voce comprehenduntur. Non enim unus erat angelus Ephesi, sed plures: nec inter istos aliquis princeps.* Brightman, *Apocalypsis Apocalypseos* 34; idem, *Revelation*, 32.

[28] Τῷ ἀγγέλῳ, id est, προεστῶτι. *Quem nimirum oportuit imprimis de his rebus admoneri, ac per eum caeteros collegas, totamque adeo ecclesiam.* Theodore Beza, *Annotationes Maiores in Novum DN. Nostri Iesu Christi Testamentum*, 2 vols ([Geneva], 1594), 2:635.

[29] John Rainolds, *The Summe of the Conference between Iohn Rainoldes and Iohn Hart touching the Head and the Faith of the Church* (London, 1584), 535.

the fathers called bishop, may further be made manifest, not only by the succession of the first bishops of that church, but also by the clear testimony of Ignatius, who, within no greater compass of time than twelve years afterwards, distinguisheth the singular and constant president thereof, from the rest of the number of the presbyters, by appropriating the name of bishop unto him.

As for the former, we find it openly declared in the general council of Chalcedon, by Leontius, Bishop of Magnesia, that from Timothy (and so from the days of the apostles) there had been a continued succession of seven and twenty bishops, all of them ordained in Ephesus.[30] Of which number the angel of the church of Ephesus, mentioned in the Revelation, must needs be one, whether it were Timothy himself, as some conceive,[31] or one of his next successors, as others rather do imagine.

For that Timothy had been sometime the προεστὼς[32](which is the appellation that Justin Martyr, in his *Second Apology* for Christians,[33] and Dionysius of Corinth not long after him, in his epistle to the church of Athens,[34] and Marcellus, Bishop of Ancyra, in his letters to Julius, Bishop of

---

[30] Ἀπὸ τοῦ ἁγίου Τιμοθέου μέχρι νῦν εἴκοσι ἑπτὰ ἐπίσκοποι ἐγένοντο, πάντες ἐν Ἐφέσῳ ἐχειροτονήθησαν. Council of Chalcedon, Session 11 [Giovanni Domenico Mansi, *Sacrorum Conciliorum Nova et Amplissima Collectio*, repr. ed., 53 vols in 60 (Paris: Welter, 1901–27), 7:293; *The Acts of the Council of Chalcedon*, ed. and trans. Richard Price and Michael Gaddis, 3 vols (Liverpool: Liverpool University Press, 2005), 3:16].

[31] Benedict Pereira, *Tertius Tomus Selectarum Disputationum in Sacram Scripturam,* ... *super libro Apocalypsis B. Ioannis Apostoli* (Lyon, 1606), 77–79; Luis del Alcázar, *Vestigatio Arcani Sensus in Apocalypsi* (Antwerp, 1619), 214–16; Pierre Halloix, 'Notationes ad Vitam S. Polycarpi,' in *Illustrium Ecclesiae Orientalis Scriptorum* (Douai, 1633), 558.

[32] *Notandum est ex hoc loco, Timotheum in Ephesino presbyterio tum fuisse* προεστωτὰ *(id est antistitem) ut vocat Junstinus* ["It should be noted out of this place [1 Tim. 5:19] that in the presbytery of Ephesus Timothy had been at that time προεστωτὰ (that is, president), as Justin calls him"]. Theodore Beza, *Annotationes* 2:459. [The reference is to Justin's *Apologia Prima* 67 (*PG* 6:429B). Ussher would have known this as the second apology, but the order has been reversed in modern editions as this longer work appears to be quoted in the shorter of the two.]

[33] *Qui politiae causa reliquis fratribus in coetu praeerat (quem Justinus* τὸν προεστῶτα *vocat) peculiariter dici episcopus coepit.* ["He who took charge of the rest of the brothers in the assembly for the sake of order (whom Justin calls 'president') began to be called 'bishop' specifically"]. Beza, *Annotationes* 2:384.

[34] *Dionysius Corinthiensis in epist. ad Athenienses, eodem sensu Publium martyrem nominat* προεστῶτα αὐτῶν, *quo proximus ejus successorem Quadratum* ἐπίσκοπον αὐτῶν ["Di-

Rome,[35] do give unto a bishop), or *Antistes*, or president of the Ephesian presbytery, is confessed by Beza himself; and that he was ordained the first bishop of the church of the Ephesians, we do not only read in the subscription of the second Epistle to Timothy,[36] and the *Ecclesiastical History* of Eusebius,[37] but also in two ancient treatises concerning the martyrdom of Timothy; the one nameless in the library of Photius,[38] the other bearing the name of Polycrates,[39] even of that Polycrates, who was not only himself bishop of this church of Ephesus, but born also within six or seven and thirty years after St. John wrote the forenamed epistle unto the angel of that church, as it appears by the years he was of, when he wrote that epistle unto Victor, Bishop of Rome, wherein he maketh mention of "seven kinsmen of his who had been bishops," he himself being the eighth.[40]

I come now to the testimony of Ignatius, whom Theodoret,[41] and Felix, Bishop of Rome,[42] and John, the chronographer of Antioch,[43] report to

---

onysius of Corinth in an epistle to the Athenians, in the same sense calls the martyr Publius their president [προεστῶτα αὐτῶν], as he names his immediate successor Quadratus their bishop [ἐπίσκοπον αὐτῶν]"]. Eusebius, *Historia Ecclesiastica* 4.23.3 [*PG* 20:384B–C; *NPNF2* 1:200].

[35] Δεινὰ κατά τε τῶν τοῦ Θεοῦ ἐκκλησιῶν χαὶ ἡμῶν τῶν προεστώτων αὐτῶν τετολμήκασιν ["they have dared dreadful ventures against the churches of God and us who head them"]. Marcellus of Ancyra, in Epiphanius, *Panarion* 72.2.2 [*PG* 42:384C; *The Panarion of Epiphanius of Salamis, Books II and III. De Fide*, trans. Frank Williams, 2nd rev. ed. (Leiden: Brill, 2013), 434].

[36] [In its fullest form this includes the expression της Εφεσιων εκκλησιας επισκωπον πρωτον. See critical editions of the Greek New Testament.]

[37] Eusebius, *Historia Ecclesiastica* 3.4.6 [*PG* 20:220B; *NPNF2* 1:136].

[38] Ὅτι πρῶτον Τιμόθεον ἡ παροῦσα συγγραφή φησιν Ἐφέσου ἐπισκοπῆσαι. *Et post*. Ὅτι ὁ ἀπόστολος Τιμόθεος ὑπὸ τοῦ μεγάλου Παύλου καὶ χειροτονεῖται τῆς Ἐφεσίων μητροπόλεως ἐπίσκοπος καὶ ἐνθρονίζεται ["The history declares Timothy to have been first bishop of Ephesus ... that the Apostle Timothy was ordained and enthroned bishop of the metropolis of Ephesus by the great Paul"]. Photius, *Bibliotheca* 254 [*PG* 104:101C, 104A].

[39] Polycrates, *De Martyrio Timothei*, in *Historiae Plurimorum Sanctorum* (Louvain, 1485), fols xvi(r)–xvii(r).

[40] Ἑπτὰ μὲν ἦσαν συγγενεῖς μου ἐπίσκοποι, ἐγὼ δὲ ὄγδοος. Eusebius, *Historia Ecclesiastica* 5.24 [*PG* 20:496B; *NPNF2* 1:242].

[41] Theodoret, *Eranistes*, Dialogus I [*PG* 83:81A].

[42] Felix III, *Epist. ad Zenonem*, read at the fifth [general] Council of Constantinople [553; *ACO*, tom. 3, 24, where gathered with the documents of that held under John the Cappadocian in 518; *PL* 58:919A].

have been ordained bishop of Antioch by St. Peter in special, Chrysostom (who was a presbyter of the same church) by the apostles in general,[44] and without all controversy did sit in that see, the very same time wherein that epistle unto the angel of the Church of Ephesus was commanded to be written.

In the Isle of Patmos had St. John his Revelation manifested unto him, "toward the end of the empire of Domitian," as Irenaeus testifieth;[45] or the fourteenth year of his government, as Eusebius and Jerome specify it.[46] From thence there are but twelve years reckoned unto the tenth of Trajan, wherein Ignatius, in that last journey which he made for the consummation of his glorious martyrdom at Rome, wrote another epistle unto the self same church of Ephesus. In which he maketh mention of their then bishop Onesimus, as it appears both by Eusebius citing this out of it,[47] and by the epistle itself yet extant.

In this epistle to the Ephesians, Ignatius having acknowledged that their numerous multitude was received by him in the person of their bishop Onesimus, and blessed God for granting unto them such a bishop as he was,[48] doth afterwards put them in mind of their duty in concurring with

---

[43] Johannes Malela Antiochenus, "Chronicle," lib. 10. MS. [Ussher here cites the *Chronographia* of John Malalas, the manuscript of which was purchased for the Bodleian Library by William Herbert, third Earl of Pembroke and Chancellor of Oxford University, as part of a large collection assembled by Francesco and Iacopo Barozzi of Venice. It is now Bodleian MS Barocci 182 (in which, see fol. 154r–v). As a source of otherwise lost material this sixth-century work was used by Ussher, John Selden and John Pearson in their historical research but it was not published until 1691. *PG* 97:384B–C; *The Chronicle of John Malalas*, trans. Elizabeth Jeffreys, Michael Jeffreys, and Roger Scott (Melbourne: Australian Association for Byzantine Studies, 1986), 134.]

[44] Παρὰ τῶν ἁγίων ἐκείνων τὴν ἀρχὴν ταύτην ἐνεχειρίσθη, καὶ αἱ τῶν μακαρίων Ἀποστόλων χεῖρες τῆς ἱερᾶς ἐχείνης ἥψαντο κεφαλῆς ["He obtained this office from those saints, and the hands of the blessed apostles touched that sacred head"]. John Chrysostom, *Hom. in S. Martyrem Ignatium* 2 [*PG* 50:588].

[45] Πρὸς τῷ τέλει τῆς Δομετιανοῦ ἀρχῆς. Irenaeus, *Adversus Haereses* 5.30.3 [*PG* 7:1207B; *ANF* 1:559–60].

[46] Eusebius, *Chronicorum* 2 [*PG* 19:551–52]; Jerome, *De Viris Illustribus* 9 [*PL* 23:625A {655B}; *NPNF2* 3:364].

[47] Eusebius, *Historia Ecclesiastica* 3.36.5 [*PG* 20:288C; *NPNF2* 1:167–68].

[48] Τὴν πολυπλήθειαν ὑμῶν ἐν ὀνόματι Θεοῦ ἀπείληφα ἐν Ὀνησίμῳ ... Εὐλογητὸς ὁ θεὸς, ὁ χαρισάμενος ὑμῖν τοιούτοις οὖσι τοιοῦτον ἐπίσκοπον. Igna-

him, as he showeth their worthy presbytery did, being "so conjoined," as he saith, "with their bishop, as the strings are with the harp";[49] and toward the end exhorteth them to "obey both the bishop and the presbytery, with an undivided mind."[50]

In the same journey wrote Ignatius also an epistle unto the church of Smyrna, another of the seven, unto whom those letters are directed in St. John's Revelation, wherein he also saluteth their bishop and presbytery,[51] exhorting all the people to "follow their bishop, as Christ Jesus did his Father, and the presbytery, as the apostles,"[52] and telling them that no man ought either to administer the sacraments, or do any thing appertaining to the church, without the consent of the bishop.[53]

Who this bishop, and what that presbytery was, appeareth by another epistle written a little after from Smyrna, by "Polycarpus and the presbyters that were with him,"[54] unto the Philippians. And that the same Polycarpus was then also bishop there, when St. John wrote unto "the angel of the

---

tius, *Ad Ephesios* 1 [*PG* 5:732B–733A (see 645A); *ANF* 1:49; the Greek cited here and in the following is that of the longer, interpolated Ignatian text].

[49] Ὅθεν ὑμῖν πρέπει συντρέχειν τῇ τοῦ ἐπισκόπου γνώμῃ ... Τὸ γὰρ ἀξιονόμαστον πρεσβυτέριον, ἄξιον ὂν τοῦ θεοῦ, οὕτως συνήρμοσται τῷ ἐπισκόπῳ, ὡς χορδαὶ κιθάρᾳ. Ignatius, *Ad Ephesios* 4 [*PG* 5:733C, 736A (see 648A–B); *ANF* 1:50].

[50] Ὑπακούοντες τῷ ἐπισκόπῳ καὶ τῷ πρεσβυτερίῳ ἀπερισπάστῳ διανοίᾳ. Ignatius, *Ad Ephesios* 20 [*PG* 5:756A (see 661A); *ANF* 1:57–58].

[51] Ἀσπάζομαι τὸν ἀξιόθεον ἐπίσκοπον (ὑμῶν Πολύκαρπον) καὶ τὸ θεοπρεπὲς πρεσβυτέριον ["I salute the most worthy bishop (your Polycarp) and the godly presbytery"]. Ignatius, *Ad Smyrnaeos* 12 [*PG* 5:857A (see 717A); *ANF* 1:92].

[52] Πάντες τῷ ἐπισκόπῳ ἀκολουθεῖτε, ὡς ὁ Χριστὸς Ἰησοῦς τῷ Πατρί, καὶ τῷ πρεσβυτερίῳ ὡς τοῖς ἀποστόλοις. Ignatius, *Ad Smyrnaeos* 8 [*PG* 5:852A (see 713B); *ANF* 1:89].

[53] Μηδεὶς χωρὶς ἐπισκόπου τι πρασσέτω τῶν ἀνηκόντων εἰς τὴν ἐκκλησίαν, ἐκείνη βεβαία εὐχαριστία ἡγείσθω, ἡ ὑπὸ τὸν ἐπίσοπον οὖσα, ἢ ᾧ ἂν αὐτὸς ἐπιτρέψῃ [...] Οὐκ ἐξόν ἐστι χωρὶς τοῦ ἐπισκόπου οὔτε βαπτίζειν, etc. ["Let no man do anything connected with the church without the bishop. Let that be deemed a proper Eucharist which is administered either by the bishop, or by one to whom he has entrusted it ... It is not lawful without the bishop either to baptize, etc..."] Ignatius, *Ad Smyrnaeos* 8 [*PG* 5:852A (see 713B); *ANF* 1:89–90].

[54] Πολύκαρπος, καὶ οἱ σὺν αὐτῷ πρεσβύτεροι τῇ ἐκκλησίᾳ τοῦ Θεοῦ τῇ παροικούσῃ Φιλίπποις. Polycarp, *Ad Phillipenses*, Address [*PG* 5:1905A; *ANF* 1:33].

church of Smyrna," who can better inform us than Irenaeus, who did not only know those worthy men "who succeeded Polycarpus in his see,"[55] but also was present, when he himself did discourse of his conversation with St. John, and of those things which he heard from those who had seen our Lord Jesus?[56]

"Polycarpus," saith he, "was not only taught by the apostles, and conversed with many of those that had seen Christ, but also was by the apostles constituted in Asia bishop of the church which is in Smyrna: whom we ourselves also did see in our younger age; for he continued long, and being very aged, he most gloriously and nobly suffering martyrdom departed this life."[57]

Now being ordained bishop of Smyrna by the apostles, who had finished their course, and departed out of this life before St. John, the last survivor of them, did write his Revelation, who but he could there be meant by "the angel of the church in Smyrna"? In which that he still held his episcopal office unto the time of his martyrdom, which fell out seventy-four years afterward, may sufficiently appear by this testimony, which the brethren of the church of Smyrna, who were present at his suffering, gave unto him: "He was the most admirable man in our times, an apostolical and prophetical doctor, and bishop of the catholic church which is in Smyrna."[58] Whereunto we may add the like of Polycrates, Bishop of Ephesus, who lived also in his time and in his neighbourhood, affirming Polycarpus to

---

[55] Οἱ μέχρι νῦν διαδεδεγμένοι τὸν τοῦ Πολυκάρπου θρόνον. Irenaeus, *Adversus Haereses* 3.3.4 [*PG* 7:852B, and see n. 83 which dismisses the θρόνον variant reading; *ANF* 1:416].

[56] Irenaeus, *Ad Florinum*, in Eusebius, *Historia Ecclesiastica* 5.20.6 [*PG* 20:485B; *NPNF2* 1:239]; Irenaeus, *Ad Victorem*, in Eusebius, *Historia Ecclesiastica* 5.24.16 [*PG* 20:508A; *NPNF2* 1:244].

[57] Καὶ Πολύκαρπος δὲ οὐ μόνον ὑπὸ ἀποστόλων μαθητευθεὶς, καὶ συναναστραφεὶς πολλοῖς τοῖς τὸν Χριστὸν ἑωρακόσιν, ἀλλὰ καὶ ὑπὸ ἀποστόλων κατασταθεὶς εἰς τὴν Ἀσίαν ἐν τῇ ἐν Σμύρνῃ ἐκκλησίᾳ ἐπίσκοπος, ὃν καὶ ἡμεῖς ἑωράκαμεν ἐν τῇ πρώτῃ ἡμῶν ἡλικίᾳ. ἐπὶ πολὺ γὰρ παρέμεινεν καὶ πάνυ γηραλέος ἐνδόξως καὶ ἐπιφανέστατα μαρτυρήσας ἐξῆλθεν τοῦ βίου. Irenaeus, *Adversus Haereses* 3.3.4 [*PG* 7:851B–852A; *ANF* 1:416]. See also Eusebius, *Historia Ecclesiastica* 3.36.1 [*PG* 20:288B; *NPNF2* 1:166].

[58] Οὗτος γέγονεν ὁ θαυμασιώτατος ἐν τοῖς καθ' ἡμᾶς χρόνοις διδάσκαλος ἀποστολικὸς καὶ προφητικός, γενόμενος ἐπίσκοπος τῆς ἐν Σμύρνῃ καθολικῆς ἐκκλησίας. *Smyrnensis Ecclesiae Epist. de Martyrio Polycarpi*, in Eusebius, *Historia Ecclesiastica* 4.15.39 [*PG* 20:356C; *NPNF2* 1:191].

have been "both bishop and martyr in Smyrna."[59] So he saith in his synodical epistle, directed unto Victor, Bishop of Rome, about twenty-seven years after the martyrdom of Polycarpus, he himself being at that time sixty-five years of age.

About the very same time wherein Polycrates[60] wrote this epistle unto Victor, did Tertullian publish his book of *Prescriptions against Heretics*, wherein he avoucheth against them, that "as the church of Smyrna had Polycarpus placed there by John, and the church of Rome Clement ordained by Peter, so the rest of the churches also did show what bishops they had received by the appointment of the apostles, to traduce the apostolical seed unto them."[61] And so before him did Irenaeus urge against them "the successions of bishops, unto whom the apostles committed the charge of the church in every place."[62] "For all the heretics," saith he, "are much later than those bishops, unto whom the apostles committed the churches."[63] And, "we are able to number those who by the apostles were ordained bishops in the churches, and their successors unto our days, who neither taught nor knew any such thing as these men dream of."[64]

For proof whereof, he bringeth in the succession of the bishops of Rome, from Linus (unto whom the blessed apostles committed that episcopacy) and Anacletus (by others called Cletus) and Clement (who did both see the apostles, and conferred with them)[65] unto Eleutherius, who when

---

[59] Πολύκαρπος, ὁ ἐν Σμύρνῃ καὶ ἐπίσκοπος καὶ μάρτυς. Polycrates, *Ad Victorem*, in Eusebius, *Historia Ecclesiastica* 5.24.4 [*PG* 20:496A; *NPNF2* 1:242].

[60] Elrington mistakenly gives as "Polycarpus."

[61] *Sicut Smyrnaeorum ecclesia Polycarpum ab Johanne conlocatum refert; sicut Romanorum Clementem a Petro ordinatum edit; proinde* (or, *perinde*) *utique et caeterae exhibent quos, ab apostolis in episcopatum constitutos, apostolici seminis traduces habeant.* Tertullian, *De Praescriptionibus Adversus Haereticos* 32 [*PL* 2:45A {53A}; *ANF* 3:258]; See idem, *Adversus Marcionem* 4.5 [*PL* 2:366C–368A {395B–397A}; *ANF* 3:349–51].

[62] *Successiones episcoporum, quibus apostolicam quae in unoquoque loco est ecclesiam tradiderunt.* Irenaeus, *Adversus Haereses* 4.33.8 [*PG* 7:1077B; *ANF* 1:508].

[63] *Omnes enim ii valde posteriores sunt quam episcopi, quibus apostoli tradiderunt ecclesias.* Irenaeus, *Adversus Haereses* 5.20.1 [*PG* 7:1177A; *ANF* 1:547].

[64] *Habemus annumerare eos qui ab apostolis instituti sunt episcopi in ecclesiis, et successores eorum usque ad nos; qui nihil tale docuerunt, neque cognoverunt quale ab his deliratur.* Irenaeus, *Adversus Haereses* 3.3.1 [*PG* 7:848A; *ANF* 1:415].

[65] Θεμελιώσαντες οὖν καὶ οἰκοδομήσαντες οἱ μακάριοι ἀπόστολοι τὴν ἐκκλησίαν, Λίνῳ τὴν τῆς ἐπισκοπῆς λειτουργίαν ἐνεχείρισαν. (τούτου τοῦ Λίνου Παῦλος ἐν ταῖς πρὸς Τιμόθεον ἐπιστολαῖς μέμνηται.) διαδέχεται δ᾽ αὐτὸν

Irenaeus wrote, "had the charge of that bishopric in the twelfth place after the apostles."⁶⁶ Concerning whom, and the integrity which then continued in each other succession from the apostles' days, Hegesippus, who at the same time published his history of the church, saith thus: "Soter succeeded Anicetus, and after him was Eleutherius. Now, in every succession, and in every city, all things so stand, as the law and the prophets and our Lord do preach."⁶⁷

And more particularly concerning the church of Corinth, after he had spoken of the epistle written unto them by Clement,⁶⁸ for the repressing of some factions wherewith they were at that time much troubled, which gave him occasion to tell them that the apostles, of whom he himself was an hearer, had perfect intelligence from our Lord Jesus Christ, of the "contention that should arise about the name of episcopacy,"⁶⁹ he declareth, that after the appeasing of this tumult, "the church of the Corinthians continued in the right way, until the days of Primus, whom he did visit in his sailing

---

Ἀνέγκλητος, μετὰ τοῦτον δὲ τρίτῳ τόπῳ ἀπὸ τῶν ἀποστόλων τὴν ἐπισκοπὴν κληροῦται Κλήμης, ὁ καὶ ἑωρακὼς τοὺς μακαρίους ἀποστόλους, καὶ συμβεβληκὼς αὐτοῖς ["The blessed apostles, then, having founded and built up the Church, committed into the hands of Linus the office of the episcopate. Of this Linus, Paul makes mention in the Epistles to Timothy. To him succeeded Anacletus; and after him, in the third place from the apostles, Clement was allotted to the bishopric, who both had seen the blessed apostles and conversed with them"]. Irenaeus, *Adversus Haereses* 3.3.3 [*PG* 7:849A–B; *ANF* 1:416].

⁶⁶ Νῦν δωδεκάτῳ τόπῳ τὸν τῆς ἐπισκοπῆς ἀπὸ τῶν ἀποστόλων κατέχει κλῆρον Ἐλεύθερος. Irenaeus, *Adversus Haereses* 3.3.3 [*PG* 7:851A; *ANF* 1:416].

⁶⁷ Παρὰ Ἀνικήτου διαδέχεται Σωτήρ, μεθ' ὃν Ἐλεύθερος. Ἐν ἑκάστῃ δὲ διαδοχῇ καὶ ἐν ἑκάστῃ πόλει οὕτως ἔχει ὡς ὁ νόμος κηρύττει καὶ οἱ προφῆται καὶ ὁ κύριος. Hegesippus, *Memoranda*, in Eusebius, *Historia Ecclesiastica* 4.22.3 [*PG* 20:377D, 380A; *NPNF2* 1:199].

⁶⁸ Μετά (*ita enim ex MS. legendum, non* μεγάλα) τινα περὶ τῆς Κλήμεντος πρὸς Κορινθίους ἐπιστολῆς αὐτῷ εἰρημένα. Hegesippus, *Memoranda*, in Eusebius, *Historia Ecclesiastica* 4.22.1 [*PG* 20:377C, and note 11; *NPNF2* 1:198].

⁶⁹ Καὶ οἱ ἀπόστολοι ἡμῶν ἔγνωσαν διὰ τοῦ κυρίου ἡμῶν Ἰησοῦ Χριστοῦ, ὅτι ἔρις ἔσται ἐπὶ τοῦ ὀνόματος τῆς ἐπισκοῆς. διὰ ταύτην οὖν τὴν αἰτίαν, πρόγνωσιν εἰληφότες τελείαν, κατέστησαν τοὺς προειρημένους. ["Our apostles also knew, through our Lord Jesus Christ, that there would be strife on account of the office of the episcopate. For this reason, therefore, inasmuch as they had obtained a perfect fore-knowledge of this, they appointed those already mentioned."] Clement of Rome, *Ad Corinthios* 44 [*PG* 1:296C–297A; *ANF* 1:17].

toward Rome."[70] Which Primus had for his successor that famous Dionysius, whose epistle to the church of the Athenians hath been before nominated; wherein he put them in mind of "the first bishop" that had been placed over them,[71] even Dionysius the Areopagite, St. Paul's own convert,[72] a thing whereof they could at that time have no more cause to doubt, than we should have, if any question were now made of the bishops that were here in King Edward the VI or Queen Mary's days: I might also say, in the middle of the reign of Queen Elizabeth herself, if with Baronius I would produce[73] the Areopagite's life unto the government of the emperor Hadrian.[74]

This Hegesippus, living next after "the first succession of the apostles," as Eusebius noteth,[75] and being himself a Christian of the race of the Hebrews,[76] was careful to record unto posterity the state of the church of Jerusalem in the days of the apostles, and the alteration that followed after their departure out of this life. Where first he showeth that James the brother of our Lord, surnamed the Just, did govern that church together with the apostles;[77] yet so, as Clement of Alexandria, who wrote some

---

[70] Καὶ ἐπέμενεν ἡ ἐκκλησία τῶν Κορινθίων ἐν τῷ ὀρθῷ λόγῳ μέχρι Πρίμου ἐπισκοπεύοντος ἐν Κορίνθῳ, ᾧ (ita MS. non οἷς) συνέμιξα πλέων εἰς Ῥώμην. Hegesippus, Memoranda, in Eusebius, Historia Ecclesiastica 4.22.2 [PG 20:377C; NPNF2 1:198].

[71] According to Dionysius of Corinth, related in Eusebius, Historia Ecclesiastica 3.4.11 [PG 20:221A; NPNF2 1:138]. Cf. 4.22.2 [PG 20:377C; NPNF2 1:198].

[72] Acts 17:34.

[73] [As in "prolong" or "extend."]

[74] [Ussher's reference here, "Baron. Annal. tom. 2. ann. 120," would appear to be erroneous. A very brief discussion of the Athenian episcopal succession comes under "Annus 125," and a more wide-ranging discussion of Dionysius and his survival into the reign of Hadrian can be found in Baronius's martyrology under "Octobris 9." See Caesar Baronius, Annales Ecclesiastici, 12 vols (Rome 1588–1607), 2:72; idem, Martyrologium Romanum (Cologne, 1603), 645.]

[75] Ὁ Ἡγήσιππος (non, ut vulgo legitur, Ἰώσηπος) ἐπὶ τῆς πρώτης τῶν ἀποστόλων γενόμενος διαδοχῆς. Egesippus qui post ipsas statim primas apostolorum successiones fuit: ut Rufinus locum expressit. Eusebius, Historia Ecclesiastica 2.23.3 [PG 20:196D, and note 92 which gives the Latin rendering of Rufinus, also supplied by Ussher; NPNF2 1:125].

[76] Eusebius, Historia Ecclesiastica 4.22.7 [PG 20:384A; NPNF2 1:200].

[77] Διαδέχεται τὴν ἐκκλησίαν μετὰ τῶν ἀποστόλων ὁ ἀδελφὸς τοῦ κυρίου Ἰάκωβος, ὁ ὀνομασθεὶς ὑπὸ πάντων δίκαιος. Hegesippus, Memoranda 5, in Eusebius, Historia Ecclesiastica 2.23.4 [PG 20:197A; NPNF2 1:125].

twenty years after him, further addeth, that he had this preferment even before the three prime apostles, Peter and the two sons of Zebedee, James and John, to be chosen the peculiar Bishop of Jerusalem, the then mother church of the world.[78]

After the death of James the Just, Hegesippus declareth that Symeon, the son of Clopas or Cleophas, was constituted bishop, and so continued until the days of the emperor Trajan, under whom he suffered a glorious martyrdom about the same time that Ignatius did, being then an hundred and twenty years of age, and by that account born before the Incarnation of our blessed Saviour.[79] Where, the observation of this prime historian is not to be passed over, that until these times the Church was called a virgin, as being not yet corrupted with the overspreading of heretical doctrine. For howsoever heresies did spring up before, yet they were so kept down by the authority of the apostles and the disciples who had heard our Lord himself preach; that the authors and fautors thereof were not able to get any great head, being forced, by the authority of such opposites, to lurk in obscurity.[80]

But as soon as all that generation was gathered unto their fathers, and none of those were left who had the happiness to hear the gracious words that proceeded from the Lord's own mouth, the heretics, taking that advantage, began to enter into a kind of combination, and with open face

---

[78] Πέτρον καὶ Ἰάκωβον καὶ Ἰωάννην μετὰ τὴν ἀνάληψιν τοῦ σωτῆρος, ὡς ἂν καὶ ὑπὸ τοῦ κυρίου προτετιμημένους μὴ ἐπιδικάζεσθαι δόξης, ἀλλ᾽ Ἰάκωβον τὸν δίκαιον ἐπίσκοπον Ἱεροσολύμων ἑλέσθαι. Clement, *Hypotyposes* 6, in Eusebius, *Historia Ecclesiastica* 2.1.3 [*PG* 20:136A; *NPNF2* 1:104].

[79] Hegesippus, *Memoranda*, in Eusebius, *Historia Ecclesiastica* 4.22.4 [*PG* 20:380A; *NPNF2* 1:199]; cf. 3.11.2 [*PG* 20:245B; *NPNF2* 1:146]; 3.32.1–6 [*PG* 20:281B–284B; *NPNF2* 1:163–64].

[80] Ὡς ἄρα μέχρι τῶν τότε χρόνων παρθένος καθαρὰ καὶ ἀδιάφθορος ἔμεινεν ἡ ἐκκλησία, ἐν ἀδήλῳ που σκότει φωλευόντων εἰσέτι τότε τῶν, εἰ καί τινες ὑπῆρχον, παραφθείρειν ἐπιχειρούντων τὸν ὑγιῆ κανόνα τοῦ σωτηρίου κηρύγματος· ὡς δ᾽ ὁ ἱερὸς τῶν ἀποστόλων χορὸς διάφορον εἰλήφει τοῦ βίου τέλος παρεληλύθει τε ἡ γενεὰ ἐκείνη τῶν αὐταῖς ἀκοαῖς τῆς ἐνθέου σοφίας ἐπακοῦσαι κατηξιωμένων, τηνικαῦτα τῆς ἀθέου πλάνης τὴν ἀρχὴν ἐλάμβανεν ἡ σύστασις, διὰ τῆς τῶν ἑτεροδιδασκάλων ἀπάτης, οἳ καὶ ἅτε μηδενὸς ἔτι τῶν ἀποστόλων λειπομένου, γυμνῇ λοιπὸν ἤδη τῇ κεφαλῇ, τῷ τῆς ἀληθείας κηρύγματι τὴν ψευδώνυμον γνῶσιν ἀντικηρύττειν ἐπεχείρουν. Hegesippus in Eusebius, *Historia Ecclesiastica* 3.32.7–8 [*PG* 20:284B–285A; *NPNF2* 1:164].

publicly to maintain the "oppositions of their science falsely so called,"[81] from whence they assumed unto themselves the name of Gnostics, or men of knowledge, against the preaching of that truth, which by those who were eye-witnesses[82] and ministers of the Word had been "ONCE delivered unto the saints."[83] The first beginner of which conspiracy was one Thebuthis, who had at the first been bred in one of the seven sects, into which the people of the Jews were in those days divided, but afterwards, because he missed of a bishopric unto which he had aspired (this of Jerusalem, as it may seem, whereunto Justus, after the death of Symeon, was preferred before him) could think of no readier a way thoroughly to revenge himself of this disgrace, than by raising up the like distractions among the Christians.[84] Which as, in the *effect*, it showeth the malignity of that ambitious sectary, so doth it, in the *occasion*, discover withal the great esteem that in those early days was had of episcopacy.

When Hegesippus wrote this ecclesiastical history, the ancientest of any since the Acts of the Apostles, Eleutherius as we heard before, was bishop of the church of Rome; unto whom "Lucius, King of the Britons," as our Bede relateth, "sent an epistle, desiring that by his means he might be made Christian. Who presently obtained the effect of his pious request, and the Britons kept the faith then received sound and undefiled in quiet peace, until the times of Diocletian the emperor."[85] By whose bloody persecution the faith and discipline of our British churches was not yet so quite extinguished, but that within ten years after, and eleven before the first general council of Nicea, three of our bishops were present and subscribed unto the Council of Arles: Eborius of York, Restitutus of London, and Adelfius

---

[81] Ἀντιθέσεις τῆς ψευδωνύμου γνώσεως. 1 Tim. 6:20.

[82] Luke 1:2.

[83] Jude 3.

[84] Διὰ τοῦτο ἐκάλουν τὴν ἐκκλησίαν παρθένον. οὔπω γὰρ ἔφθαρτο ἀκοαῖς ματαίαις· Ἄρχεται δ᾽ ὁ Θέβουθις, διὰ τὸ μὴ γενέσθαι αὐτὸν ἐπίσκοπον, ὑποφθείρειν, Ἀπὸ τῶν ἑπτὰ αἱρέσεων, εἷς καὶ αὐτὸς ἦν ἐν τῷ λαῷ. Hegesippus, *Memoranda*, in Eusebius, *Historia Ecclesiastica* 4.22.4–5 [*PG* 20:380A; *NPNF2* 1:199].

[85] *Misit ad eum Lucius Britannorum rex epistolam, obsecrans: ut per eius mandatum Christianus efficeretur. Et mox effectum piae postulationis consecutus est: susceptamque fidem Britanni usque in tempora Diocletiani principis inviolatam integramque quieta in pace servabant.* Bede, *Historia Ecclesiastica* 1.4 [*PL* 95:30B; Bede, *The Ecclesiastical History of the English People*, ed. Judith McClure and Roger Collins (Oxford: Oxford University Press, 1994), 14].

of Colchester,[86] if that be it, which is called there *Colonia Londinensium*. The first root of whose succession we must fetch beyond Eleutherius, and as high as St. Peter himself, if it be true, that he "constituted churches here, and ordained bishops, presbyters, and deacons" in them,[87] as Symeon Metaphrastes relateth out of some part of Eusebius, as it seemeth, that is not come unto our hands.[88]

But, to return unto the "angels of the seven churches," mentioned in the Revelation of St. John: by what hath been said, it is apparent that seven singular bishops, who were the constant presidents over those churches, are pointed at under that name. For other sure they could not be, if all of them were cast into one mould, and were of the same quality with Polycarpus, the then angel of the church in Smyrna, who without all question was such, if any credit may be given herein unto those that saw him and were well acquainted with him.

And as Tertullian in express terms affirmeth him to have been placed there by St. John himself, in the testimony before alleged out of his *Prescriptions*,[89] so doth he elsewhere, from the order of the succeeding bishops, not obscurely intimate, that the rest of that number were to be referred unto the same descent. "We have," saith he, "the churches that were bred by John.

---

[86] Jacques Sirmond, *Concilia Antiqua Galliae*, 3 vols (Paris, 1629), 1:9 [see *PL* 84:241B, 242A].

[87] Ἐπιμείνας τε ἐν Βρετανίᾳ ἡμέρας τινὰς, καὶ πολλοὺς τῷ λόγῳ φωτίσας τῆς χάριτος, ἐκκλησίας τε συστησάμενος, ἐπισκόπους τε καὶ πρεσβυτέρους καὶ διακόνους χειροτονήσας, δωδεκάτῳ ἔτει τοῦ Καίσαρος Νέρωνος αὖθις εἰς Ῥώμην παραγίνεται. Metaphrastes, *Commentarius de Petro et Paulo, ad diem 29 Junii* ["After remaining in Britain for some time, illuminating many people with words of grace, founding churches, and ordaining bishops, presbyters, and deacons, he came to Rome in the twelfth year of the Emperor Nero." This work, which is no longer numbered among those of Symeon Metaphrastes can be found in *Acta Sanctorum Junii ... Tomus V* (Antwerp, 1709), 416E.]

[88] Εὐσέβιος ὁ Παμφίλου δώδεκα μὲν ἔτη διατρίψαι Πέτρον λέγει ἐν τῇ ἀνατολῇ, εἴκοσι δὲ καὶ τρία πεποιηκέναι εἴς τε Ῥώμην καὶ τὴν Βρετανίαν καὶ τὰς περὶ τὴν δύσιν πόλεις. Metaphrastes, *Commentarius* ["Eusebius of Pamphylia says that Peter stayed twelve years in the east, and spent twenty-three years in Rome, and Britain, and the cities of the west." *Acta Sanctorum* 423C.]

[89] Tertullian, *De Praescriptionibus Adversus Haereticos* 32 [*PL* 2:45A {53A}; *ANF* 3:258]; cf. Jerome, *De Viris Illustribus* 17 [*PL* 23:635B {667B}; *NPNF2* 3:367]; Nicephorus Callistus, *Historia Ecclesiastica* 3.2 [*PG* 145:893D].

For although Marcion do reject his Revelation, yet the order of the bishops reckoned up unto their original, will stand for John to be their founder."[90]

Neither doth the ancient writer of the martyrdom of Timothy, mentioned by Photius, mean any other by those seven bishops, whose assistance he saith St. John did use, after his return from Patmos, in the government of the metropolis of the Ephesians. For "being revoked from his exile," saith he, "by the sentence of Nerva, he betook himself to the metropolis of Ephesus, and being assisted with the presence of SEVEN bishops, he took upon him the government of the metropolis of the Ephesians, and continued, preaching the word of piety, until the empire of Trajan."[91]

That he remained with the Ephesians and the rest of the brethren of Asia, until the days of Trajan, and that during the time of his abode with them, he published his Gospel, is sufficiently witnessed by Irenaeus.[92] That upon his return from the island, after the death of Domitian, he applied himself to the government of the churches of Asia, is confirmed likewise both by Eusebius,[93] and by Jerome,[94] who further addeth that at the earnest entreaty of the bishops of Asia he wrote there his Gospel.[95]

And that he himself also, being free from his banishment, did ordain bishops in divers churches, is clearly testified by Clement of Alexandria, who lived in the next age after, and delivereth it as a certain truth, which he had received from those who went before him, and could not be far from

---

[90] *Habemus et Johannis alumnas ecclesias. Nam etsi apocalypsim ejus Marcion respuit; ordo tamen episcoporum ad originem recensus, in Johannem stabit auctorem. Sic et caeterarum generositas recognoscitur.* Tertullian, *Adversus Marcionem* 4.5 [PL 2:366C {395C}; *ANF* 3:350].

[91] Ψηφίσματι Νέρβα τῆς ὑπερορίας ἀνακληθεὶς τῇ Ἐφεσίων ἐπέστη μητροπόλει, καὶ αὐτὸς δι' ἑαυτοῦ, ἑπτὰ συμπαρόντων ἐπισκόπων τῆς Ἐφεσίων ἀντιλαμβάνεται μητροπόλεως, καὶ διήρκεσε τὸν τῆς εὐσεβείας κηρύσσων λόγον ἄχρι τῆς βασιλείας Τραϊανοῦ. Photius, *Bibliotheca* 254 [PG 104:103A, 104A].

[92] Irenaeus, *Adversus Haereses* 2.22.5 [the original reference of 2.39, reproduced by Elrington, corresponds to the numbering in early modern editions such as those of Nicolas des Gallars (Geneva, 1570) and François Feuardent (Cologne, 1596); *PG* 7:785A; *ANF* 1:392]; cf. *Adversus Haereses*, 3.1.1; 3.3.4 [PG 7:845A–B, 854B–855A; *ANF* 1:414, 416].

[93] Eusebius, *Historia Ecclesiastica* 3.23.1–6 [PG 20:256C–257B; *NPNF2* 1:150].

[94] Jerome, *De Viris Illustribus* 9 [PL 23:625A {656B–657A}; *NPNF2* 3:364–65].

[95] Jerome, *De Viris Illustribus* 9 [PL 23:623A {653B–C}; *NPNF2* 3:364]; idem, *Commentariorum in Evangelium Matthaei*, preface [PL 26:18B–19A; *NPNF2* 6:495].

the time wherein the thing itself was acted. "When St. John," saith he, "Domitian the tyrant being dead, removed from the island of Patmos unto Ephesus, by the entreaty of some he went also unto the neighbouring nations; in some places constituting bishops, in others founding whole churches."[96]

Among these neighbouring churches was that of Hierapolis, which had Papias placed bishop therein.[97] That this man was "a hearer of St. John, and a companion of Polycarpus,"[98] is testified by his own scholar Irenaeus;[99] and that he conversed with the disciples of the apostles,[100] and of Christ also, he himself doth thus declare, in the proem of the five books which he entitled, "A declaration of the words of the Lord": "If upon occasion, any of the presbyters which had accompanied the apostles did come, I diligently enquired what were the speeches which the apostles used, what Andrew or what Peter did say, or what Philip, or Thomas, or James, or John, or Matthew, or some other of the disciples of the Lord; and the things that Aristion and John the elder, our Lord's disciples, did speak."[101]

---

[96] Ἐπειδὴ τοῦ τυράννου τελευτήσαντος ἀπὸ τῆς Πάτμου τῆς νήσου μετῆλθεν ἐπὶ τὴν Ἔφεσον, ἀπῄει παρακαλούμενος καὶ ἐπὶ τὰ πλησιόχωρα τῶν ἐθνῶν, ὅπου μὲν ἐπισκόπους καταστήσων, ὅπου δὲ ὅλας ἐκκλησίας ἁρμόσων. Clement of Alexandria, *Quis Dives Salvetur* 42 [*PG* 9:648B; *ANF* 2:603. Ussher disputes the attribution of this work to Origen by Michele Ghislieri, later Pius V, in *Michaelis Ghislerii ... in Ieremiam Prophetam Commentariorum*, 3 vols (Lyon, 1623), 3:262–282. He notes Eusebius, *Historia Ecclesiastica* 3.23.5 in support of Clement's authorship (*PG* 20:257A–B; *NPNF2* 1:150)].

[97] Eusebius, *Historia Ecclesiastica* 3.36.2 [but given as 3.35 in original; *PG* 20:288B; *NPNF2* 1:166]; Jerome, *De Viris Illustribus* 18 [*PL* 23:637A {669A}; *NPNF2* 3:367]; idem, *Eusebii Chronicorum*, ann. 2 Trajani [*PL* 27:461].

[98] Παπίας Ἰωάννου μὲν ἀκουστὴς, Πολυκάρπου δὲ ἑταῖρος γεγονὼς, ἀρχαῖος ἀνήρ. Irenaeus, *Adversus Haereses* 5.33.4 [*PG* 7:1214A; *ANF* 1:563].

[99] *Irenaeus, vir apostolicorum temporum et Papiae auditoris evangelistae Johannis discipulus, episcopus ecclesiae Lugdunensis* ["Irenaeus, bishop of the church of Lyons, a man of the apostolic times, who was a disciple of Papias the hearer of the evangelist John"]. Jerome, *Epist. ad Theodoram* 75.3 [given in original as 53, corresponding to the Benedictine edition; *PL* 22:687; *NPNF2* 6:156]

[100] *Hi sunt presbyteri apostolorum discipuli* ["These are the presbyters, the disciples of the apostles"]. Cf. Irenaeus, *Adversus Haereses* 5.36.2 [*PG* 7:1223B; *ANF* 1:567].

[101] Εἰ δέ που καὶ τὶς τῶν πρεσβυτέρων παρηκολουθηκὼς τοῖς ἀποστόλοις ἔλθοι, τοὺς τῶν ἀποστόλων ἀνέκρινον λόγους (*ita enim ex Graecis MSS. et vetere Rufini versione locus est restituendus*) τί Ἀνδρέας, ἢ τί Πέτρος εἶπεν, ἢ τί Φίλιππος, ἢ τί Θωμᾶς, ἢ Ἰάκωβος, ἢ τί Ἰωάννης, ἢ Ματθαῖος, ἢ τις ἕτερος τῶν τοῦ κυρίου μαθητῶν,

The two last of whom he often cited by name in the process of the work, relating the passages in this kind which he had heard from them.[102]

Neither can any man be so simple as to imagine, that in the language of Clement of Alexandria the name of a bishop should import no more than a bare presbyter; if he consider, that not the difference only betwixt presbyters, bishops, and deacons is by him acknowledged,[103] but further also, that the disposition of their three offices, in his judgment, doth carry with it an "imitation of the angelical glory";[104] to say nothing of the emperor Hadrian, who, hard upon the time of the forenamed Papias, writing unto the consul Servianus touching the state of things in Egypt, maketh distinct mention in his letter of the "presbyters of the Christians,"[105] and of those "who call themselves bishops of Christ."[106]

And thus having deduced episcopacy from the apostolical times, and declared that the angels of the seven churches were no other, but such as in the next age after the apostles were by the fathers termed bishops, we are now further to enquire, why these churches are confined unto the number of seven, in the superscription of that apostolical epistle prefixed before the

---

ἅτε Ἀριστίων καὶ ὁ πρεσβύτερος Ἰωάννης, οἱ τοῦ κυρίου μαθηταὶ, λέγουσιν. Papias, Λογίων Κυριακῶν ἐξηγήσεως ["Explanation of the Lord's Discourses"], proem, in Eusebius, *Historia Ecclesiastica* 3.39.4 [against the textual tradition on which Ussher relies here, the generally accepted reading is εἰ δέ που καὶ παρηκολουθηκώς τις τοῖς πρεσβυτέροις ἔλθοι, τοὺς τῶν πρεσβυτέρων ἀνέκρινον λόγους; *PG* 20:297A; *NPNF2* 1:171].

[102] Ἀριστίωνος δὲ καὶ τοῦ πρεσβυτέρου Ἰωάννου αὐτήκοον ἑαυτόν φησι γενέσθαι· ὀνομαστὶ γοῦν πολλάκις αὐτῶν μνημονεύσας ἐν τοῖς αὐτοῦ συγγράμμασι τίθησιν αὐτῶν παραδόσεις. Eusebius, *Historia Ecclesiastica* 3.39.7 [*PG* 20:297C; *NPNF2* 1:171–72].

[103] Μυρίαι δὲ ὅσαι ὑποθῆκαι, εἰς πρόσωπα ἐκλεκτὰ διατείνουσαι ἐγγεγράφαται ταῖς βίβλοις ταῖς ἁγίαις, αἱ μὲν πρεσβυτέροις, αἱ δὲ ἐπισκόποις, διακόνοις· ἄλλαι, χήραις ["Innumerable commands such as these are written in the holy Bible appertaining to chosen persons, some to presbyters, some to bishops, some to deacons, others to widows"]. Clement of Alexandria, *Paedagogus* 3.12 [*PG* 8:676D–677A; *ANF* 2:294].

[104] Αἱ ἐνταῦθα κατὰ τὴν ἐκκλησίαν προκοπαί, ἐπισκόπων, πρεσβυτέρων, διακόνων, μιμήματα οἶμαι τῆς ἀγγελικῆς δόξης. Clement of Alexandria, *Stromata* 6.13 [*PG* 9:328C; *ANF* 2:505].

[105] *Nemo Christianorum presbyter.* Hadrian Augustus to Servianus, in Flavius Vopiscus, *Vita Saturnini* 8 [*LCL* 263:398–99].

[106] *Qui se Christi episcopos dicunt.* Hadrian, in Vopiscus, *Vita Saturnini* 8.

book of the Revelation: "John to the seven churches in Asia: Grace be unto you and peace,"[107] where St. John directing his letters unto them thus indefinitely, without any mention of their particular names, cannot by common intendment be conceived to have understood any other thereby, but such as by some degree of eminency were distinguishable from all the rest of the churches that were in Asia, and in some sort also did comprehend all the rest under them.

For taking Asia here in that stricter sense, wherein the New Testament useth it, as denoting the Lydian Asia alone, of the circuit whereof I have treated elsewhere more particularly,[108] it is not to be imagined, that after so long pains taken by the apostles and their disciples in the husbanding of that part of the Lord's vineyard, there should be found no more but seven churches therein, especially since St. Paul, that "wise masterbuilder"[109] professeth that he had here "a great door and effectual opened" unto him;[110] and St. Luke testifieth accordingly, that "all they which dwelt in Asia heard the word of the Lord Jesus, both Jews and Greeks; so mightily grew the word of God and prevailed."[111] Which extraordinary blessing of God upon his labours, moved the apostle to make his residence in those parts "for the space of three years," wherein he "ceased not to warn every one night and day with tears."[112]

So that in all reason we are to suppose, that these seven churches, comprising all the rest within them, were not bare parochial ones, or so many particular congregations, but diocesan churches, as we use to call them, if not metropolitical rather. For that in Laodicea,[113] Sardis, Smyrna, Ephesus, and Pergamum,[114] the Roman governors held their courts of justice, to which all the cities and towns about had recourse for the ending of their suits, is noted by Pliny. And besides these, which were the greatest,

---

[107] Rev. 1:4.

[108] James Ussher, *A Geographicall and Historicall Disquisition, Touching the Asia Properly So Called* (Oxford, 1643), 8–13 [*WJU*, 7:13–18].

[109] 1 Cor. 3:10.

[110] 1 Cor. 16:8–9.

[111] Acts 19:10, 20.

[112] Acts 20:31.

[113] Pliny, *Historia Naturalis* 5.29 [*LCL* 352:298–99].

[114] Pliny, *Historia Naturalis* 5.33 [given in original as 5.30 corresponding to chapter divisions in early modern editions; *LCL* 352:314–15].

Thyatira is also by Ptolemy expressly named a metropolis,[115] as Philadelphia also is, in the Greek acts of the council of Constantinople, held under Menas.[116] Which giveth us good ground to conceive, that the seven cities, in which these seven churches had their seat, were all of them metropolitical, and so had relation unto the rest of the towns and cities of Asia, as unto daughters rising under them.

This Lydian Asia was separated from Caria by the river Maeander, upon the banks whereof Magnesia and Trallis were seated; to the Christians whereof Ignatius directed two of his epistles, wherein he maketh mention of Damas, bishop of the one church, and Polybius, bishop (or "ruler,"[117] as Eusebius calleth him) of the other, whom they had sent to visit him at Smyrna, adding withal in that to the Trallians, his usual admonitions: "Be subject to the bishop, as to the Lord," and "to the presbytery, as to the apostles of Jesus Christ our hope."[118] "He that doth any thing without the bishop and the presbyters and the deacons, such a one is defiled in conscience."[119] "Fare you well in Jesus Christ, being subject to the bishop, and likewise to the presbyters."[120]

Wherein we may note, that within twelve years after mention of the seven churches made in the Apocalypse (for then, as hath been shown, were these epistles of Ignatius written), other episcopal cities are found in the same Lydian Asia; and two such, as in after times are well own to have

---

[115] Ptolemy, *Geographia*, lib. 5 [see, for example, *Geographia Cl. Ptolemaei Alexandrini* (Venice, 1562), 159].

[116] Council of Constantinople under Menas, Session 5 [*ACO*, tom. 3, 65; though gathered with the documents of the Council of 536 presided over by Menas, this subscription list is from that held under John the Cappadocian in 518].

[117] Ἄρχοντα. Eusebius, *Historia Ecclesiastica* 3.36.5 [given as 3.35 in original; *PG* 20:288C; *NPNF2* 1:168].

[118] Τῷ ἐπισκόπῳ ὑποτάσσεσθε, ὡς τῷ Κυρίῳ ... ὑποτάσσεσθε καὶ τῷ πρεσβυτερίῳ, ὡς ἀποστόλοις Ἰησοῦ Χριστοῦ τῆς ἐλπίδος ἡμῶν. Ignatius, *Ad Trallianos* 2 [*PG* 5:777C, 780A (see 676B); *ANF* 1:66].

[119] Ὁ χωρὶς τοῦ ἐπισκόπου καὶ τῶν πρεσβυτέρων καὶ τῶν διακόνων τι πράσσων, ὁ τοιοῦτος μεμίανται τῇ συνειδήσει. Ignatius, *Ad Trallianos* 7 [*PG* 5:785B (see 681A); *ANF* 1:69].

[120] Ἔρρωσθε ἐν Ἰησοῦ Χριστῷ, ὑποτασσόμενοι τῷ ἐπισκόπῳ, ὁμοίως καὶ τοῖς πρεσβυτέροις, etc. Ignatius, *Ad Trallianos* 13 [*PG* 5:800B (see 684C–685A); *ANF* 1:72].

been under the government of the metropolitan of Ephesus.[121] But whether this subordination were as ancient as the days of Ignatius, whose epistles are extant unto these three churches, and Damas the then bishop of Magnesia,[122] with Polybius of Trallis, were at that time subject to Onesimus the bishop of Ephesus, might well be doubted, but that the same Ignatius directeth one of his epistles unto the church "which had presidency in the place of the region of the Romans,"[123] and in the body thereof doth attribute unto himself the title of the bishop of Syria. Whereby, as he intimateth himself to have been not only the bishop of Antioch, but also of the rest of the province of Syria, which was under that metropolis, so doth he likewise not obscurely signify that the bishop of Rome had at that time a presidency over the churches that were in the Urbicarian region,[124] as the imperial constitutions, or the Roman province, as the acts of the first council of Arles call it.[125]

What that Urbicarian region was, I will not now stand to discuss: whether Tuscia only, wherein Rome itself was situated, which in the days of Ignatius was one entire region, but afterwards divided into Tuscia Suburbicaria and Annonaria; or the territory wherein the *praefectus urbis* [prefect of the city] did exercise his jurisdiction, which was confined within the compass of a hundred miles about the city, or with that, those other provinces also whereunto the authority of the *vicarius urbis* [deputy or sheriff of the city] did extend; or lastly the circuit within which those sixty-nine bishoprics were contained that were immediately subject to the bishop of Rome, and frequently called to his synods, the names whereof are found registered in

---

[121] See "Ordo Metropolitarum" in the "Notitiae Antiquae" appended to Carolus a Sancto Paulo, *Geographia Sacra* (Paris, 1641), appendix, 11; see *Iuris Graeco-Romani*, ed. Johannes Leunclavius, 2 vols (Frankfurt, 1596), 1:90.

[122] Eusebius, *Historia Ecclesiastica* 3.36.5 [given as 3.35 in original; *PG* 20:288C; *NPNF2* 1:167–68].

[123] Ἥτις προκάθηται ἐν τόπῳ χωρίου Ῥωμαίων. Ignatius, *Ad Romanos*, address [*PG* 5:810A (see 685B); *ANF* 1:73].

[124] *Ex urbicaria regione*. *Codicis Theodosiani libri XVI* (Paris and Geneva, 1586), 303 (lib. 11, tit. 2, leg. 3).

[125] *Ex provincia Romana, civitate Portuen[sis], &c. In nominibus quae concilio Arelatensi 1. praefixa leguntur* ["From the Roman province, from the city of Portus." From the names which preface the decrees of the first Council of Arles. For this specific form of Bishop Gregory's title see, for example, Severin Binius, *Concilia Generalia, et Provincialia*, 4 vols (Cologne, 1606), 1:265].

the records of that church.[126] The antiquity of which number as it may in
some sort receive confirmation from the Roman synod of seventy bishops
held under Gelasius, so for the distinction of the bishops which belonged
to the city of Rome, from those that appertained to Italy, we have a far
more ancient testimony from the edict of the emperor Aurelian, who in the
controversy that arose betwixt Paulus Samosatenus and Domnus for the
house which belonged unto the church of Antioch, commanded that it
should be delivered to them, to whom the bishops of Italy and Rome
should by their letters declare that it ought to be given;[127] which distinction,
as well in the forecited acts of the council of Arles,[128] as in the epistles of
the Sardican synod[129] and Athanasius may likewise be observed,[130] the name
of Italy being in a more strict sense applied therein to the seven provinces,
which were under the civil jurisdiction of the *vicarius* or lieutenant of Italy,
and the ecclesiastical of the bishop of Milan.

And it is well worth the observing, that the fathers of the great council of Nicea, afterwards confirming this kind of primacy, in the bishops of
Alexandria, Rome, and Antioch, and in the metropolitans of other provinces,[131] do make their entrance into that canon with "Τὰ ἀρχαῖα ἔθη

---

[126] *Insuper praeter septem collaterales episcopos erant alii episcopi, qui dicuntur suffraganei Romani pontificis, nulli alii primati vel archiepiscopo subjecti; qui frequenter ad synodos vocarentur.*
["In addition to seven collateral bishops there were other bishops, who were called
suffragans to the Roman pontiffs, subject to no other primate, even the archbishop; who were frequently called to synods."] From a Vatican manuscript cited in
Baronius, *Annales Ecclesiastici* 11:237 (ann. 1057).

[127] Οἷς ἂν οἱ Ῥώμης ἐπίσκοποι ἐπιστέλλοντες εὐδοκήσαιεν saith Nicephorus Callistus, *Historia Ecclesiastica* 6.29 [*PG* 145:1185B], but Eusebius, *Historia Ecclesiastica*
7.30.19 [*PG* 20:720A; *NPNF2* 1:316] more fully: οἷς ἂν οἱ κατὰ τὴν Ἰταλίαν καὶ
τὴν Ῥωμαίων πόλιν ἐπίσκοποι τοῦ δόγματος ἐπιστέλλοιεν.

[128] *Ex provincia Italiae, civitate Mediolanen[sis], &c. Ex provincia Romana, civitate Portuen[sis]* ["From the Italian province, from the city of Milan ... From the Roman
province, from the city of Portus"; Binius, *Concilia Generalia, et Provincialia* 1:265].

[129] Ἡ ἁγία σύνοδος συναχθεῖσα ἀπό Ῥώμης καὶ Ἰταλίας ["The holy council assembled from Rome and Italy." Ussher abbreviates the passage and omits the many
other place names in the source]. *Epist. Synodi Sardicae*, address, in Athanasius, *Apologia Contra Arianos* [*PG* 25:312A; *NPNF2* 4:119].

[130] Ἀπό τε τῆς μεγάλης Ῥώμης καὶ τῆς Ἰταλίας πάσης ["From great Rome and all
Italy"]. Athanasius, *Historia Arianorum ad Monachos* 28 [*PG* 25:725A; *NPNF2* 4:279].

[131] Ὁμοίως δὲ καὶ κατὰ τὴν Ἀντιόχειαν, καὶ ἐν ταῖς ἄλλαις ἐπαρχίαις, τὰ
πρεσβεῖα σώζεσθαι ταῖς ἐκκλησίαις, καθόλου δὲ πρόδηλον ἐκεῖνο, ὅτι εἴ τις
χωρὶς γνώμης μητροπολίτου γένοιτο ἐπίσκοπος, τὸν τοιοῦτον ἡ μεγάλη σύνοδος

κρατείτω, Let the *ancient* customs continue." Which as it cleareth the antiquity of the metropolitical jurisdiction of the bishop of Rome, so doth it likewise confirm the opinion of those who conceive the metropolitan of Alexandria to be meant in that passage of the emperor Hadrian's epistle unto Servianus: "Even the very patriarch himself, when he cometh into Egypt, is by some compelled to adore Serapis, and by others to worship Christ,"[132] as if, upon his returning into Egypt, either from his visitation of Libya and Pentapolis, which this same Nicene canon showeth to have of old belonged unto his care, or from his flight in that present time of persecution, he should suffer this distraction: the heathen labouring to compel him to the worship of Serapis, and his own Christian flock on the other side striving to keep him constant in the service of Christ. For that either the heathen had will, or the Christians power at that time to force the Jewish patriarch, of whom some do understand the place, to the adoration of Christ, has no manner of probability in it.

That part also of the canon, which ratifieth the ancient rights of metropolitans of all other provinces, may serve to open unto us the meaning of that complaint which, some threescore and ten years before the time of this synod, St. Cyprian made against Novatian for the confusion which by his schism he brought upon the churches of God: that "whereas long since in all provinces, and in all cities, bishops had been ordained, in age ancient, sound in faith, tried in affliction, proscribed in persecution; yet took he the boldness to create other false bishops over their heads,"[133] namely, subordinate bishops in every city, and metropolitans in every province.

In Africa at that time, although there were many civil provinces, yet was there but one ecclesiastical, whereof Cyprian himself was archbishop,

---

ὥρισε μὴ δεῖν εἶναι ἐπίσκοπον. ["Likewise in Antioch and the other provinces, let the churches retain their privileges. And this is to be universally understood, that if any one be made bishop without the consent of the metropolitan, the great synod has declared that such a man ought not to be a bishop."] Council of Nicea, Can. 6 [*Decrees of the Ecumenical Councils*, ed. Norman P. Tanner, 2 vols (London: Sheed and Ward, 1990), 1:9; *NPNF2* 14:15].

[132] *Ipse ille patriarcha quum Aegyptum venerit, ab aliis Serapidem adorare, ab aliis cogitur Christum.* Hadrian Augustus to Servianus, in Flavius Vopiscus, *Vita Saturnini* 8 [*LCL* 263:398–401].

[133] *Cum jampridem per omnes provincias, et per urbes singulas, ordinati sint episcopi in aetate antiqui, in fide integri, in pressura probati, in persecutione proscripti; ille super eos creare alios pseudo-episcopos audeat.* Cyprian to Antonianus, in Cyprian, *Epist.* 52.24 [*PL* 3:790B {815B} (see 4:345B–346A {355A–B}); *ANF* 5:333 where numbered 51.24].

as the fathers of the Trullan synod call him.[134] It pleased, saith he in one of his epistles, "all the bishops constituted either in our province or beyond the sea,"[135] intimating thereby, that all the bishops which were on his side [of] the sea did belong unto one province. "For our province," saith he in another place, "is spread more largely; having Numidia also, and both the Mauritaniaes, annexed unto it."[136] Whence that great council assembled by him for determining the question touching the baptizing of those that had been baptized by heretics, is said to be gathered "out of the province of Africa, Numidia, and Mauritania."[137] For howsoever in the civil government, the proconsular Africa, wherein Carthage was seated, Numidia, and both the Mauritanies, Sitifensis and Caesariensis, were accounted three distinct provinces, yet in the ecclesiastical administration they were joined together and made but one province, immediately subject to the metropolitical jurisdiction of the prime see of Carthage.

Some threescore years before this African council was held by Cyprian, those other provincial synods were assembled by the metropolitans of sundry nations, for the composing of the paschal controversy, then hotly pursued, and among the rest, that in our neighbour country, out of "the parishes" (for so, in the ancient language of the Church, those precincts were named, which now we call dioceses), "of which Irenaeus had the superintendency";[138] whence also he wrote that free epistle unto Victor, bishop of Rome, "in the person of those brethren over whom he was president,"[139] at which time, and before, the most famous metropoles of

---

[134] Τοῦ Κυπριανοῦ τοῦ γενομένου ἀρχιεπισκόπου τῆς Ἄφρων χώρας ["Cyprian, Archbishop of the country of the Africans"]. Council of Constantinople in Trullo [Quinisext Council, 692], Can. 2 [*PG* 137:521D; *NPNF2* 14:361].

[135] *Universis episcopis, vel in nostra provincia vel trans mare constitutis.* Cyprian to the People, in Cyprian, *Epist.* 40.3 [*PL* 4:334B–335A {344A}; *ANF* 5:317 where numbered 39.3].

[136] *Quoniam latius fusa est nostra provincia; habet etiam Numidiam et Mauritanias duas sibi cohaerentes.* Cyprian to Cornelius, in Cyprian, *Epist.* 45.3 [*PL* 3:710C–711A {733B} (see 4:341A–B {350B–C}); *ANF* 5:322 where numbered 44.3].

[137] *Ex provincia Africa, Numidia, Mauritania.* Council of Cyprian [Carthage, 257; *PL* 3:1052A {1090B}; *NPNF2* 14:517].

[138] Τῶν κατὰ Γαλλίαν παροικιῶν ἃς Εἰρηναῖος ἐπεσκόπει. Eusebius, *Historia Ecclesiastica* 5.23.2 [*PG* 20:493A; *NPNF2* 1:242].

[139] Ἐκ προσώπου ὧν ἡγεῖτο κατὰ τὴν Γαλλίαν ἀδελφῶν. Irenaeus, *Ad Victorem*, in Eusebius, *Historia Ecclesiastica* 5.24.11 [*PG* 20:497B; *NPNF2* 1:243].

that country,[140] and so the most eminent churches therein,[141] were Lyons and Vienna [Vienne]; in the one whereof Irenaeus was then no less renowned a prelate, than Cyprian was afterwards in Africa.[142]

Dionysius, the famous bishop of Corinth, was elder than they; who among many other epistles, directed one to the church of Gortyna, and all the rest of the churches of Crete, wherein he saluted their bishop Philip,[143] whereby it appeareth that at that time, as well as in the ages following, Gortyna was the metropolis, and the bishop thereof the metropolitan of all the rest of that whole island.[144] Which kind of superintendancy there, Eusebius, the ancientest ecclesiastical historian now extant, deriveth from the very times of Titus; whom, out of the histories that were before his time, he relateth to have held "the bishopric of the churches in Crete."[145] With whom the Grecians of after times do fully concur, as appeareth both by the subscription annexed by them unto the epistle of St. Paul to Titus, "ordained," as there they say, "the first bishop of the church of the Cretians,"[146] and by the argument prefixed by them before the same, speaking of him to the same effect: that "he was by Paul ordained bishop of that great country," and "had commission to ordain the bishops that were under

---

[140] Ἧς μητροπόλεις ἐπίσημοι καὶ παρὰ τὰς ἄλλας τῶν αὐτόθι διαφέρουσαι, βεβόηνται Λούγδουνος καὶ Βίεννα. Eusebius, *Historia Ecclesiastica* 5.1.1 [*PG* 20:408C; *NPNF2* 1:211].

[141] Αἱ τῇδε διαφανέσταται ἐκκλησίαι. Eusebius, *Historia Ecclesiastica* 5.1.2 [*PG* 20:408C; *NPNF2* 1:212].

[142] Ὃς τῆς Πολυκάρπου διδασκαλίας ἀπήλαυσεν, ἐγεγόνει δὲ φωστὴρ Γαλατῶν τῶν ἑσπερίων ["who enjoyed the teaching of Polycarp, and became a light of the western Gauls"]. Theodoret, *Eranistes*, Dialogus I [*PG* 83:81A; *NPNF2* 3:175].

[143] Τῇ ἐκκλησίᾳ τῇ παροικούσῃ Γόρτυναν, ἅμα ταῖς λοιπαῖς κατὰ Κρήτην παροικίαις ἐπιστείλας, Φίλιππον ἐπίσκοπον αὐτῶν ἀποδέχεται. Eusebius, *Historia Ecclesiastica* 4.23.5 [*PG* 20:385A; *NPNF2* 1:201].

[144] Subscriptions. Council of Chalcedon, Session 6 [*ACO*, tom. 2, vol. 1, pars altera, 143]; Council of Constantinople under Menas [536], Session 5 [*ACO*, tom. 3, 115]; fifth general council, Constantinople [553], collat. 8 [*ACO*, tom. 4, vol. 1, 225].

[145] Τιμόθεός τῆς ἐν Ἐφέσῳ παροικίας ἱστορεῖται πρῶτος τὴν ἐπισκοπὴν εἰληχέναι ὡς καὶ Τίτος τῶν ἐπὶ Κρήτης ἐκκλησιῶν ["It is recorded that Timothy was the first appointed bishop of the parish in Ephesus, as was Titus of the churches of Crete"]. Eusebius, *Historia Ecclesiastica* 3.4.6 [*PG* 20:220B; *NPNF2* 1:136].

[146] Πρός Τίτον τῆς Κρητῶν ἐκκλησίας πρῶτον ἐπίσκοπον χειροτονηθέντα.

him,"[147] which they gather out of those words of St. Paul unto him: "For this cause left I thee in Crete, that thou shouldest set in order the things that are wanting, and ordain elders in every city, as I had appointed thee."[148] Out of which M. Calvin collecteth this doctrine unto us for the general: "We learn out of this place, that there was not then such an equality betwixt the ministers of the church, but that there was some one who was president over the rest both in authority and in counsel."[149] And St. Chrysostom, for the particular of Titus: "Had he not been an approved man, he would not have committed that whole island unto him; he would not have commanded him to supply the things that were defective; he would not have committed unto him the judgment of so many bishops, if he had not had very great confidence in the man."[150] And Bishop Jewell upon him again: "Having the government of many bishops, what may we call him but an archbishop?"[151]

Which is not so much to be wondered at, when we see that the bishops of another island stick not, and that without any control, to deduce the ordination of their metropolitan from the apostolic times, in the face of the whole general council of Ephesus. For whereas the patriarch of Antioch did claim an interest in the ordaining of the metropolitan of Cyprus, the bishops of that island prescribed to the contrary, that from the time of "the holy apostles it could never be showed, that the bishop of Antioch was ever present at any such ordination, or did ever communicate the grace of ordi-

---

[147] Ἐπίσκοπος τῆς Κρήτης, μεγίστης οὔσης, κεχειροτόνητο ὑπὸ τοῦ Παύλου. ἐπετέτραπτο δὲ τοὺς ὑπ' αὐτὸν ἐπισκόπους χειροτονῆσαι. *Argumentum* attributed to Theodoret in Oecumenius Triccae, *Comment. in Epist. ad Titum* [PG 119:241C].

[148] Tit. 1:5.

[149] *Discimus ex hoc loco, non eam fuisse tunc aequalitatem inter ecclesiae ministros quin unus aliquis autoritate et consilio praeesset.* John Calvin, *Comment. in Epist. ad Titum*, on 1:5 [CO 52:409; *Commentaries on the Epistles to Timothy, Titus, and Philemon*, trans. William Pringle (Edinburgh: Calvin Translation Society, 1856), 291].

[150] Εἰ μὴ γὰρ ἦν δόκιμος, οὐκ ἂν αὐτῷ τὴν νῆσον ὁλόκληρον ἐπέτρεψεν, οὐκ ἂν τὰ ἐλλειφθέντα ἀναπληρῶσαι προσέταξεν (Ἵνα γάρ, φησι, τὰ λείποντα ἐπιδιορθώσῃ) οὐκ ἂν τοσούτων ἐπισκόπων κρίσιν ἐπέτρεψεν, εἰ μὴ σφόδρα ἐθάρρει τῷ ἀνδρί. Chrysostom, *In Epist. ad Titum*, Homily 1 [PG 62:663; NPNF1 13:519].

[151] [John Jewel, "Certain Frivolous Objections against the Government of the Church of England," in *The Works of John Jewel, D.D., Bishop of Salisbury*, ed. Richard William Jelf, 8 vols (Oxford: Oxford University Press, 1848), 8:264].

nation to that island";[152] and that the former bishops of Constantia (the metropolis of Cyprus), Troilus, Sabinus, Epiphanius, and "all the holy and orthodox bishops which were before them, ever since the holy apostles, were constituted by those which were in Cyprus,"[153] and therefore desired that "as in the beginning from the times of the apostles, and by the constitutions and canons of the most holy and great synod of Nicea, the synod of the Cyprian bishops remained untouched and superior to privy underminings and open power";[154] so they might still be continued in the possession of their ancient right. Whereupon the council, condemning the attempt of the bishop of Antioch as an "innovation brought in against the ecclesiastical laws and the canons of the holy fathers,"[155] did not only order, that "the governors of the churches which were in Cyprus should keep their own right entire and inviolable, according to the canons of the holy fathers and their ancient custom,"[156] but also for all other dioceses and provinces wheresoever, that no bishop should intrude himself into any other province, which had not formerly and *from the beginning* been under him or his predecessors.[157]

---

[152] *A sanctis apostolis nunquam possunt ostendere quod adfuerit Antiochenus et ordinaverit, vel communicaverit unquam insulae ordinationis gratiam, neque alius quisquam.* Council of Ephesus, Session 7 [*ACO*, tom. 1, vol. 5, pars altera, fasc. v, 359].

[153] *Et nunc memorati episcopi, et qui a sanctis apostolis erant omnes orthodoxi, ab his qui in Cypro constituti sunt.* Council of Ephesus, Session 7 [*ACO*, tom. 1, vol. 5, pars altera, fasc. v, 359].

[154] *Sicut initio a temporibus apostolorum et constitutionibus et canonibus sanctissimae et magnae synodi Nicaenae; illaesa et superior insidiis et potentia permansit nostra Cypriorum synodus.* Council of Ephesus, Session 7 [p. 358].

[155] Πρᾶγμα παρὰ τοὺς ἐκκλησιαστικοὺς θεσμοὺς καὶ τοὺς κανόνας τῶν ἁγίων πατέρων καινοτομούμενον. Council of Ephesus, Session 7 [*ACO*, tom. 1, vol. 1, pars septima, 122].

[156] Ἕξουσι τὸ ἀνεπηρέαστον καὶ ἀβίαστον οἱ τῶν ἁγίων ἐκκλησιῶν τῶν κατὰ τὴν Κύπρον, προεστῶτες, κατὰ τοὺς κανόνας τῶν ὁσίων πατέρων, καὶ τὴν ἀρχαίαν συνήθειαν. Council of Ephesus, Session 7 [*ACO*, tom. 1, vol. 1, pars septima, 122].

[157] Τὸ δὲ αὐτὸ καὶ ἐπὶ τῶν ἄλλων διοικήσεων, καὶ τῶν ἀπανταχοῦ ἐπαρχιῶν παραφυλαχθήσεται· ὥστε μηδένα τῶν θεοφιλεστάτων ἐπισκόπων ἐπαρχίαν ἑτέραν, οὐκ οὖσαν ἄνωθεν καὶ ἐξ ἀρχῆς ὑπὸ τὴν αὐτοῦ ἤγουν τῶν πρὸ αὐτοῦ χεῖρα, καταλαμβάνειν ... Ἔδοξε τοίνυν τῇ ἁγίᾳ καὶ οἰκουμενικῇ συνόδῳ, σώζεσθαι ἑκάστῃ ἐπαρχίᾳ καθαρὰ καὶ ἀβίαστα τὰ αὐτῇ προσόντα δίκαια αὐτῇ ἐξ ἀρχῆς ἄνωθεν, κατὰ τὸ πάλαι κρατῆσαν ἔθος. Council of Ephesus, Session 7 [*ACO*, tom. 1, vol. 1, pars septima, 122].

The *beginning* of which kind of subordination of many bishops unto one chief, if it were not to be derived from apostolical right, yet it is by Beza fetched from the same light of nature and enforcement of necessity, whereby men were at first induced to enter into consociations, subjected one unto another,[158] and by Bucer acknowledged to have "been consentaneous to the law of Christ," and to have "been done by the right of the body of Christ,"[159] and by all men must be confessed to be conformable to the pattern delivered by God unto Moses. For having set apart the three families of the Levites for his own service, and constituted a chief, as we have heard, over every of them, he placed immediately over them all, not Aaron the high priest, but Eleazar his son, saying, "Eleazar, the son of Aaron the priest, shall be chief over the chief of the Levites, and have the oversight of them that keep the charge of the sanctuary."[160]

In respect of which oversight, as he hath by the Septuagint (warrantably enough by the Word of God) given unto him the name of a bishop,[161] so the Holy Ghost having vouchsafed to honour him with the title of נשיא הלוי נשיאי, ὁ ἄρχων ἐπὶ τῶν ἀρχόντων τῶν Λευϊτῶν, "the president of the presidents of the Levites,"[162] none that without prejudice did take the matter into consideration, would much stick to afford unto him the name of an archbishop. At least he would be taught hereby to retain that reverend opinion of the primitive bishops of the Christian Church, who so willingly sub-

---

158 *Neque vero magis existimandum est, hunc externum ordinem fuisse* [Ussher here omits two complete lines of Beza's text through eyeskip from *initio* to *initio*, a mistake replicated in every edition from 1641 to Elrington: *initio ab aliquo coëuntium omnium Patrum consilio & decreto profectum, quam quod*] *initio humani generis. Pagi enim ex familiis, et ex pagis urbes, et ex urbibus civitates ipsae, suadente natura et necessitate flagitante, sensum coierunt; aliis aliorum exemplum sequutis* ["Nor ought it be thought that this external order was in the beginning to progress from some agreement of all the Fathers by counsel and decree, more than what was in the beginning from the families of the human race. For districts unite in judgement out of families, and cities out of districts, and states themselves out of cities; with nature recommending it and necessity requiring it; with some having followed the example of others."] Theodore Beza, *Ad Tractationem de Ministrorum Evangelii Gradibus, ab Hadriano Saravia Belga editam. Theodori Bezae Responsio* (Geneva, 1592), 166.

159 *Atque hoc consentiebat legi Christi, fiebatque ex jure corporis Christi.* Martin Bucer, *De Vi et Usu Sacri Minsterii*, in *Scripta Anglicana* (Basle, 1577), 565.

160 Num. 3:32.

161 Ἐπίσκοπος Ἐλεάζαρ ['bishop Eleazar'], LXX, Num. 4:16.

162 Num. 3:32.

mitted themselves, not only to the archiepiscopal, but also to a patriarchical government, which Calvin professed he did; that in all this, they were far from having a thought, "to devise another form of church government, than that which God had prescribed in his Word."[163]

The writers which, in the next age after the Apostles, have here given testimony for episcopacy.

In the fourteenth year of Domitian, about the ninety-fifth year of our Lord, according to the vulgar account, St. John wrote his Revelation; and in it, the epistle directed by our Saviour "to the angel of the church in Philadelphia."[164] No longer than twelve years after that time, Ignatius, St. John's scholar, writeth his letters unto the same church. In the beginning whereof, he giveth this testimony unto their bishop: that "he knew him to have been promoted, not of himself, nor by men, unto that ministry, pertaining to the public weal of the Church,"[165] which is every whit as much as if he had called him their angel. Afterwards he telleth them, that there is but "one bishop," joined "with the presbytery and the deacons,"[166] and that he delivered this as the voice of God; "Take heed unto your bishop, and to the presbytery and the deacons,"[167] calling him to witness, for whom he was bound, and for whom he went then unto his last martyrdom, that he had

---

[163] *Reperiemus veteres episcopos non aliam regendae ecclesiae formam voluisse fingere ab ea quam Deus verbo suo praescripsit.* Calvin, *Institutes* 4.4.4 [*CO* 2:790; *Institutes of the Christian Religion*, trans. Ford Lewis Battles, and ed. John T. McNeill, 2 vols (Philadelphia, PA: Westminster Press, 1960), 2:1072].

[164] [Rev. 3:7].

[165] Ἔγνων ὅτι οὐκ ἀφ' ἑαυτοῦ, οὐδὲ δι' ἀνθρώπων, ἠξιώθη τὴν διακονίαν τὴν εἰς τὸ κοινὸν ἀνήκουσαν ἐγχειρισθῆναι. Ignatius, *Ad Philadelphenses* 1 [In these citations Ussher again follows the longer version as found at *PG* 5:820A (cf. 697A); *ANF* 1:79].

[166] Εἷς ἐπίσκοπος, ἅμα τῷ πρεσβυτερίῳ καὶ τοῖς διακόνοις. Ignatius, *Ad Philadelphenses* 4 [*PG* 5:824A (see 700B); *ANF* 1:81].

[167] Οὐκ ἐμὸς ὁ λόγος ἀλλὰ Θεοῦ. Τῷ ἐπισκόπῳ προσέχετε, καὶ τῷ πρεσβυτερίῳ καὶ τοῖς διακόνοις. Ignatius, *Ad Philadelphenses* 7 [*PG* 5:832C–833A (see 701C); *ANF* 1:83].

not this from human flesh, or from the mouth of men, but that the Spirit spoke it: "Without the bishop do nothing."[168] So that from St. John's time, we have this continued succession of witnesses, in the age next following, for episcopacy:

In the year

107. Ignatius, Bishop of Antioch, where first they were called Christians.

130. Hadrian the Emperor, touching the bishops of Egypt.

150. Justin Martyr, from Samaria.

169. The church of Smyrna.

175. Dionysius, Bishop of Corinth.

180. Hegesippus, from Judaea.

Irenaeus, Bishop of Lyons, near unto us.

195. Tertullian, from Africa.

Polycrates, Bishop of Ephesus.

200. Clemens, Presbyter of Alexandria.

---

[168] Μάρτυς μοι, δι' ὃν δέδεμαι, ὅτι ἀπὸ στόματος ἀνθρώπου (al. ἀπὸ σαρκὸς ἀνθρωπίνης) οὐκ ἔγνων· τὸ δὲ πνεῦμα ἐκήρυξε (μοι,) λέγον τάδε· Χωρὶς ἐπισκόπου μηδὲν ποιεῖτε. Ignatius, *Ad Philadelphenses* 7 [PG 5:833A (see 704A); ANF 1:83–84]; cf. Antiochus Monachus, *Pandectes* 124 [PG 89:1820D].

THE REDUCTION OF EPISCOPACY (1657)

The reduction of episcopacy unto the form of synodical government, received in the ancient Church; proposed in the year 1641 as an expedient for the prevention of those troubles, which afterwards did arise about the matter of church government.

To the reader.

The original of this was given me by the most reverend Primate, some few years before his death, wrote throughout with his own hand, and of late I have found it subscribed by himself, and Doctor Holsworth, and with a marginal note at the first proposition, which I have also added.[1] If it may now answer the expectation of many pious, and prudent persons, who have

---

[1] [The text followed here is that found in *The Judgement of the Late Arch-Bishop of Armagh, … Of the Extent of Christs death, and satisfaction, &c.* (ed. Nicholas Bernard; London, 1657; published again in 1658). Bernard had already issued *The Reduction of Episcopacie* as a separate treatise in 1656 on the heels of another edition from earlier the same year. Bernard's 1656 preface assures the reader that his copy of the manuscript was in Ussher's own hand "according to his own last correction." His most serious complaint about the earlier edition is the lack of chronological reference. The reader could be easily misled into thinking that these proposals spoke to the problems of 1656 rather than the crisis of 1641, "as an expedient of the prevention of what fell out afterwards." Amongst other changes he removes the marginal notes pointing out the parallels with the Scottish system of church government from the proposals in line with Ussher's wishes: "these by his orders to me were to be wholly left out, if ever they should be thought fit to be published." This, of course, is an admission that these notes were present in the manuscript copies that were circulating, presumably part of the original. The tract was published again in London (1679, as *Episcopal and Presbyterial Government Conjoyned*), and Edinburgh (1689, 1703, and 1706), and also in Latin with extensive commentary by Johannes Hoornbeek at Utrecht (*De Reductione Episcopatus, ad formam regiminis synodici, in antiqua ecclesia recepti*, 1661). It can be found in *WJU*, 12:527–36.]

desired the publishing of it, as a seasonable preparative to some moderation in the midst of those extremes, which this age abounds with, it will attain the end intended by the author; and it is likely to be more operative, by the great reputation he had, and hath in the hearts of all good men, being far from the least suspicion to be biased by any private ends, but only aiming at the reducing of order, peace, and unity, which God is the author of, and not of confusion.[2] For the recovery of which, it were to be wished, that such as do consent in substantials for matter of doctrine, would consider of some conjunction in point of discipline, that private interests and circumstantials, might not keep them thus far asunder.

N. Bernard

Gray's Inn

Octob. 13th. 1657.

Episcopal and Presbyterial Government Conjoined

BY ORDER of the Church of England, all presbyters are charged "to administer the doctrine and sacraments, and the discipline of Christ, as the Lord hath commanded, and as this realm hath received the same";[3] and that they might the better understand what the "Lord hath commanded" therein, the exhortation of St. Paul to the elders of the church of Ephesus is appointed to be read unto them at the time of their ordination: "Take heed unto your selves, and to all the flock among whom the Holy Ghost hath made you overseers to rule[4] the congregation of God, which he hath purchased with his blood."[5]

Of the many elders, who in common thus ruled the church of Ephesus, there was one president, whom our Saviour in his epistle unto this

---

[2] [1 Cor. 14:33.]

[3] The book of ordination ['The Form of Ordering Priests' (1559), in *Liturgical Services: Liturgies and Occasional Forms of Prayer Set Forth in the Reign of Queen Elizabeth*, ed. William Keatinge Clay (Cambridge: Parker Society, 1847), 290].

[4] ποιμαίνειν so taken in Matt. 2:6 and Rev. 12:5 and 19:15.

[5] Acts 20:28 [See Clay, ed., *Liturgical Services*, 284].

church in a peculiar manner styleth "the angel of the Church of Ephesus";[6] and Ignatius in another epistle, written about twelve years after unto the same church, calleth the bishop thereof. Betwixt the bishop and the presbytery[7] of that church, what an harmonious consent there was in the ordering of the church government, the same Ignatius doth fully there declare,[8] by the presbytery, with St. Paul,[9] understanding the community of the rest of the presbyters, or elders, who then had a hand not only in the delivery of the doctrine, and sacraments, but also in the administration of the discipline of Christ. For further proof of which, we have that known testimony of Tertullian in his general *Apology* for Christians: "In the church are used exhortations, chastisements, and divine censure; for judgment is given with great advice as among those who are certain they are in the sight of God, and it is the chiefest foreshowing of the judgment which is to come, if any man have so offended, that he be banished from the communion of prayer, and of the assembly, and of all holy fellowship. The presidents that bear rule therein are certain approved elders, who have obtained this honour not by reward, but by good report,"[10] who were no other, as he himself intimates elsewhere, but those from whose hands they used to receive the sacrament of the Eucharist.[11]

For with the bishop, who was the chief president (and therefore styled by the same Tertullian in another place, *Summus Sacerdos* ["chief priest"] for distinction's sake),[12] the rest of the dispensers of the word and

---

[6] Rev. 2:1.

[7] [Elrington gives as "presbyter," in *WJU*, 12:532.]

[8] [Ignatius, *Ad Ephesios* 4; *PG* 5:648A–B; *ANF* 1:50–51.]

[9] 1 Tim. 4:14.

[10] *Ibidem etiam exhortationes, castigationes et censura divina; nam et judicatur magno cum pondere, ut apud certos de Dei conspectu, summumque futuri judicii praejudicium est, si quis ita deliquerit, ut a communicatione orationis, et conventus, et omnis sancti commercii relegetur; praesident probati quique seniores, honorem istum non pretio, sed testimonio adepti.* Tertullian, *Apologeticus Adversus Gentes Pro Christianis* 39 [*PL* 1:469A–70A {532A–533A}; *ANF* 3:46].

[11] *Nec de aliorum manibus quam praesidentium sumimus* ["We receive [the sacrament of the Eucharist] from the hands of none but the presidents"]. Idem, *De Corona Militis* 3 [*PL* 2:79A–B {99A}; *ANF* 3:94; *manu* in original].

[12] *Dandi quidem baptismi habet jus summus sacerdos, qui est episcopus, dehinc presbyteri et diaconi* ["The chief priest, who is the bishop, has, of course, the right of conferring baptism, then the presbyters and deacons"]. Idem, *De Baptismo*, 17 [*CCSL* 1:291; *ANF* 3:677].

sacraments joined in the common government of the church; and therefore, where in matters of ecclesiastical judicature, Cornelius bishop of Rome used the received form of "gathering together the presbytery,"[13] of what persons that did consist, Cyprian sufficiently declareth, when he wisheth him to read his letters "to the flourishing clergy, which there did preside," or rule, "with him";[14] the presence of the clergy being thought to be so requisite in matters of episcopal audience, that in the fourth council of Carthage it was concluded, "That the bishop might hear no man's cause without the presence of the clergy: and that otherwise the bishop's sentence should be void, unless it were confirmed by the presence of the clergy";[15] which we find also to be inserted into the canons of Egbert, who was Archbishop of York in the Saxon times,[16] and afterwards into the body of the canon law itself.[17]

True it is, that in our church this kind of presbyterial government hath been long disused, yet seeing it still professeth that every pastor hath a right to rule the church (from whence the name of rector[18] also was given at first unto him) and to administer the discipline of Christ, as well as to dispense the doctrine and sacraments, and the restraint of the exercise of that right proceedeth only from the custom now received in this realm, no man can doubt, but by another law of the land, this hindrance may be well removed. And how easily this ancient form of government by the united suffrages of the clergy might be revived again, and with what little show of alteration the synodical conventions of the pastors of every parish might be accorded with the presidency of the bishops of each diocese and province,

---

[13] *Omni actu ad me perlato placuit contrahi presbyterium* ["The news being brought before me of all these proceedings, I decided to gather together the presbytery"]. Cornelius to Cyprian, in Cyprian, *Epistolae* 46.2 [*PL* 4:341B {351A}; See 3:719B–720A {742A}; *ANF* 5:323, where numbered 45.2].

[14] *Florentissimo illic clero tecum praesidenti*. Cyprian to Cornelius, in Cyprian, *Epistolae* 55.20 [*PL* 4:348B–C {358B–C}; See 3:828A {854A}; *ANF* 5:346, where numbered 54.20].

[15] *Ut episcopus nullius causam audiat absque praesentia clericorum suorum, alioquin irrita erit sententia episcopi nisi clericorum praesentia confirmetur.* Fourth Council of Carthage, 23 [e.g. *PL* 84:202B].

[16] Egbertus Eboracensis, *Excerptiones* 45 [*PL* 89:385C].

[17] Gratian, *Decreti Pars Secunda* 15, q. 7 [*PL* 187:987A].

[18] [Rector (a guider, leader, director, ruler, master), from *rego* (to keep straight or from going wrong, to lead straight; to guide, conduct, direct). *A Latin Dictionary*, ed. Charlton T. Lewis and Charles Short (Oxford: Clarendon Press, 1879), s.v. rector, rego.]

the indifferent reader may quickly perceive by the perusal of the ensuing propositions.

I

In every parish,[19] the rector, or incumbent pastor, together with the church-wardens and sidesmen, may every week take notice of such as live scandal-ously in that congregation, who are to receive such several admonitions and reproofs, as the quality of their offence shall deserve; and if by this means they cannot be reclaimed, they may be presented to the next monthly syn-od, and in the mean time debarred by the pastor from access unto the Lord's table.

II

Whereas by a statute in the six-and-twentieth year of King Henry the eighth, revived in the first year of Queen Elizabeth, suffragans are appoint-ed to be erected in 26 several places of this kingdom,[20] the number of them might very well be conformed unto the number of the several rural deaner-ies, into which every diocese is subdivided; which being done, the suffragan supplying the place of those, who in the ancient church were called *chore-piscopi*,[21] might every month assemble a synod of all the rectors,[22] or incum-bent pastors within the precinct, and according to the major part of their voices, conclude all matters that shall be brought into debate before them.

To this synod the rector and church-wardens might present such im-penitent persons, as by admonitions and suspension from the sacrament would not be reformed; who if they should still remain contumacious and

---

[19] How the Church might synodically be governed, archbishops and bishops being still retained. [Bernard's marginal note. But in the first edition of 1656 one finds instead the first of a series of notes setting forth parallels between Ussher's scheme and the presbyterian government of the Scottish church: "The parochial govern-ment answerable to the church session in Scotland."]

[20] [*The Statutes: Revised Edition*, Vol. 1. Henry III to James II, A.D. 1235/6–1685 (London: Eyre and Spottiswoode, 1870), 447–49, 578.]

[21] [Once numerous, these were bishops of country districts, in full episcopal orders but with limited powers and acting under their diocesans. ODCC, s.v. chorepisco-pus.]

[22] [Margin of first 1656 edition: "The presbyterial monthly synods answer to the Scottish presbyteries or ecclesiastical meetings."]

incorrigible, the sentence of excommunication might be decreed against them by the synod, and accordingly be executed in the parish where they lived. Hitherto also all things that concerned the parochial ministers might be referred, whether they did touch their doctrine, or their conversation, as also the censure of all new opinions, heresies, and schisms, which did arise within that circuit, with liberty of appeal, if need so require, unto the diocesan synod.

III

The diocesan synod[23] might be held once or twice in the year, as it should be thought most convenient. Therein all the suffragans, and the rest of the rectors, or incumbent pastors, or a certain select number of every deanery within the diocese, might meet, with whose consent, or the major part of them, all things might be concluded by the bishop, or superintendent[24] (call him whether you will), or in his absence, by one of the suffragans, whom he shall depute in his stead to be moderator of that assembly.

Here all matters of greater moment might be taken into consideration, and the orders of the monthly synods revised, and, if need be, reformed; and if here also any matter of difficulty could not receive a full determination, it might be referred to the next provincial, or national synod.

IV

The provincial synod[25] might consist of all the bishops and suffragans, and such other of the clergy as should be elected out of every diocese within the province. The archbishop of either province might be the moderator of this meeting, or in his room some one of the bishops appointed by him, and all matters be ordered therein by common consent as in the former assemblies.

---

[23] [Margin of first 1656 edition: "Diocesan synods answerable to the provincial synods in Scotland."]

[24] Ἐπισκοποῦντες, *id est, superintendentes; unde et nomen episcopi tractum est* ["Επισκοποῦντες, that is, overseeing, and from which the name overseer [or bishop, ἐπίσκοπος] is derived"]. Jerome, *Epist. ad Evagrium* [the recipient has more recently been identified as Evangelus; *PL* 22:1193; *NPNF2* 6:288].

[25] [Margin of first 1656 edition: "The provincial and national synod answerable to the General Assembly in Scotland."]

This synod might be held every third year, and if the parliament do then sit, according to the act of a triennial parliament, both the archbishops and provincial synods of the land might join together, and make up a national council, wherein all appeals from inferior synods might be received, all their acts examined and all ecclesiastical constitutions which concern the state of the church of the whole nation established.

We are of the judgment that the form of government here proposed is not in any point repugnant to the Scripture, and that the suffragans mentioned in the second proposition may lawfully use the power both of jurisdiction and ordination, according to the word of God, and the practice of the ancient Church.

Ja. Armachanus.
Rich. Holdsworth.[26]

[Bernard:] After the proposal of this, An. 1641, many queries were made, and doubts in point of conscience resolved by the Primate, diverse passages of which he hath left under his own hand, showing his pious endeavours to peace and unity, which how far it then prevailed is out of season now to relate; only I wish it might yet be thought of, to the repairing of the breach, which this division hath made, and that those, who are by their office messengers of peace, and whose first word to each house should be peace,[27] would earnestly promote it, within the walls of their mother church, wherein they were educated, and not thus by contending about circumstantials[28] lose the substance, and make our selves a prey to the adversary of both, who rejoice in their hearts, saying, "so would we have it."[29]

---

[26] [Richard Holdsworth (1590–1649), Master of Emmanuel College, Cambridge from 1637 to 1643. Later Lady Margaret Professor of Divinity and Vice-Chancellor, and a member of the Westminster Assembly.]

[27] [Luke 10:5.]

[28] [Matters incidental, not essential.]

[29] [Ps. 35:25, the words of those who delight in David's distress.]

BIBLIOGRAPHY

MANUSCRIPTS

Balliol College, Oxford

MS 259 — Ussher sermons, 1620s

Bodleian Library, Oxford

MS Add. C299 — Ussher papers

MS Barlow 13 — Ussher papers

MS Barocci 182 — *Chronographia* of John Malalas

MS e Mus. 86 — Historical papers

MS Eng.th.e.25 — Ussher sermons, 1626

MS Perrot 9 — Sermon at the Temple Church

MS Rawlinson D1290 — Ussher notes and sermon outlines

MS Tanner 74 — Correspondence

Cambridge University Library, Cambridge

MS Add. 69 — Ussher sermon, 1624

MS Dd.v.31 — Ussher sermon, 1626

MS Mm.6.55 — Ussher sermons, 1641–42, 1647–52

Essex Record Office, Chelmsford

D/Dba F5/1   Sermons by Ussher and John Preston, 1625

Northamptonshire Record Office, Northampton

Finch Hatton MS 247   Ussher sermon, 1626

Trinity College, Dublin

MS 2940   Ambrose Ussher's translation of *De Successione*

WORKS BY JAMES USSHER

Ussher, James. *Gravissimae Quaestionis, de Christianarum Ecclesiarum, in Occidentis praesertim partibus, Ab Apostolicis Temporibus ad nostram usq[ue] aetatem, continuâ successione & statu, Historica Explicatio.* 1613.

———— *The Substance of That VVhich Was Delivered in a Sermon before the Commons House of Parliament, in St. Margarets Church at Westminster, the 18. of February, 1620.* 1621.

———— *An Epistle VVritten By The Reverend Father in God, James Ussher Bishop of Meath, concerning the religion anciently professed by the Irish and Scottish; Shewing it to be for substance the same with that which is at this day by publick authoritie established in the Church of England,* in Christopher Sibthorpe, *A Friendly Advertisement to the pretended Catholickes of Ireland: Declaring, for their satisfaction; That both the Kings Supremacie, and the Faith whereof his Majestie is the Defender, are consonant to the doctrine delivered in the holy Scriptures, and writings of the ancient Fathers. And Consequently, That the Lawes and Statutes enacted in that behalfe, are dutifully to be observed by all his Majesties subjects within that Kingdome.* Dublin, 1622.

———— *A Sermon Preached before the Commo[n]s-House of Parliament, in Saint Margarets Church at Westminster, the 18. of February. 1620.* 1624.

———— *An Answer to a Challenge Made by a Iesuite in Ireland. Wherein the Iudgement of Antiquity in the Points Questioned is Truely Delivered, and the Noveltie of the Now Romish Doctrine Plainly Discovered.* Dublin, 1624.

———— *A Briefe Declaration of the Universalitie of the Church of Christ, and the Unitie of the Catholike Faith professed therein: Delivered in a Sermon before His Majestie the 20th of Iune, 1624. at Wansted.* 1624.

———— *A Briefe Declaration of the Universalitie of the Church of Christ, and the Unitie of the Catholike Faith professed therein: Delivered in a Sermon before His Majestie the 20th of Iune, 1624. at Wansted,* second impression, appended to *An Answer to a Challenge Made by a Iesuite in Ireland.* 1625.

———— *A Briefe Declaration of the Universalitie of the Church of Christ, and the Unitie of the Catholike Faith professed therein: Delivered in a Sermon before His Majestie the 20th of Iune, 1624. at Wansted,* third impression, 'corrected and amended'. 1629.

———— *The Workes of the Most Reverend Father in God, Iames Ussher, Archbishop of Armagh, and Primate of Ireland. Containing, I. An Answer to a Challenge made by a Iesuite in Ireland: wherein the iudgement of Antiquity in the points questioned is delivered, and the Novelty of the now Romish Doctrine is plainly discovered. II. A Sermon preached before the Commons house of Parliament, Febr. 18. 1620. III. A briefe Declaration of the Universality of the Church of Christ, in a Sermon before his Maiestie, Anno 1624. IV. A Discourse of the Religion anciently professed by the Irish and Brittish. V. A Speech delivered in the Castle-Chamber at Dublin, concerning the Oath of Supremacie. All newly revised and published with priviledge.* 1631.

———— *Gotteschalci, et praedestinatianae controversiae ab eo motae, historia.* Dublin, 1631.

———— *Britannicarum Ecclesiarum Antiquitates quibus inserta est pestiferae adversùs Dei gratiam à Pelagio Britanno in Ecclesiam inductae Haereseos Historia.* Dublin, 1639.

———— *The Original of Bishops and Metropolitans,* in *Certain Briefe Treatises Written by Diverse Learned Men, Concerning the Ancient and Moderne Government of the Church.* Oxford, 1641.

———— *A Geographicall and Historicall Disquisition, touching the Lydian or Procon-sular Asia; and the seven Metropolitical Churches contained therein,* in *Certain Briefe Treatises Written by Diverse Learned Men, Concerning the Ancient and Moderne Government of the Church.* Oxford, 1641.

———— *The Iudgement of Doctor Rainoldes Touching the Originall of Episcopacy.* 1641.

———— *A Geographicall and Historicall Disquisition, touching the Asia properly so called, the Lydian Asia … the Proconsular Asia and the Asian Diocese.* Oxford, 1643.

———— *The Originall of Bishops and Metropolitans,* in *Confessions and Proofes of Protestant Divines of Reformed Churches, that Episcopacy is in respect of the Office according to the Word of God, and in respect of the Use the Best.* Oxford, 1644.

———— *Polycarpi et Ignatii Epistolae.* Oxford, 1644.

———— *A Body of Divinitie, or The Summe and Substance of Christian Religion, Catechistically propounded, and explained, by way of Question and Answer: Methodically and familiarly handled. Composed long since by James Usher B. Of Armagh, And at the earnest desires of divers godly Christians now Printed and Published; VVhereunto is adjoyned a Tract, intituled Immanuel, or The Mystery of the Incarnation of the Son of God Heretofore written and published by the Same Authour.* Edited by John Downame. 1645.

———— *Annales Veteris Testamenti, a prima mundi origine deducti: una cum rerum Asiaticarum et Aegyptiacarum chronico, a temporis historici principio usque ad Maccabaicorum initia producto.* 1650.

———— *Jacobi Usserii armachani Annalium pars posterior: in qua, praeter Maccabaicam et Novi Testamenti historiam imperii Romanourm caesarum sub C. Julio & Octaviano ortus, rerúmque in Asiâ & Ægypto gestarum continetur chronicon : ab Antiochi Epiphanis regni exordio, usque ad Imperii Vespasiani inita atque extremum templi & reipublicae Judaicae deductum.* 1654.

———— *The Reduction of Episcopacie unto the Form of Synodical Government Received in the Antient Church: Proposed as an Expedient for the compremising of the now Differences, and preventing of those Troubles that may arise about the matter of Church-Government.* London: T.N. for G.B. and T.C., 1656.

——— *The Reduction of Episcopacie unto the Form of Synodical Government Received in the Ancient Church: Proposed in the year 1641. as an Expedient for the prevention of those Troubles, which afterwards did arise about the matter of Church-Government … A true Copy set forth by Nicholas Bernard, D.D. Preacher to the Honourable Society of Grayes Inne occasioned by an imperfect Copy lately printed.* London: E.C. for R. Royston at the Angel in Ivie-lane, 1656.

——— *The Judgement of the Late Arch-Bishop of Armagh, and Primate of Ireland, 1. Of the Extent of Christs death, and satisfaction, &c. 2. Of the Sabbath, and observation of the Lords day. 3. Of the Ordination in other reformed Churches. With a Vindication of him from a pretended change of Opinion in the first; Some Advertisements upon the latter; And, in prevention of further injuries, A Declaration of his judgement in several other subjects.* Edited by Nicholas Bernard. 1657.

——— *The Judgement of the Late Arch-Bishop of Armagh and Primate of Ireland, 1. Of the extent of Christs death and satisfaction, &c. 2. Of the Sabbath, and observation of the Lords day. 3. Of the ordination in other reformed churches.* Edited by Nicholas Bernard. 1658.

——— *The Judgement of the late Arch-Bishop of Armagh, and Primate of Ireland. Of Babylon (Rev. 18. 4.) being the present See of Rome. (With a Sermon of Bishop Bedels upon the same words.) Of laying on of hands (Heb. 6. 2.) to be an ordained Ministery. Of the old Form of words in Ordination. Of a Set Form of Prayer.* Edited by Nicholas Bernard. 1659.

——— *De Reductione Episcopatus, ad formam regiminis synodici, in antiqua ecclesia recepti.* Edited by Johannes Hoornbeek. Utrecht, 1661.

——— *The Originall of Bishops and Metropolitans,* in *Confessions and Proofes of Protestant Divines of Reformed Churches, that Episcopacy is in respect of the Office according to the Word of God, and in respect of the Use the Best.* [London?], 1662.

——— *Episcopal and Presbyterial Government Conjoyned. Proposed as an Expedient for the compremising of the Differences, and preventing of those about the matter of Church-Government.* 1679.

——— *A Sermon Preached before the Commons House of Parliament in Saint Margarets Church at Westminster, the 18 of February 1620.* 1681.

———— *A Brief Declaration of the Universality of the Church of Christ; and the Unitie of the Catholick Faith professed therein. Delivered in a Sermon before the King's Majesty the 20th. of Iune, 1624.* at Wansted, appended to *An Answer to a Challenge Made by a Iesuite in Ireland.* Fourth impression. 1687.

———— *Britannicarum Ecclesiarum Antiquitates quibus inserta est Pestiferae adversùs Dei Gratiam à Pelagio Britanno in Ecclesiam inductae Haereseos Historia. Accedit Gravissimae Quaestionis de Christianarum Ecclesiarum Successione & Statu Historica Explicatio.* 1687.

———— *Jacobi Usserii Archiepiscopi Armachani, Opuscula Duo.* 1687.

———— *Jacobi Usserii Archiepiscopi Armachani, Opuscula Duo.* 1688.

———— *The Reduction of Episcopacy unto the Form of Synodical Government, Received in the Ancient Church, proposed in the Year 1641. as an Expedient for the Prevention of those Troubles, which afterwards did arise about the matter of Church Government.* Edinburgh, 1689.

———— *The Reduction of Episcopacy unto the form of Synodical Government, Received in the antient Church, proposed in the Year 1641. as an Expedient for the prevention of those Troubles, which afterwards did arise about the matter of Church Government ... Proposed now again, Anno 1703. for removing the Differences in the Church of Scotland, By the Author of the Essay for promoving National Love and Unity. This may be altered according to the different circumstances of the National Church of Scotland.* Edinburgh, 1703.

———— *The Reduction of Episcopacy unto the form of Synodical-Government, Received in the Ancient Church, proposed in the Year 1641. As an Expedient for the Prevention of those Troubles, which afterwards did arise about the Matter of Church-Government ... Proposed now again, Anno 1706; for removing the Differences in the Church of Scotland, By the Author of the Essay for promoving National Love and Unity. This may be altered according to the different Circumstances of the National Church of Scotland.* Edinburgh, 1706.

———— *The Whole Works of the Most Rev. James Ussher, D.D., Lord Archbishop of Armagh, and Primate of All Ireland.* Edited by Charles R. Elrington and J. H. Todd. 17 vols. Dublin: Hodges and Smith, 1829–64.

——— *The Annals of the World: James Ussher's Classic Survey of World History*. Edited by Larry Pierce and Marion Pierce. Green Forest: Master Books, 2003.

——— *The Puritan Pulpit: James Ussher, 1581–1656*. Orlando: Soli Deo Gloria Publications, 2006.

——— *A Body of Divinity*. Birmingham, AL: Solid Ground Christian Books, 2007.

——— *The Correspondence of James Ussher, 1600–1656*. Edited by Elizabethanne Boran. 3 vols. Dublin: Irish Manuscripts Commission, 2015.

OTHER PRIMARY SOURCES

Acta Sanctorum Junii ... Tomus V. Antwerp, 1709.

Ancient Christian Writers: The Works of the Fathers in Translation. 63 vols. Mahwah, NJ: Paulist Press, 1946–.

Biblia: The Byble, that is, the Holy Scrypture of the Olde and New Testament, faithfully translated in to Englyshe. "Coverdale Bible", 1535.

The Byble, which is all the holy Scripture: In whych are contayned the Olde and Newe Testament truly and purely translated into Englysh by Thomas Matthew. "Matthew Bible", 1537.

Codicis Theodosiani libri XVI. Paris and Geneva, 1586.

Corpus Christianorum, Series Latina. 212 vols. Turnhout: Brepols, 1953–.

The Fathers of the Church (Patristic Series). 138 vols. Washington, DC: Catholic University of America Press, 1947–.

Historiae Plurimorum Sanctorum. Louvain, 1485.

The Holy Bible, Conteyning the Old Testament, and the New: Newly Translated out of the Originall tongues: & with the former Translations diligently compared and revised, by his Maiesties speciall Comandement. "King James Version", 1611.

Index Librorum Prohibitorum Alexandri VII Pontificis Maximi: Iussu editus. Rome, 1664.

Journal of the House of Commons: Volume 1, 1547–1629. London, 1802.

Journal of the House of Commons: Volume 2, 1640–1643. London, 1802.

Journal of the House of Commons: Volume 5, 1646–1648. London, 1802.

Journal of the House of Lords: Volume IV, 1629–42. London, 1771.

The Kings Majesties Answer to the Paper Delivered in by the Reverend Divines. 1648.

Loeb Classical Library. 534 vols. Cambridge, MA: Harvard University Press, 1911–.

Pontificale Romanum Clementis VIII Pont. Max. Iussu restitutum atque editum. Rome, 1595.

A Proclamation for the Establishing of the Peace and Quiet of the Church of England. 1626.

Report on the Manuscripts of the Right Honourable Viscount De L'Isle & Dudley. 6 vols. London: Historical Manuscripts Commission, 1925–66.

The Statutes: Revised Edition, Vol. 1. Henry III to James II, A.D. 1235/6–1685. London: Eyre and Spottiswoode, 1870.

Aretius, Benedictus. *Commentarii in Apocalypsin D. Joannis Apostoli*. Morges, 1581.

Augustinus Triumphus [Augustine of Ancona]. *Summa de Potestate Ecclesiastica*. Rome, 1584.

Azor, Juan. *Institutiones Morales*. 3 vols. Cologne, 1613–18.

Bacon, Francis. *The Essayes or Counsels, Civill and Morall*. Edited by M. Kiernan. Oxford: Clarendon Press, 1985.

Baillie, Robert. *The Letters and Journals of Robert Baillie*. Edited by David Laing. 3 vols. Edinburgh: Bannatyne Club, 1841–43.

Báñez, Domingo. *De Fide, Spe & Charitate ... Commentaria in Secundam Secundae Angelici Doctoris*. Salamanca, 1584.

Baronius, Caesar. *Annales Ecclesiastici*. 12 vols. Rome, 1588–1607.

——— *Martyrologium Romanum*. Cologne, 1603.

Barrough, Philip. *The Method of Physick*. 6th ed. London: Richard Field, 1624.

Bede. *The Ecclesiastical History of the English People*. Edited by Judith McClure and Roger Collins. Oxford: Oxford University Press, 1994.

Bellarmine, Robert. *Opera Omnia*. 6 vols. Naples: Giuliano, 1856–62.

——— *De Controversiis: On the Roman Pontiff*. Translated by Ryan Grant. Mediatrix Press, 2016.

——— *De Notis Ecclesiae: On the Marks of the Church*. Translated by Ryan Grant. Mediatrix Press, 2015.

Bernard, Nicholas. *The Life & Death of the Most Reverend and Learned Father of our Church Dr. James Usher, Late Arch-Bishop of Armagh, and Primate of all Ireland. Published in a Sermon at His Funeral at the Abby of Westminster, Aprill 17. 1656. And now re-viewed with some other Enlargements*. London: E. Tyler, 1656.

——— *Clavi Trabales; Or, Nailes Fastned by some Great Masters of Assemblyes. Confirming the Kings Supremacy. The Subjects Duty. Church Government by Bishops. The Particulars of which are as followeth I. Two Speeches of the late Lord Primate Ushers. The one of the Kings Supremacy, the other of the Duty of Subjects to supply the Kings Necessities. II. His Judgment and Practice in Point of Loyalty, Episcopacy, Liturgy and Constitutions of the Church of England, III. Mr. Hookers Judgment of the Kings Power in matters of Religion, advancement of Bishops &c. IV. Bishop Andrews of Church-Government &c. both confirmed and enlarged by the said Primate. V. A Letter of Dr Hadrianus Saravia of the like Subjects. Unto which is added a Sermon of Regal Povver, and the Novelty of the Doctrine of Resistance, Also a Preface by the Right Reverend Father in God, the Lord Bishop of Lincolne*. London: R. Hodgkinson, 1661.

Beza, Theodore. *Ad Tractationem de Ministrorum Evangelii Gradibus, ab Hadriano Saravia Belga editam. Theodori Bezae Responsio*. Geneva, 1592.

——— *Annotationes Maiores in Novum DN. Nostri Iesu Christi Testamentum*. 2 vols. [Geneva], 1594.

Binius, Severin. *Concilia Generalia, et Provincialia*. 4 vols. Cologne, 1606.

Brightman, Thomas. *Apocalypsis Apocalypseos*. Frankfurt, 1609.

——— *A Revelation of the Apocalyps*. Amsterdam, 1611.

——— *A Revelation of the Revelation*. Amsterdam, 1615.

Bristow, Richard. *A Briefe Treatise of Diverse Plaine and Sure Wayes to find out the Truthe in this Doubtful and Dangerous Time of Heresie.* Antwerp, 1574.

Bucer, Martin. *Scripta Anglicana.* Basle, 1577.

Calvin, John. *Commentaries on the Epistles to Timothy, Titus, and Philemon.* Translated by William Pringle. Edinburgh: Calvin Translation Society, 1856.

———— *Ioannis Calvini Opera Quae Supersunt Omnia.* Edited by G. Baum, E. Cunitz and E. Reuss. 59 vols. Brunswick and Berlin: C. A. Schwetschke, 1863–1900.

———— *Institutes of the Christian Religion.* Translated by Ford Lewis Battles, and edited by John T. McNeill. 2 vols. Philadelphia: Westminster Press, 1960.

Cano, Melchior. *De Locis Theologicis libri duodecim.* Louvain, 1564.

Carolus a Sancto Paulo. *Geographia Sacra.* Paris, 1641.

Chamberlain, John. *The Letters of John Chamberlain.* Edited by Norman E. McClure. 2 vols. Philadelphia: The American Philosophical Society, 1939.

Clay, William Keatinge, ed. *Liturgies and Occasional Forms of Prayer Set Forth in the Reign of Queen Elizabeth.* Cambridge: Parker Society, 1847.

Coke, Edward. *Quinta Pars Relationum Edwardi Coke Equitis Aurati, Regii Atturnati Generalis.* London: [Adam Islip], 1607.

Coster, Francis. *Enchiridion Controversiarum Praecipuarum Nostri Temporis de Religione.* Cologne, 1608.

d'Ailly, Pierre. *Quaestio Vesperiarum,* in *Quaestiones super I, III et IV libros Sententiarum. Recommendati o Sacrae Scripturae. Principium in cursum Bibliae, praesertim in Evangelium Marci. Quaestio insuis vesperis. Quaestio de resumpta. Recommendatio doctrinae evangelicae.* Strasbourg, 1490.

del Alcázar, Luis. *Vestigatio Arcani Sensus in Apocalypsi.* Antwerp, 1619.

de Serres, Jean [Serranus]. *De Fide Catholica, sive Principiis Religionis Christianae.* Paris, 1607.

Evelyn, John. *Diary and Correspondence of John Evelyn.* Edited by William Bray. 4 vols. London, 1859–62.

Fisher, John. *Opusculum de Fiducia & Misericordia Dei*. Cologne, 1556.

Fitzherbert, Thomas. *Apology of T.F. in Defence of Himself and Other Catholics, falsly charged with a fayned conspiracy against her Majesties person, for the which one Edward Squyre was wrongfully condemned and executed in the yeare of our Lorde 1598*, appended to *A Defence of the Catholyck Cause*. Antwerp, 1602.

Gardiner, S. R., ed. *Letters and Other Documents Illustrating the Relations Between England and Germany at the Commencement of the Thirty Years' War: Second Series*. London: Camden Society, 1868.

——— *Constitutional Documents of the Puritan Revolution, 1625–1660*. 3rd ed. Oxford: Clarendon Press, 1906.

Ghislieri, Michele. *Michaelis Ghislerii... in Ieremiam Prophetam Commentariorum*. 3 vols. Lyon, 1623.

Gregory of Valencia. *De Idololatria Contra Sectariorum Contumelias Disputatio; una cum Apologetico adversus Iacobum Heerbrandum Lutheranum*. Ingolstadt, 1580.

——— *Commentariorum Theologicorum*. 4 vols. Lyon, 1609.

Griffiths, John, ed. *The Two Books of Homilies Appointed to Be Read in Churches*. Oxford: Oxford University Press, 1859.

H[acket], R[oger]. *A Sermon Needful for These Times*. Oxford, 1591.

Halloix, Pierre. 'Notationes ad Vitam S. Polycarpi', in *Illustrium Ecclesiae Orientalis Scriptorum*. Douai, 1633.

Henderson, Alexander. *The Unlawfulness and Danger of Limited Prelacie, or Perpetual Precidencie in the Church, Briefly Discovered*. S.l. [London?], 1641.

Hoyle, Joshua. *A Reioynder to Master Malone's Reply Concerning Reall Presence*. Dublin, 1641.

Hozjusz, Stanisław [Hosius]. *Confessio Catholicae Fidei Christiana: vel potius explicatio quaedam confessionis a patribus factae in synodo provinciali, quae habita est Petrikoviae*. Mainz, 1557.

Jewel, John. *The Works of John Jewel, D.D.* Edited by Richard William Jelf. 8 vols. Oxford: Oxford University Press, 1848.

John Malalas. *The Chronicle of John Malalas*. Translated by Elizabeth Jeffreys, Michael Jeffreys, and Roger Scott. Melbourne: Australian Association for Byzantine Studies, 1986.

Juan de Mariana. *De Rege et Regis Institutione*. Hanau, 1611.

Lapide, Cornelius à. *Commentaria in Quatuor Prophetas Maiores*. Paris, 1622.

Leunclavius, Johannes, ed. *Iuris Graeco-Romani*. 2 vols. Frankfurt, 1596.

Lipsius, Justus. *Diva Virgo Hallensis: beneficia eius et miracula fide atque ordine descripta*. Antwerp, 1604.

Mansi, Giovanni Domenico. *Sacrorum Conciliorum Nova et Amplissima Collectio*. Reprinted edition. 53 vols in 60. Paris: Welter, 1901–27.

Mazzolini, Silvestro [Prierias]. *Sylvestrinae Summae, Quae Summa Summarum Merito Nuncupatur*. 2 vols. Lyon, 1553.

Migne, J.-P., ed. *Patrologia Latina*. 221 vols. Paris, 1844–64.

———— ed. *Patrologia Graeca*. 161 vols. Paris, 1857–66.

Monceaux, Franciscus (Moncaeus). *Aaron Purgatus, sive De Vitulo Aureo*. Arras, 1606.

Napier, John. *A Plaine Discovery of the Whole Revelation of S. John*. 1611.

Numan, Philippe. *Miracles Lately VVrought by the Intercession of the Glorious Virgin Marie, at Mont-aigu, nere unto Siché in Brabant*. Antwerp, 1606.

Ortelius, Abraham. *Parergon, sive Veteris Geographiae Aliquot Tabulae*. Antwerp, 1601.

Pacenius, Bartholus. Ἐξετασις, *Epistola Nomine Regis Magnae Britanniae, Ad Omnes Christianos Monarchos, Principes, & Ordines, scriptae: quae, praefationis monitoriae loco, ipsius Apologiae pro iuramento fidelitatis, praefixa est*. Mons [Mainz?], 1609.

Paraeus, David. *In Divinam Apocalypsin S. Apostoli et Evangelistae Johannis Commentarius*. Heidelberg, 1618.

Parr, Richard. *The Life of the Most Reverend Father in God, James Usher, Late Lord Arch-Bishop of Armagh, Primate and Metropolitan of all Ireland. With a Collection of Three Hundred Letters between the said Lord Primate and most of the Eminentest Persons for Piety and Learning in his time*. 1686.

Pereira, Benedict. *Tertius Tomus Selectarum Disputationum in Sacram Scripturam, ... super libro Apocalypsis B. Ioannis Apostoli.* Lyon, 1606.

Person, David. *Varieties: Or, A Surveigh of Rare and Excellent Matters.* 1635.

Peter Lombard. *The Sentences: Book 4: On the Doctrine of Signs.* Translated by Giulio Silano. 4th ed. Toronto: Pontifical Institute of Mediaeval Studies, 2010.

Postel, Guillaume. *De nativitate mediatoris ultima, nunc futura, et toti orbi terrarum in singulis ratione praeditis manifestanda.* Basel, 1547.

Price, Richard, and Michael Gaddis, eds. *The Acts of the Council of Chalcedon.* 3 vols. Liverpool: Liverpool University Press, 2005.

Ptolemy, *Geographia Cl. Ptolemaei Alexandrini.* Venice, 1562.

Pusey, E. B., et al, eds. *A Library of Fathers of the Holy Catholic Church.* 51 vols. London: G. & F. Rivington, and Oxford: John Henry Parker, 1838–85.

Rainolds, John. *The Summe of the Conference between Iohn Rainoldes and Iohn Hart touching the Head and the Faith of the Church.* London, 1584.

Ribera, Francisco. *In Sacram b. Iohannis Apostoli & Euangelistae Apocalypsin Commentarii.* Salamanca, 1591.

Richter, Aemilius Ludovicus, ed. *Corpus Iuris Canonici.* Revised by Aemilius Friedberg. 2 vols. Leipzig: Tauchnitz, 1879–81.

Roberts, Alexander, and James Donaldson, eds. *The Ante-Nicene Fathers.* 9 vols. Buffalo and New York: Christian Literature Company, 1885–96.

Sanders, Nicholas. *The Supper of Our Lord, Set Foorth According to the Truth of the Gospell and the Catholicke Faith.* Louvain, 1566.

Schaff, Philip, ed. *The Creeds of Christendom: With a History and Critical Notes.* 6th ed. 3 vols. New York: Harper, 1931; repr. Grand Rapids, MI: Baker, 1998.

———, ed. *A Select Library of the Nicene and Post-Nicene Fathers of the Christian Church.* 14 vols. Buffalo and New York: Christian Literature Company, 1886–90.

———— and Henry Wace, eds. *A Select Library of the Nicene and Post-Nicene Fathers of the Christian Church, Second Series.* 14 vols. Buffalo and New York: Christian Literature Company, 1890–1900.

Schwartz, E., and J. Straub, eds. *Acta Conciliorum Oecumenicorum.* 4 tomes in 15 vols. Berlin: de Gruyter, 1914–.

Searle, Arthur, ed. *Barrington Family Letters, 1628–1632.* Camden Society. 4th series, 28. London: Royal Historical Society, 1983.

Shakespeare, William. *King Henry IV, Part 1.* Edited by David Scott Kastan. Arden Shakespeare: 3rd series. London: Thomson, 2002.

Shirley, Walter W., ed. *Fasciculi Zizaniorum Magistri Johannis Wyclif cum tritico.* Rolls Series. London: Longman, Brown, Green, Longmans, and Roberts, 1858.

Sirmond, Jacques. *Concilia Antiqua Galliae.* 3 vols. Paris, 1629.

Smith, Thomas. *V[iri] Cl[arissimi] Guilielmi Camdeni et Illustrium Virorum ad G. Camdenum Epistolae.* London, 1691.

Sodi, Manlio, and Achille Maria Triacca, eds. *Pontificale Romanum: Editio Princeps (1595–1596).* Vatican: Libreria Editrice Vaticana, 1997.

Stapleton, Thomas. *Principiorum Fidei Doctrinalium Demonstratio Methodica.* Paris, 1582.

Suárez, Francisco. *Commentariorum ac Disputationum in Tertiam Partem Divi Thomae.* 5 vols. Venice, 1604–1606.

———— *Defensio Fidei Catholicae et Apostolicae adversus Anglicanae Sectae Errores.* Cologne, 1614.

Tanner, Norman P., ed. *Decrees of the Ecumenical Councils.* 2 vols. London: Sheed and Ward, 1990.

Theodoret. *Theodoret of Cyrus: Commentaries on the Letters of St. Paul.* Edited by Robert C. Hill. 2 vols. Brookline, MA: Holy Cross Orthodox Press, 2001.

Thomas Aquinas. *Summa Theologiae.* Edited by Thomas Gilby, Blackfriars edition. 61 vols. London: Eyre & Spottiswoode, 1964–81.

Topsell, Edward. *Times Lamentation.* London, 1599.

Ulenbergius, Casparus. *Graves et iustae causae, cur Catholicis in communione veteris, eiusque veri Christianismi, constanter usque ad vitae finem permanendum sit; cur item omnibus iis, qui se vocant Evangelicos, relictis erroribus, ad eiusdem Christianismi consortium, vel postliminio sit redeundum.* Cologne, 1589.

van Prinsterer, G. Groen, ed. *Archives ou Correspondance inédite de la Maison d'Orange-Nassau, Deuxième Série, Tome III, 1625–1642.* Utrecht: Kemink et Fils, 1859.

Vásquez, Gabriel. *De Cultu Adorationis.* Mainz, 1601.

Veridicus, Paulus [Paul Harris]. *A Briefe Confutation of Certaine Absurd, Heretical and Damnable Doctrines, delivered by Mr. James Usher, in a sermon, preached before King James our late soveraigne, at Wansted, Iune 20. anno domini 1624.* St. Omer, 1627; republished in *English Recusant Literature 1558–1640.* Vol. 161. [Menston: Scolar Press, 1973]; 2nd edition, Antwerp, 1639.

Viseur, Robert [Visorius]. *Aaronis Purgati, seu Pseudo-Cherubi ex aureo vitulo recens conflati destructio.* Paris, 1609.

Williams, Frank, ed. *The Panarion of Epiphanius of Salamis, Books II and III. De Fide.* 2nd revised edition. Leiden: Brill, 2013.

SECONDARY SOURCES

Abbott, William M. "The Issue of Episcopacy in the Long Parliament, 1640–1648: The Reasons for Abolition." Unpublished doctoral dissertation, University of Oxford, 1981.

——— "James Ussher and 'Ussherian' Episcopacy, 1640–1656: The Primate and His Reduction Manuscript." *Albion* 22 (1990): 237–59.

Adams, S. L. "The Protestant Cause: Religious Alliance with the West European Calvinist Communities as a Political Issue in England, 1585–1630." Unpublished doctoral dissertation, University of Oxford, 1973.

Adlington, Hugh. "Gospel, Law, and *Ars Prædicandi* at the Inns of Court." In *The Intellectual and Cultural World of the Early Modern Inns of Court*, edited by Jayne Archer, Elizabeth Goldring, and Sarah Knight, 51–74. Manchester: Manchester University Press, 2011.

Beckwith, Roger. *Elders in Every City: The Origin and Role of the Ordained Ministry*. Carlisle: Paternoster, 2003.

Benn, Wallace. *Ussher on Bishops: A Reforming Ecclesiology*. London: St. Antholin's Lectureship Charity, 2002.

Blake-Knox, Jamie. "High-Church History: C. R. Elrington and His Edition of James Ussher's Works." In *The Church of Ireland and its Past: History, Interpretation and Identity*, edited by Mark Empey, Alan Ford, and Miriam Moffitt, 74–94. Dublin: Four Courts Press, 2017.

Boran, Elizabethanne. "An Early Friendship Network of James Ussher, Archbishop of Armagh, 1626–1656." In *European Universities in the Age of Reformation and Counter Reformation*, edited by Helga Robinson-Hammerstein, 116–34. Dublin: Four Courts Press, 1998.

Bottigheimer, Karl S., and Ute Lotz-Heumann. "The Irish Reformation in European Perspective." *Archiv für Reformationsgeschichte* 87 (1998): 268–309.

Brass, Maynard F. "Moderate Episcopacy, 1640–1662." Unpublished doctoral dissertation, State University of Iowa, 1962.

Capern, Amanda Louise. "The Caroline Church: James Ussher and the Irish Dimension." *Historical Journal* 39 (1996): 57–85.

Cole, Emily V. "The State Apartment in the Jacobean Country House, 1603–1625." Unpublished doctoral dissertation, University of Sussex, 2010.

Collier, Jay T. *Debating Perseverance: The Augustinian Tradition in Post-Reformation England*. New York: Oxford University Press, 2018.

Collinson, Patrick. "Episcopacy and Reform in England in the Later Sixteenth Century." In *Godly People: Essays on English Protestantism and Puritanism*, 155–89. London: Hambledon Press, 1983.

Cross, F. L., ed. *The Oxford Dictionary of the Christian Church*. 3rd ed. Revised by E. A. Livingstone. Oxford: Oxford University Press, 2005.

Cunningham, Jack P. "The *Eirenicon* and the 'Primitive Episcopacy' of James Ussher: An Irish Panacea for Britannia's Ailment." *Reformation and Renaissance Review* 8 (2006): 128–46.

de Quehen, Hugh. "Politics and Scholarship in the Ignatian Controversy." *Seventeenth Century* 13 (1998): 69–84.

Elrington, Charles R. "The Life of James Ussher, D.D., Archbishop of Armagh." In *The Whole Works of the Most Rev. James Ussher, D.D., Lord Archbishop of Armagh, and Primate of All Ireland. With the Life of the Author, and an Account of His Writings*, edited by Charles R. Elrington and J. H. Todd, 1:1–324. 17 vols. Dublin: Hodges and Smith, 1829–64.

Firth, Katherine R. *The Apocalyptic Tradition in Reformation Britain, 1530–1645*. Oxford: Oxford University Press, 1979.

Ford, Alan. *The Protestant Reformation in Ireland, 1590–1641*. 2nd impression. Frankfurt am Main: Peter Lang, 1987.

——— "Dependent or Independent? The Church of Ireland and Its Colonial Context, 1536–1649." *Seventeenth Century* 10 (1995): 163–87.

——— "James Ussher and the Creation of an Irish Protestant Identity." In *British Consciousness and Identity: The Making of Britain, 1533–1707*, edited by Brendan Bradshaw and Peter Roberts, 185–212. Cambridge: Cambridge University Press, 1998.

——— "'That Bugbear Arminianism': Archbishop Laud and Trinity College, Dublin." In *British Interventions in Early Modern Ireland*, edited by Ciaran Brady and Jane Ohlmeyer, 135–60. Cambridge: Cambridge University Press, 2005.

——— *James Ussher: Theology, History, and Politics in Early-Modern Ireland and England*. Oxford: Oxford University Press, 2007.

Geyl, Pieter. *The Netherlands in the Seventeenth Century, 1609–1648*. London: E. Benn, 1961.

Goodman, Godfrey. *The Court of King James the First*, edited by J. S. Brewer. 2 vols. Richard Bentley: London, 1839.

Greengrass, Mark. *Christendom Destroyed: Europe 1517–1648*. London: Allen Lane, 2014.

Gribben, Crawford. *The Puritan Millennium: Literature & Theology, 1550–1682*. Dublin: Four Courts Press, 2000.

———— *The Irish Puritans: James Ussher and the Reformation of the Church*. Darlington: Evangelical Press, 2003.

Hendrix, Scott H. *Recultivating the Vineyard: The Reformation Agendas of Christianization*. Louisville: Westminster John Knox Press, 2004.

Hill, Christopher. *Antichrist in Seventeenth-Century England*. London: Oxford University Press, 1971.

Jefferies, Henry A. *The Irish Church and the Tudor Reformations*. Dublin: Four Courts Press, 2010.

Keulemans, Michael. *Bishops: The Changing Nature of the Anglican Episcopate in Mainland Britain*. Bloomington, IN: Xlibris, 2012.

Knox, R. Buick. *James Ussher: Archbishop of Armagh*. Cardiff: University of Wales Press, 1967.

Lake, Peter. "The Laudian Style: Order, Uniformity and the Pursuit of the Beauty of Holiness in the 1630s." In *The Early Stuart Church, 1603–1642*, edited by Kenneth Fincham, 161–85. Basingstoke, United Kingdom: Macmillan, 1993.

Lewis, Charlton T., and Charles Short. *A Latin Dictionary*. Oxford: Clarendon Press, 1879.

Lotz-Heumann, Ute. "The Protestant Interpretation of History in Ireland: The Case of James Ussher's *Discourse*." In *Protestant History and Identity in Sixteenth-Century Europe*, edited by Bruce Gordon, 2:107–20. 2 vols. Aldershot: Scolar Press, 1996.

———— "'The Spirit of Prophecy Has Not Wholly Left the World': The Stylisation of Archbishop James Ussher as a Prophet." In *Religion and Superstition in Reformation Europe*, edited by Helen Parish and W. G. Naphy, 119–32. Manchester: Manchester University Press, 2002.

Matthew, H. C. G., and Brian Howard Harrison, eds. *Oxford Dictionary of National Biography*. 60 vols. Oxford: Oxford University Press, 2004.

McCullough, Peter E. *Sermons at Court: Politics and Religion in Elizabethan and Jacobean Preaching*. Cambridge: Cambridge University Press, 1998.

Milton, Anthony. *Catholic and Reformed: The Roman and Protestant Churches in English Protestant Thought, 1600–1640*. Cambridge: Cambridge University Press, 1995.

———— "The Creation of Laudianism: A New Approach." In *Politics, Religion and Popularity in Early Stuart Britain*, edited by Thomas Cogswell, Richard Cust and Peter Lake, 162–84. Cambridge: Cambridge University Press, 2002.

Milward, Peter. *Religious Controversies of the Jacobean Age: A Survey of Printed Sources*. London, Scolar Press, 1978.

Patterson, W. B. *King James VI and I and the Reunion of Christendom*. Cambridge: Cambridge University Press, 1997.

Perkins, Harrison. "Manuscript and Material Evidence for James Ussher's Authorship of 'A Body of Divinitie' (1645)." *Evangelical Quarterly* 89 (2018): 133–61.

Petry, Yvonne. *Gender, Kabbalah and the Reformation: The Mystical Theology of Guillaume Postel*. Leiden: Brill, 2004.

Scott, David. *Politics and War in the Three Stuart Kingdoms, 1637–49*. Basingstoke: Palgrave Macmillan, 2004.

Sharpe, Kevin. *The Personal Rule of Charles I*. New Haven, CT: Yale University Press, 1992.

Snoddy, Richard. *The Soteriology of James Ussher: The Act and Object of Saving Faith*. New York: Oxford University Press, 2014.

Spalding, James C., and Maynard F. Brass. "Reduction of Episcopacy as a Means to Unity in England, 1640–1662." *Church History* 30 (1961): 414–32.

Stewart, Alistair C. *The Original Bishops: Office and Order in the First Christian Communities*. Grand Rapids: Baker Academic, 2014.

Trevor-Roper, Hugh. "James Ussher, Archbishop of Armagh." In *Catholics, Anglicans and Puritans: Seventeenth Century Essays*, 120–65. London: Secker & Warburg, 1987.

Tyacke, Nicholas. "Puritanism, Arminianism and Counter-Revolution." In *The Origins of the English Civil War*, edited by Conrad Russell, 119–43. London: Macmillan, 1973.

———— *Anti-Calvinists: The Rise of English Arminianism c.1590–1640*. Oxford: Clarendon Press, 1987.

VanGemeren, Willem, ed. *New International Dictionary of Old Testament Theology and Exegesis*. 5 vols. Carlisle: Paternoster, 1996.

Vout, Caroline. *The Hills of Rome: Signature of an Eternal City*. Cambridge: Cambridge University Press, 2012.

Wadkins, Timothy H. "The Percy-'Fisher' Controversies and the Ecclesiastical Politics of Jacobean Anti-Catholicism, 1622–1625." *Church History* 57 (1988): 153–69.

Walsham, Alexandra. "Miracles in Post-Reformation England." *Studies in Church History* 41 (2005): 273–306.

White, Peter. "The Rise of Arminianism Reconsidered." *Past & Present* 101 (1983): 34–53.

———— *Predestination, Policy and Polemic: Conflict and Consensus in the English Church from the Reformation to the Civil War*. Cambridge: Cambridge University Press, 1992.

———— "The *Via Media* in the Early Stuart Church." In *The Early Stuart Church, 1603–1642*, edited by Kenneth Fincham, 211–30. Basingstoke: Macmillan, 1993.

Wilson, Peter. *Europe's Tragedy: A History of the Thirty Years' War*. London: Allen Lane, 2009.

Windsor, Graham. "The Reunion Views of Archbishop Ussher and his Circle." *The Churchman* 77 (1963): 163–74.

Woolrych, Austin. *Britain in Revolution, 1625–1660*. Oxford: Oxford University Press, 2002.

ABOUT THE DAVENANT INSTITUTE

The Davenant Institute aims to retrieve the riches of classical Protestantism in order to renew and build up the contemporary church: building networks of friendship and collaboration among evangelical scholars committed to Protestant resourcement, publishing resources old and new, and offering training and discipleship for Christians thirsting after wisdom.

We are a nonprofit organization supported by your tax-deductible gifts. Learn more about us, and donate, at www.davenantinstitute.org.

MORE FROM DAVENANT PRESS

RICHAR HOOKER MODERNIZATION PROJECT
Radicalism: When Reform Becomes Revolution
Divine Law and Human Nature
The Word of God and the Words of Man

INTRODUCTION TO THE PROTESTANT REFORMATION
Reformation Theology: A Reader of Primary Sources with Introductions

DAVENANT GUIDES
Jesus and Pacifism: An Exegetical and Historical Investigation
The Two Kingdoms: A Guide for the Perplexed
Natural Law: A Brief Introduction and Biblical Defense

DAVENANT RETRIEVALS
People of the Promise: A Mere Protestant Ecclesiology

DAVENANT ENGAGEMENTS
Enduring Divine Absence: The Challenge of Modern Atheism

CONVIVIUM PROCEEDINGS
For the Healing of the Nations: Essays on Creation, Redemption, and Neo-Calvinism
For Law and for Liberty: Essays on the Trans-Atlantic Legacy of Protestant Political Thought
Beyond Calvin: Essays on the Diversity of the Reformed Tradition
God of Our Fathers: Classical Theism for the Contemporary Church

MONTHLY PUBLICATIONS
Ad Fontes: A Journal of Protestant Resourcement
Davenant Digests: Protestant Wisdom in Focus for the Whole Church

Made in the USA
Middletown, DE
23 September 2018